THE MANAGEMENT OF ARCHIVES

Number Fourteen
Columbia University Studies
in Library Service

THE MANAGEMENT

OF ARCHIVES

T. R. Schellenberg

COLUMBIA UNIVERSITY PRESS

New York

T. R. Schellenberg was Assistant Archivist of the United States until his retirement in 1963. He is also the author of *Modern Archives: Principles and Techniques.*

7.00

Copyright © 1965 Columbia University Press

ISBN 0-231-02812-1

Library of Congress Catalog Card Number: 65-14409
Printed in the United States of America
10 9 8 7 6 5

COLUMBIA UNIVERSITY STUDIES
IN LIBRARY SERVICE

TO ALMA GROENING SCHELLENBERG

PREFACE

While teaching courses in archival principles and techniques at the National Archives and during summer sessions at the American University, the University of Texas, and the University of Washington, I became aware of the gaps in the literature and in the documental knowledge of the archival profession. I therefore attempted to define the principles and techniques of arranging and describing documentary material. In this attempt I proceeded on the assumption that the principles and techniques now applied to public records may be applied also, with some modification, to private records, especially to private manuscript material of recent origin, much of which has the organic character of archival material.

In my definition of archival principles and techniques I took into account the distinctive characteristics of documentary material. These characteristics differ from those of library material; for this reason, archival arrangement and description differ from library classification and cataloging.

I believe archival principles and techniques should be systematized and, to a very large extent, standardized, if work with records, whether public or private, is to become truly professional. While contributions to developing principles and techniques can be made individually, standardization can come only through collaborative effort. Once archival methodology has been clearly and fully defined, it can be taught effectively in training courses. The places in which such courses can be given most systematically, in my opinion, are library schools, which are concerned with methodological training. Systematic training is likely to bring about a standardization of method.

The principles and techniques I discuss relate to the arrangement and description of records for research use, not current use. They are thus archival, rather than record management, principles and techniques. The book is therefore directed primarily to custodians of research material—archivists, manuscript curators, and librarians.

The records with which I am concerned fall into three major classes—textual, cartographic, and pictorial. The textual record class includes both public records and private records; the former are customarily designated as archives, the latter as historical manuscripts. I do not discuss the management of motion picture films, aerial films, and microfilms.

A Portuguese version of this book has been issued under the auspices of the Brazilian National Archives, under the title *Arquivos Privados e Publicos: Arranjo e Descrição* (Rio de Janeiro, 1963). It lacks the chapters on the arrangement and description of cartographic and pictorial records.

Some of the information in this book is derived from articles and books previously written by me. The sections on the arrangement and description of textual records are revised versions of manuals I wrote for the first Inter-American Archival Seminar held in Washington, D.C., in October, 1961. The section on description was issued in near-print form in English, under the title "Draft of a Manual on Archival Descriptive Techniques," by the Texas State Historical Survey Committee, in June, 1961; and in Spanish, under the title "Principios archivisticos de ordenacion," by the National Archives, in September, 1961. The section on description was published, under the title *Tecnicas para descrivir archivos*, by the University of Cordoba, Argentina, in 1961.

The manuals, in turn, are based on a number of articles, which include the following:

"European Archival Practices in Arranging Records," National Archives, *Staff Information Circular No. 5* (July, 1939);

"The Preparation of Preliminary Inventories," National Archives, *Staff Information Circular No. 14* (May, 1950);

"The Preparation of Lists of Record Items," National Archives, *Staff Information Paper No. 17 Revised* (December, 1960);

"Principles of Arrangement," National Archives, *Staff Infor-*

mation Paper No. 18 (June, 1951);

"Arrangement of Private Papers," *Archives and Manuscripts: The Journal of the Archives Section of the Library Association of Australia*, II (Canberra, A.C.T., June, 1957), 1-19;

"Description of Private Papers," *Archives and Manuscripts: The Journal of the Archives Section of the Library Association of Australia*, II (Canberra, A.C.T., August, 1958), 1-19; and

"Archival Principles of Arrangement," *American Archivist*, XXIV (January, 1961), 11-24.

The articles on the arrangement and description of private papers, published in the Australian archival journal, also appear as added chapters in the Spanish, German, and Hebrew versions of my book on *Modern Archives: Principles and Techniques* (Melbourne, 1956; Chicago, 1956), which were published respectively in Havana, in 1958; in Munich, in 1960; and in Tel Aviv, in 1966.

In the preparation of this book I thoroughly revised all my previous writings that relate to arrangement principles and descriptive techniques. By analyzing such principles and techniques in a comprehensive manner, I was often able to bring my views, expressed in earlier writings, into better focus. Also, I was able to fill gaps in these writings. I thus added much that is new, as, for example, information on methodological developments in the library and archival fields, the arrangement of record items, physical arrangements, record attributes, the preparation of guides, the arrangement and description of cartographic and pictorial records, and notational systems. The method of subject cataloging that I discuss is also new, though the method itself was suggested by the procedure followed by Hubert H. Bancroft, noted American historian, in organizing his source material for historical exploitation.

The responsibility for all statements in this book is my own. Although many of the views expressed are derived from official publications that I wrote while employed in the federal government of the United States, they are here produced as expressions of my personal views—not as the official views of any federal agency with which I have been associated.

For help in writing this book I am especially indebted to those who reviewed my manuscript from specialized points of view: Curtis W. Garrison, as a manuscript curator; Robert R. Douglass as a librarian; Herman R. Friis, Alfred P. Muntz, and Franklin W. Burch, as map curators; Josephine Cobb, as an expert in pictorial records; and Herman G. Goldbeck, as an editor. I am also indebted to the following staff members of the National Archives, who helped me in an unofficial capacity in various ways: Julia B. Carroll, Cleveland E. Collier, Grace Quimby, James B. Rhoads, Morris Rieger, and Jane F. Smith. I especially appreciate the encouragement given me by Dorman H. Winfrey, State Librarian of Texas; Richard C. Berner, Manuscript Curator of the Libraries of the University of Washington; and George S. Ulibarri, who assisted me in directing the Inter-American Archival Seminar, for which much of the material in this book was produced.

T. R. SCHELLENBERG

June, 1964

CONTENTS

EXPLANATION OF TERMS

Records—a generic term, used synonymously with the term *material*, that includes both *archives*, a term customarily used to refer to material of public origin, and *historical records*, customarily used to refer to material of private origin.

Record classes—refers to three major kinds of records:

(1) *Textual records*, which appear in written form. The term includes papers that are both public and private in origin. It is thus more inclusive than the terms *historical documents* and *historical manuscripts*, which refer only to papers of private origin.

(2) *Cartographic records*, which appear in graphic form.

(3) *Pictorial records*, which appear in the form of pictures.

Record types—the kinds of records within the three major classes. Types are both generic and specific. In the *textual* record class, *generic terms* are records, papers, and manuscripts; *specific types* are letters, reports, diaries, and the like. In the *cartographic* record class, *general types* are maps, charts, diagrams, and the like; *specific types* are cadastral, geological, topographic, and other kinds of maps; hydrographic, aeronautical, and other kinds of charts; and various kinds of diagrams. In the *pictorial* record class, *general types* are photographs, original productions, and press productions; *specific types* are photographic prints and negatives, paintings and drawings, lithographs, etchings, engravings, and the like.

Types are established in the three major record classes on the basis of varying factors, as follows: in the textual record class, chiefly on the basis of *activity;* in the cartographic record class, chiefly on the basis of *subject content;* and in the pictorial record class, chiefly on the basis of the *method of production.*

Record forms—the kind of copy of a record type. The main kinds of textual record forms are typescripts, photoprints, and microfilms; the main kinds of cartographic forms are manuscript as distinguished from printed maps and charts. The term "form" is not useful in respect to pictorial record types, since such types are established chiefly on the basis of the method of production.

Record units—refers to physical entities, which are distinguished on the basis of provenance and size, as follows:

(1) *Archival groups and subgroups,* used synonymously with the terms *record groups and subgroups,* which are established by a consideration of their organizational, as distinct from their functional, origins. An *archival group* is the largest physical unit established in an archival institution. It is comprised of records created by a public agency that has separate or distinct functional responsibilities and that can, for this reason, be dealt with separately. An *archival subgroup* is comprised of records created by an organizational subdivision of the public agency that created an archival group.

(2) *Manuscript collection,* used synonymously with the term *manuscript group,* to refer to large physical units established in a manuscript repository. A collection is comprised, usually, of manuscripts derived from a particular source; but it may also be comprised of single manuscripts, or small groups of manuscripts, from various sources brought together in a repository or by a collector. If brought together in a repository, such manuscripts are designated as a *collection of miscellany;* if brought together by a collector, as an *artificial collection.*

(3) *Series and subseries* are physical units, within archival groups or manuscipt collections, that are established by a consideration of their functional, as distinct from their organizational, origins. The units may be either *archival series or subseries* or *manuscript series or subseries,* depending on whether they were created by a public or a private body.

(4) *Items* are the smallest physical units that are found in a series. An item may be either (1) a single document or (2) many documents that were brought together, usually in the course of their current use, into volumes, binders, folders, or other containers.

(5) *Piece* is a single sheet of paper.

Part 1

DEVELOPMENT OF PRINCIPLES AND TECHNIQUES

The question of the future, so far as the material of history is concerned, relates to getting at what has been accumulated,—the ready extraction of the marrow. In other words, it is a problem of differentiation, selection, arrangement, indexing and cataloguing. To-day we are like men wandering in a vast wilderness, which is springing up in every direction with tropical luxuriance. The one great necessity is to have paths carried through it on some intelligible plan, which will at once enable us to find our way whither we would go, or tell us in what directions further research would be futile.

Charles Francis Adams, April 13, 1899

I

DEVELOPMENT OF LIBRARY METHODOLOGY

The role of historians in the development of the American archival profession is well known, but that of librarians has received relatively little attention. After historians organized the American Historical Association, they fostered the growth of institutions that collected and preserved documentary material; surveyed such material, both in the United States and abroad; and, in annual meetings, discussed archival principles and techniques. They worked chiefly through two commissions, one concerned with private, and the other with public, records.

While librarians have not played as conspicuous a role as historians, the two stellar figures in the archival movement during the nineteenth century—Justin Winsor and William F. Poole—were librarians as well as historians. Both became presidents of the American Library Association and of the American Historical Association. And librarians, during the present century, organized a committee that engaged in activities that paralleled those of the two commissions of the American Historical Association. The Committee on Public Archives, established by the National Association of State Libraries, met annually between 1913 and 1918 and interested itself especially in the methods that should be employed in an archival institution. In recent years, librarians have taken the lead in collecting and preserving private records.

Justin Winsor (1831–97), first president of the American Library Association, helped develop archival techniques and institutions. He interested himself in archives and manuscripts generally, for his *Narrative and Critical History of America* [1] contains a comprehensive review of the historical sources available in his time. He also interested himself in the methods to be applied to archives and manuscripts. As a member of the Massachusetts Historical Society, he formulated rules for cataloging manuscripts.[2] As librarian of Harvard University, he organized the university archives and calendared the papers of Jared Sparks (1789–1866). In 1890, he visited English institutions, including the Public Record Office and the British Museum, to study their systems, in which he found "many defects." [3] He participated actively in the work of the American Historical Association in preserving historical manuscripts and making them available for use and in promoting the establishment of a national archives in the United States.

William F. Poole (1821–94), another president of the American Library Association and librarian of the Chicago Public Library, became greatly interested in the management of historical manuscripts in the State Department.[4] He worked with Winsor on a committee of the American Historical Association that sponsored the establishment of a national archives in the United States. In 1893 he wrote that he had "long believed that the chief mission of the American Historical Association was to bring the Government up to the duty of establishing and maintaining a Department of Archives." [5]

Since librarians have often interested themselves in the development of the archival profession, archivists should reciprocate and interest themselves in library techniques. A distinction is made between these techniques and those of archivists on the basis of an assumption: namely, that archival techniques relate to records and library techniques to publications. This assumption, I realize, may be questioned on the ground that librarians and archivists are concerned with the same kinds of material. To a degree they are, for archivists may concern themselves with publications, i.e., records in published form, and librarians with manuscripts, which are increasingly occupying their attention. Archivists and librarians, moreover, are both concerned with still pictures, motion pictures, and maps. A distinction between their techniques can be made only if it is assumed that they are concerned with different kinds of material, and this assumption is valid if it is qualified by the statement that librarians are *mainly* concerned with publications and archivists *mainly* with records. The analysis of archival techniques in this book rests on this basic assumption.

The reasons why archivists should interest themselves in library techniques are the following:

Library techniques have the same purpose as archival techniques, i.e., to make material available for use.

Library techniques have the same general character as archival techniques. While library material may be quite different from archival material, essentially the same action must be taken with respect to the two kinds of material, for both must be arranged and described so that they may be made available for use.

Library techniques have often been applied to documentary material that is the concern of archivists. Librarians directed work with historical manuscripts in most repositories of the last century, and at the present time are more often custodians of such manuscripts than are the members of any other professional class. And in administering historical manuscripts, librarians have often applied the techniques of their profession—techniques of classifying and cataloging publications.

Library techniques have been developed to solve a problem that is essentially similar to that facing archivists. It is the problem of mass. After the Civil War, librarians, like archivists a few decades later, had to find ways to deal with ever-increasing quantities of material. They had to evolve techniques for doing this. They, like archivists, had to concern themselves with methodology.

The growth of library material parallels somewhat the growth of documentary material. At the beginning of our national history the United States was "book poor." All the books in all libraries of the country were not as numerous as those in a single large library in Europe. At the outbreak of the Civil War, library holdings had increased considerably, amounting to about 3,000,000 volumes in the significant public libraries of the country.[6] This figure rose to 12,300,000 by 1876.[7] Various factors—social, educational, economic, and technological—led to a tremendous production of books in the period after 1876. Many new libraries were established, and their holdings increased almost in a geometric rather than an arithmetic ratio.

The growth in library holdings can best be illustrated by examining statistics in respect to a particular library, that of Harvard University. The Harvard Library was the first university library to be established in the United States (in 1636) and "for more than two centuries . . . was the largest on the American Continent."[8] It is now the largest university library in the world. John Harvard's donation of 400 volumes of classics, theology, and general literature was an important part of his bequest to the university. By 1836, the library he helped found had 47,500 volumes; by 1863, 140,000 volumes; by 1876, 227,650 volumes; by 1893, 407,989 volumes; by 1900, 900,000 volumes; by 1928, 2,750,000 volumes; by 1937, 3,863,050 volumes; and by the present day, well over 7,000,000 volumes.[9]

But perhaps the most important reason why archivists should interest themselves in library techniques is that librarians have provided an object lesson to them as to how to develop a methodology. They have shown archivists the way in which to bring a profession to a high degree of proficiency. Their systems of classification, according to Robert C. Binkley (1897–1940), "have become practically interchangeable parts of a national system of record. The next great technical problem will be in the field of control by depositories of their sources of unpublished material, and here technique stands today where the technique of book cataloging stood fifty years ago."[10]

Before 1876, library methods were ill-defined. The profession was in its infancy. Librarians, meeting in convention in New York City in 1853, had urged that a manual be written for their guidance, just as archivists, some sixty years later, were to recommend that a "Manual of Archival Economy" be compiled.[11] But the library manual, when produced, made no attempt to provide practical guidance to librarians. It simply revealed that the period in which it was written was "a primeval period in American library history." So William I. Fletcher (1844–1917) wrote, while librarian of Amherst College.[12]

The year 1876, marking the centennial of American independence, was also an epochal year for the library profession. Several important events occurred, any one of which would have made the year memorable but which in combination made it truly the beginning of a new era for librarians:

(1) a noteworthy report was issued by the United States Bureau of Education entitled *Public Libraries in the United States of America: Their History, Condition, and Management;*

(2) Charles A. Cutter's "Rules for a Printed Dictionary Catalogue" was issued as a second part of the above report;

(3) the first edition of Melvil Dewey's *Decimal Classification and Relative Index* was issued;

(4) the American Library Association was formed; and

(5) the *Library Journal* was established and publication began.

The "two and a half decades, from 1876 to 1900, and then later, may be considered a very important transition period, and a very interesting one, in the history of American librarianship," wrote Grace O. Kelley.[13]

Developments in the techniques of the library profession, which are of particular concern to us, occurred in the activities that are known in the archival profession as arrangement and description. In the library profession, arrangement is known as classification, and description as cataloging. Indexing may also be considered as part of description, though library indexes, like archival indexes, usually lack descriptive information.

Classification

Before 1876, when holdings were quite small, few libraries had developed methods of arrangement that could properly be designated as "classification systems." Books were commonly grouped into broad classes, particular alcoves and shelves were assigned to each of the classes, alcoves and shelves were identified by symbols, and books were marked to show their physical location. Each librarian established his own classes, devised his own notation, and developed his own methods of marking and placing his books.

Thelma Eaton, in an excellent article on the development of classification in America, wrote that "the 19th century was a period of intense interest in classification" and that "in that period men of stature were interested in classification and individual schemes were the rule." [14]

Early schemes of arrangement had certain features that contributed to the development of the classification systems that later found general acceptance. They related to (1) the factors to be considered in establishing classes of books, such as their relation to subject and geographical area, and their form, and (2) the use of symbols, including decimal numbers, to designate both physical location and subject class.

One of the first large libraries to introduce an arrangement scheme was the Boston Public Library. In 1856 its librarian, Nathaniel B. Shurtleff (1810–74), privately published a scheme for *A Decimal System for the Arrangement and Administration of Libraries*, which was applied in the library two years later. The large hall of the library was divided, on each of its sides, into ten alcoves, each of which had ten ranges or compartments, and each range, in turn, had ten shelves. These fixed locations— alcoves, ranges, shelves—were assigned decimal numbers. The notational system may be explained by using the number 2675 for purpose of illustration. In this number the figure 26 stands for alcove, 7 for range, and 5 for shelf. One or more alcoves were assigned to each of eighteen main subject classes, and in each alcove ranges were assigned to certain subclasses within them. Books were assigned numbers to indicate their places on shelves; thus 2675.17 refers to the seventeenth book on the shelf identified above.[15]

A few years later, in 1861, the Library of Congress adopted an arrangement scheme according to which books were placed into main classes and subclasses, both of which were numbered, the subclasses being indicated by numbers placed after the decimal point. These numbers were superimposed on numbers that referred to physical location, thus: $\frac{25.7}{5082}$, the 5082 referring to a shelf number.[16]

A variant of the above schemes was devised by Jacob Schwartz, librarian at the Brooklyn Public Library, who divided his library holdings into forty-four main classes and four hundred subclasses. He used decimal numbers in his notation, a fact that later led him to criticize Melvil Dewey for lack of originality. In his notation the number 411.01 designated the following: 4 the class "History," 11 the first shelf of range 1, and .01 the first book on the particular shelf.[17]

The scheme for the Chicago Public Library was formulated by William F. Poole, who explained it in the Bureau of Education report on *Public Libraries in the United States* (1876). Poole used symbols to indicate location as follows: in the notation "A, 24, 10-2," A referred to case A, 24 to the twenty-fourth shelf, 10 to the tenth publication, and 2 to the second volume of the tenth publication. He also placed particular subject classes in particular cases, which he gave letter symbols. Within a particular class he reserved blocks of numbers for assignment to publications that fell within subclasses. In the class "History," for example, the numbers 1–100 were reserved for "History: Philosophy and Study of," 101–150 for "History of Civilization," 151–250 for "Historical Essay," etc.[18]

The Harvard University Library scheme was devised by Justin Winsor, who used symbols mainly to show location. In his notation, the number 3825.5.3 designated the following: 38 the thirty-eighth case, 2 the second range, 5 the fifth shelf, the 5 after the first decimal point the fifth publication on the fifth shelf, and the 3 after the second decimal point the third volume of the fifth publication. Winsor also affixed numbers to physical locations, as follows: a large number over the middle of each case; a secondary number at the top of each range, i.e., 1, 2, 3, etc.; and a number to each shelf, numbering from the bottom up.[19]

Before 1876, then, various schemes of arrangement were employed, many of which were improvised by librarians to meet their particular needs. Some were admittedly unsatisfactory, e.g., that of the American Philosophical Society, introduced in 1863, which, according to its librarian, "has been in use too long to change." [20] Most of the schemes had one thing in common, i.e., that the position of books was fixed in relation to shelves. For this reason they were not suited to accommodate rapidly expanding library collections, for, as shelf space for given classes of books was exhausted, major shifts of books had to be made, nor were they readily expansible within classes and subclasses.

The problem of dealing with an expanding library collection was one that especially occupied the mind of Melvil Dewey (1851–1931) while working in the Library of Amherst College, where he was a junior in 1873. He wrote (using the simplified spelling to which he was partial) that, while listening to a sermon, "my mind absorbd in the vital problem, the solution flasht over me so that I jumpt in my seat and came very near shouting 'Eureka!' It was to get absolute simplicity by using the simplest known symbols, the arabic numerals as decimals, with the ordinary significance of nought, to number a classification of all human knowledge in print; this supplemented by the next simplest known symbols, a, b, c, indexing all heds of the tables." [21] On May 8, 1873, he explained his proposed new classification to the Library Committee of Amherst.

Dewey's classification is thus based on the theory that the classes in which publications are placed should be established in relation to human knowledge, not in relation to physical location; and that the classes, and subdivisions thereof, should be designated by decimals of Arabic numerals. He established the following main classes for publications: 000, General Works; 100, Philosophy; 200, Religion; 300, Social Sciences; 400, Philology; 500, Pure Sciences; 600, Useful Arts; 700, Fine Arts; 800, Literature; and 900, History. He established subclasses by taking into account the form or type of publication, i.e., whether dictionaries, periodicals, and the like; dividing large subject fields into smaller fields on a purely logical basis; and dividing large subject fields on a geographical basis.

Dewey's division of his classes on the basis of form, relation to subject, and relation to geographical area was not new, for various schemes in use at the time he devised his system took account of such factors in classification. Jacob Schwartz, for example, had a subclass called "General Works" under each of the main classes in a scheme devised in 1871.[22]

Dewey's use of a decimal system is also not new, and he did not claim to be the first to use it. He wrote that he did not know "*where* it has been used before, but [that he] should think some one must hav happened on so easy a solution to the worst difficulties."[23] But the feature of his system that represents a radical departure from previous schemes is that his notation is keyed to classes of knowledge in relation to which books are produced, not to fixed points at which they are deposited. His system of notation was thus expansible at all points, and retained its simplicity during an indefinite division of classes on a tenfold basis.

After he conceived his original plan in 1873, Dewey, with the help of his friend and fellow student Walter Stanley Biscoe, spent the next three years in reorganizing and classifying the Amherst Library in accordance with the plan and in improving and expanding it. "The labor involved in preparing the classification and index," he wrote, "has been wholly beyond the appreciation of any who have never attempted a similar task."[24] He was particularly grateful "for valuable suggestions and appreciative criticism" received from Charles A. Cutter (1837–1903) of the Boston Athenaeum and John Fiske (1842–1901) of the Harvard University Library.[25]

In 1876 Dewey discussed his decimal classification system at the meeting of librarians during the centennial exposition in Philadelphia[26] and published it under the title *Decimal Classification and Relative Index*. He attached a great deal of importance to the relative index, which shows by means of cross-references the relation between subjects.

Dewey's system gradually supplanted most others, not only because of its simplicity and expansibility, but also because of the care with which he developed it and the assiduousness with which he made it known. He was the first to publish and to sell a classification scheme. In 1877 he began providing supplies to libraries, under the auspices of the Co-operation Committee of the American Library Association, which later became its Supply Department. He later established a Library Bureau, which supplanted the Supply Department of the association, and which provided technical information, assistance, and supplies to libraries and distributed successive revisions of his classification scheme.[27] In revising his scheme, he obtained the collaboration of a number of librarians. He and his collaborators asked "a critic to point out in print, frankly but fairly, its weak points, for we know it has them." He sent inquiries to everyone who used his system, "urging the fullest criticism." He observed that "some faults cannot be cured, but inhere in the system" and that users must decide if "its peculiar advantages . . . outweigh its peculiar faults." [28] By constantly revising, by constantly defining more carefully the contents of the divisions and subdivisions of the classes in his system, he gradually perfected it and made it workable.

Dewey's system of classification was not accepted without very considerable opposition. Against it were brought to bear all the forces of conservatism that are found in every profession and all the forces of those who had improvised their own systems and were loath to change them. In the year in which his system was first issued, the librarian of Congress, Ainsworth R. Spofford (1825–1908), observed that attempts to apply systems for the distribution of human knowledge to the classification of libraries "have not been signally successful" and that "the first thing to be done is to get rid of the system-mongers, each of whom has a plan admirably adapted to the operations of his own mind, but quite unmanageable by those of other men." [29] Jacob Schwartz collaborated with F. B. Perkins (1828–1900), librarian at San Francisco, who had also devised a classification system of his own, in an ungracious attack on Dewey in the *Library Journal*. Schwartz and Perkins claimed that the "whole idea of close classification [which is inherent in Dewey's system] rests on a transparent fallacy," that it was "either ignorant or fraudulent," that the decimal system was not original, and that " 'that which is new in his system is not good, and that which is good is not new.' " [30] William F. Poole, whose system has already been noted, wrote that he regarded "the time and energy spent in devising artificial systems of classification and mnemonic notations as wasted energy, and I have long since ceased to give them any attention." [31] The Boston Public Library, in keeping with the conservative traditions of the community in which it is located, stated in 1893, after Dewey's system was widely accepted, that "the idea of reclassifying has never been entertained for a moment, so no examination of other systems has ever been made." [32] The library, in fact, stuck to the "fixed location" system of Shurtleff until 1937, when it was replaced by the Library of Congress system.

Shortly after Dewey's *Decimal Classification* was first published, Charles A. Cutter, librarian at the Boston Athenaeum, began work on a classification system. The earliest accounts of it appeared in 1879. He, like Dewey, was concerned with developing a system that would meet the needs of an ever-expanding library. This he sought to achieve by devising several tables of classification that would provide for the needs of a library at successive stages of its growth. His system, known as *Expansive Classification*, was published in six expansions between 1891 and 1904. The seventh expansion was never quite completed.

Cutter used mainly letters of the alphabet as the basis of his notation. He designated 26 main classes by capital letters and 26 divisions of these by small letters. The 26 divisions, in turn, were divided into small groups, e.g., countries, which were designated by numerals. His scheme provided a total capacity of more than 18,000 class numbers.

Cutter's system was very carefully developed and is one of the most logical of the classification schemes devised by the library profession. According to Ernest Cushing Richardson (1860–1939), librarian of Princeton University, "The painstaking intelligence of subdivision and the full description of exact meaning of what is intended to be included under the subdivision are of the highest order, both of scholarship and industry." [33]

Certain features of the Cutter and Dewey systems were incorporated in the Library of Congress system. The Library of Congress began a reclassification of its books in accordance with its newly developed system in 1898, a time, it should be noted, when Spofford, who was opposed to all "system-mongers," had left the library. The Library of Congress scheme was not developed according to any theory of knowledge, for it simply provided classes, and subdivisions within classes, for accumulations of books on various subjects. Its system of notation is mixed, in that letters and numbers are used in conjunction. Main classes are designated by capital letters and main divisions of such classes are given a second capital letter. The numbers 1 to 9,999 are used to designate subdivisions, and, finally, special subdivisions are designated in various ways. Schedules—or statements on the classification of books—for each class have been developed by specialists. The schedules refer to general and special tables, which make extensive use of geographical divisions and alphabetical sequences, and which indicate precisely how books should be grouped in various classes. The Library of Congress system, which, along with the Dewey and Cutter systems, is one of the three most widely used in the United States, was first published in 1901 and was widely adopted, chiefly in university libraries, in the 1920s.

By the turn of the century, then, the library profession had produced two highly developed classification systems, while a third particularly suited to the needs of very large libraries was just emerging. The Dewey decimal and the Cutter expansive systems, according to Richardson, "mark the high watermark of American library science and are the climax of its achievement." [34]

Cataloging

Before 1876, library catalogs were generally in the form of published volumes. By that date, over a thousand printed catalogs had been produced by the librarians of this country. [35] Fewer than forty of them appeared in the eighteenth century, and their number increased decade by decade in the nineteenth century, as follows:

1800–10	17
1811–20	26
1821–30	57
1831–40	79
1841–50	121
1851–60	121
1861–70	218
1871–75	328

These printed catalogs were of all types. They are described at length in an article by Charles A. Cutter in the Bureau of Education report on *Public Libraries in the United States* (1876). The earliest catalogs usually contained author entries or entries that were classed by the size of books. To these types were added the dictionary catalog, in which author, subject, and title entries were listed in alphabetical order, and the subject catalog, in which entries were arranged according to the subject of books, either alphabetically by the words selected to denote the subjects or philosophically according to the relations of the subjects. Separate title and form catalogs were also produced. The bibliographical information in an entry usually included the name of author, title of book, pages, and date of publication.

The aim of librarians was to produce printed catalogs that could be revised or supplemented as new publications were acquired. With the great increase in the number of publications in the period following the Civil War, the production of printed catalogs was no longer practicable. Methods had to be devised that would permit the intercalation of entries in a catalog as new publications were received. Two means were employed to accomplish this.

The first was affixing slips containing catalog entries to sheets of paper that were fastened into binders, a practice followed in the British Museum. Usually the slips were pasted onto the sheets. A mechanical device known as the Rudolph Indexer, which permitted the slips to be put into position without pasting, was also used. The sheets of paper were placed in various types of binders, the most common being known as the Common Sense Binder.

Cards provided another means of intercalating catalog entries. They were seemingly first employed for library purposes in France, where the Abbé Rozier, in 1775, indexed the memoirs of the Academy of Sciences, employing playing cards for the purpose. They were introduced for cataloging purposes quite early in Boston, where the Public Library began using them between 1853 and 1855, and at the Harvard University Library in 1856.[36] By 1876 some of the largest libraries of the country had adopted the card system exclusively.[37]

The Library Bureau, the work of which in promoting Dewey's *Decimal Classification* has already been noted, was particularly active in introducing the use of cards. In the first few decades after its establishment (1876), it concerned itself largely with manufacturing and distributing cards, guides, and cabinets and with developing and improving card cataloging systems. The card drawer most often used after card catalogs came into vogue was a two-row drawer. This was replaced by a single-row drawer in the 1880s, when all kinds of new containers were invented. In the 1890s the American Library Association, after mature deliberation, adopted the 3 x 5-inch card. This size, which is now the library standard, was strongly advocated by Dewey, who first recognized the importance of obtaining uniformity in cataloging supplies and practices.[38]

In 1876 Charles A. Cutter, whose work in developing a classification system has already been mentioned, produced his "Rules for a Printed Dictionary Catalogue," which was published by the Bureau of Education as a second part of its report on the *Public Libraries in the United States* (1876). Cutter's "Rules" was based, in part, on his experience in producing the printed catalog of the Boston Athenaeum, the successive volumes of which appeared in 1874–82. A second edition of his "Rules" appeared in 1889. The "Rules" is as important to the development of the techniques of cataloging as Dewey's decimal system is to the techniques of classification.

Shortly after its formation, the American Library Association concerned itself with cataloging. In 1877 it sought to standardize catalog entries, and in 1878 it published its *Condensed Rules for Cataloging*.

In 1892 the association appointed a committee to study the question of subject heads. The committee's report, recommending a plan for a list of subject heads, was approved by the association a few years later. It thus anticipated the production of the important subject lists produced many years later that greatly facilitated cataloging work.

By the turn of the century, the principles and techniques of cataloging had been firmly established and were quite generally accepted. Standard rules for cataloging, either those of Cutter or of the American Library Association, were usually followed. Cards were almost invariably used for manuscript catalogs. Suitable card drawers were commercially available and generally used. The methods of showing the subjective relation of books in catalogs had been highly refined. Lists of cataloging subjects were being compiled, later to be followed by the "List of Subject Headings for Use in Dictionary Catalogues," published by the American Library Association, and "Subject Headings Used in the Dictionary Catalogues of the Library of Congress," published by the latter institution. "The subject catalog, in its development and almost universal use, is peculiarly American," Justin Winsor observed during the World's Library Congress in 1893.[39] The commonest types of catalogs were the dictionary, the author, and the subject, though classed catalogs were still being produced. Printed catalogs, however, had "nearly had their day." [40]

Indexing

The technique of indexing was developed early by the library profession, but its importance as a means of obtaining control over special types of publications was not generally recognized until William F. Poole produced his famous *Index to Periodical Literature*.

Poole began his work in library science early in his career.

Like Dewey, he made his first contributions to it during his student days. In 1847, while a student at Yale, he began compiling an index to periodical literature. The next year the first edition of his *Index to Periodical Literature*, comprising 154 pages, appeared. Librarians who met in New York City in 1853 highly approved the plan for his *Index,* and a second edition of 521 pages was issued in that year.

At the first regular meeting of the American Library Association, in 1876, plans were laid for the issuance of a new and enlarged edition of Poole's *Index.* The new edition was produced on a cooperative basis, for at least fifty libraries contributed references to it. The enlarged *Index* appeared in 1882 and pointed the way for cooperation among libraries in similar indexing projects.

In summary, then, the library profession, which achieved a high degree of proficiency by the end of the nineteenth century, owes its development to the work of a number of eminent and gifted librarians, especially to Dewey, Cutter, and Poole. Of the three, Dewey made the most significant contributions through the development of his classification system, his management of the Library Bureau, and his educational activities.

The American Library Association also served to promote the interests of the library profession; it was not manipulated for personal ends. Its meetings, according to the Amherst librarian, have "one object constantly in view," and that is "co-operation among libraries in the interests of better and more economical administration, looking to a more efficient and satisfactory service to the public." [41] Through its committees, the association helped improve the techniques of classification, cataloging, and indexing and initiated various cooperative enterprises among librarians. Its journal was also a medium through which librarians contributed to the advancement of their profession by freely and frankly discussing their mutual problems.

The development of methodology is, obviously, a never-ending job. Classification schemes and cataloging techniques of the last century are now becoming outmoded as library material

continues to increase in quantity and complexity. New methods
of control are being developed, using new devices that are the
product of modern technology, for the methodology of a profession must be constantly revised and refined to meet its current
problems.

II

FACTORS INFLUENCING
ARCHIVAL METHODOLOGY

While the story of the growth of historical societies in the United States is quite well known, and has been ably told by Dunlap[1] and Whitehill,[2] relatively little attention has been given in historical accounts, or elsewhere, to the methods that were employed in dealing with manuscript material. One can learn about the development of such methods only by gleaning scattered and fragmentary bits of information from the innumerable reports and proceedings of historical societies and by analyzing the finding aids these societies produced.

Certain general factors that influenced the development of archival methods of arrangement and description are (1) the kind of repositories in which records were accumulated, (2) the volume of records, and (3) the character of records.

Kind of Repositories

During the colonial period of American history, the activities of collecting and preserving records were largely a matter of individual enterprise; they became an institutional matter only after the federal government was established. The institutions that became interested in records are of three types: historical societies, archival institutions, and libraries; each of these types evolved fairly distinctive methods in dealing with its holdings.

HISTORICAL SOCIETIES

Before 1800, the only historical society existing in the United States was the Massachusetts Historical Society, founded on

January 24, 1791, "to collect, preserve and communicate the materials for a complete history of this country." [3]

During the first half of the nineteenth century, a number of important historical societies arose, so that, by 1861, sixty-five of them were found in the settled parts of the nation. The first among such societies were the New-York Historical Society (1804) and the American Antiquarian Society (1812), which were followed, in a few decades, by a score of important state societies.

After the Civil War, the social, economic, and educational conditions that accounted for the great increase in library holdings, which led in turn to the development of the library profession, also stimulated professional historical activities. The centenary of American independence provided the catalyst that set these activities in motion. In 1884 historians founded the American Historical Association, an organization that, from its very beginning, concerned itself with the preservation and use of historical sources. In 1886, at one of their first meetings, historians discussed the neglect and destruction of historical material in the United States [4] and adopted resolutions pertaining to its "better preservation." [5] In their meeting a year later they established a committee to explore federal assistance "in collecting, preserving, and calendaring historical manuscripts." [6] About a decade later, in 1895, they created a Historical Manuscripts Commission, which focused attention on the need of preserving manuscripts in private hands. These activities fostered the growth of historical societies, so that by 1905 the number of such societies had risen to 223; [7] by 1944, to 1,464; [8] and by 1957, to over 1,800. [9]

Historical societies of the last century occupied themselves with collecting and preserving "antiquities," a term often used to refer to their acquisitions. In their early collecting they emphasized personal papers of historical figures and single documents that had historical significance. After antiquarians, bibliophiles, and historians began collecting manuscripts, the societies occasionally received artificial collections brought together from various sources, consisting of documents relating to a historical period, event, person, or some other matter. Their holdings included books, pamphlets, newspapers, and curios of all kinds, as well as historical manuscripts. Their collecting practices were sharply criticized by Worthington C. Ford (1858–1941), editor and librarian, who played an important role in manuscript work both in the Library of Congress and in the Massachusetts Historical Society. Ford charged that the opportunities to acquire valuable documents were often neglected by collectors, who never seemed "to have a prescience of what the writing of history would demand," and who considered "a bird, stuffed by an amateur . . . as good an accession as an old pamphlet, the file of a newspaper or an armful of old sermons." [10]

Curators in the early historical societies thus dealt with library and museum, as well as manuscript, material, and the methods they evolved were a compound of those of the librarian, museum curator, and manuscript curator. They devised their methods empirically, not on the basis of professional or technical knowledge, for such knowledge had not yet been developed.

ARCHIVAL INSTITUTIONS

Most archival institutions in the United States arose in the twentieth century, and their development is largely attributable to the activities of the American Historical Association.

One of the first matters to occupy the attention of the association was the establishment of a national archival institution. During its meeting in 1893, held in conjunction with the World's Historical Congress during the Columbian Exposition in Chicago, a committee was appointed to memorialize Congress about such an institution.[11] This committee was confronted with one of the basic questions in the management of documentary material in a nation: should a national archival institution concern itself with private as well as public records? It could consider the nature of such an institution solely on the basis of merit, for there were then no federal agencies that had a vested interest in either private or public records. The Library of Congress did not become an important repository of the former until the first decade of the next century, and the National Archives of the latter until the fourth decade.

Herbert B. Adams (1850–1901), then president of the American Historical Association, thought that a "Bureau in the State Depart. conducted under a Com^n of competent men" would adequately meet the needs of historians.[12] William F. Poole vehemently opposed Adams' rather narrow point of view, insisting that

there is one thing we do *not* want, and . . . one expression we must avoid, namely: "a Bureau of Archives," which to the average Washington intelligence will mean some little annex or appendix to one of the existing Departments—perhaps the State Department. . . . We want a separate Department like the "British Public Record Office," having a separate building and to be managed by its own officials. . . . The purpose of the Department we need is not simply to preserve and arrange the manuscript material which the Government now possesses . . . but to *collect* documents relating to American history wherever they can be found in the wide world.[13]

Poole's view that a national archival institution should administer both public and private records was shared by two of the committee members: Justin Winsor, then librarian of Harvard University, and James B. Angell (1829–1916), then president of the University of Michigan. Unfortunately, this view did not prevail.

Another matter of major interest to the American Historical Association was the collection and preservation of records, both public and private, in the various states. The association, it will be recalled, established two commissions: the first, in 1895, "to deal with collections of historical material of an essentially personal character, whether in public repositories or in private hands"; and the second, in 1899, "to limit itself to an examination of documentary material of a public or governmental nature, such as is usually classed under the head of archives, public records, or state papers." [14]

The existence of two separate commissions—the Historical Manuscripts Commission on the one hand and the Public Archives Commission on the other—served to emphasize the differences in the methods that should be followed in dealing with historical manuscripts and public records. It thus tended to separate the manuscript curator from the archivist and created a division between the two that does not exist in continental European countries, where archivists are concerned with both private and public records and apply archival principles to the management of both.

The Public Archives Commission was very influential in the archival field. It sponsored annual meetings of archivists at which basic principles and techniques of the archival profession were discussed. It made known the value of public records as research material by promoting the compilation and publication of inventories of state archives and guides to archives of the federal government and of European governments that related to American history. More than any other agency it was instrumental in fostering the establishment of state and federal archival institutions.

State archival institutions developed in various ways. Sometimes they grew out of historical societies or were made part of them. Maryland's historical society was the first to become a repository of state archives. Sometimes they were created to preserve both private and public records of a historical character. Alabama's Department of History and Archives, established in 1901, served as a model for many state archival agencies, and the archival institutions established in the South that were modeled after it usually became repositories of private papers. "The close relationship between archival materials and collections of private, unofficial papers is clearly shown in the dual nature of the contents of these southern repositories, almost without exception," observed Lester J. Cappon while archivist at the University of Virginia Library.[15]

At the present time, archival programs are administered in eighteen states by independent archival agencies or agencies concerned with historical matters, many of which are state historical societies; in eleven states by libraries; and in ten states by other governmental bodies.[16]

State archival institutions usually took different approaches in dealing with private and public records. They organized and described private manuscripts according to the methods of historical societies and public records according to archival principles, especially after these principles became known during discussions of the Public Archives Commission. In recent years their methods have been further complicated by their involvement in the techniques of managing current public records, techniques that are often as different from those of an archivist as are those of a librarian or historian.

LIBRARIES

Librarians began collecting and preserving records rather late in our national history, for they were not especially interested in them until the last decades of the nineteenth century.

During their meeting in Philadelphia, in 1876, they paid little attention to manuscripts, for they were preoccupied with evolving the methods to be applied to publications, with the techniques of classifying, cataloging, and indexing. While they devoted a chapter to manuscripts in their notable report on *Public Libraries in the United States*, produced as a result of their meeting, they stated in it "that most libraries were too young to have collected many manuscripts," that "the largest collections . . . are in the oldest libraries, as might be expected," and that "many libraries do not report any manuscripts." [17]

A decade later, Charles A. Cutter underscored the lack of interest in manuscripts among librarians. While editor of the *Library Journal*, he editorialized about a statement appearing in a German periodical that "manuscripts are the most valuable part of libraries." Hardly anything, observed Cutter in 1886, could "show more clearly the distinction between European and American libraries. Instead of being the most valuable part of American libraries, manuscripts hardly exist in them and, moreover, for their chief purposes manuscripts are not wanted there. Taken as a whole our libraries exist for the instruction of the people, an object which can best be effected by the printed page." [18]

Historical manuscripts became the concern of libraries chiefly because of the activities of collectors and historians. Justin Winsor said that "we may trace the beginning of a general interest in the preservation of our national muniments to the labors and influence of three men—Jared Sparks, Peter Force, and George Bancroft." [19]

Jared Sparks, Massachusetts historian, left his personal correspondence and his historical manuscripts and transcripts to the Harvard University Library. When he became president of Harvard University, he also subjected the university archives to a thorough examination. According to a contemporary account,

He found important and very valuable manuscript papers, which had been in loose parcels, without any methodical distribution or arrangement. . . . He wrote to the families of former Presidents and officers of the College, asking a search for other College documents. Gathering them from all sources, he arranged and classified these precious papers, and, having them disposed and bound in substantial volumes, he provided for them a fire-proof deposit. [20]

Peter Force (1790–1868), historian and editor, brought together a prodigious quantity of manuscripts, newspapers, pamphlets, broadsides, and books, which were purchased by the federal government in 1867 and deposited in the Library of Congress, thus saving "from dispersion one of the most valuable private libraries ever gathered by a single hand," according to a contemporary account. [21] Before the Force collection was received, the library was "wholly destitute of manuscripts," wrote A. R. Spofford, the librarian. It was the first of many notable collections purchased by the federal government, which included the papers and transcripts of Comte de Rochambeau, obtained in 1882; the papers transferred from the Bureau of Rolls and Library of the Department of State early in the twentieth century, including those of George Washington, James Madison, Thomas Jefferson, Alexander Hamilton, and Benjamin Franklin (collected by Henry Stevens); and the records of the Continental Congress. [22]

George Bancroft's (1800–1891) collection of manuscripts and transcripts, which he accumulated for his historical writings, was one of the major early acquisitions of the Manuscript Division of the New York Public Library. It was purchased by the Lenox Library (part of the New York Public) in 1893.

Many other historians and collectors followed the example of Sparks, Force, and Bancroft. Mellen Chamberlain (1821–1900), librarian and historian, who was "an indefatigable searcher of old garrets and out-of-the-way repositories," [23] deposited the Colonial and Revolutionary War papers he had collected with the Boston Public Library. Clarence M. Burton, American lawyer, gave the Detroit Public Library its start in collecting manuscripts.

A number of libraries are, in fact, named after the persons whose donations form the central portion of their manuscript holdings. Among them are the Bancroft Library of the University of California, named after historian Hubert H. Bancroft (1832–1918); the Clements Library of the University of Michigan, named after William L. Clements, American industrialist; the Hoover Library on War, Revolution and Peace at Stanford University, named after the former President of the United States; and the Huntington Library at San Marino, California, named after Henry E. Huntington, American railway executive and financier.

University libraries, like public libraries, started to collect historical manuscripts late in our national history. While a few eastern university libraries, notably those of Harvard, Yale, Princeton, Columbia, and Brown, acquired manuscript material in the nineteenth century, most university libraries did not begin programs of collecting such material until the third and fourth decades of this century. This fact is stressed by Robert B. Downs, American librarian, who wrote that manuscripts "formerly neglected in all except a few institutions, are now in some regions of the country, at least, being pursued even more actively than printed matter." [24] In recent decades the libraries of the universities of California, Chicago, Cornell, Duke, Louisiana State, Michigan, Mississippi, Missouri, Oklahoma, Pennsylvania, Texas, Virginia, and Washington became especially active in collecting manuscript material.

The extent to which libraries have entered the field of manuscript collecting is strikingly revealed in the *Guide to Archives and Manuscripts in the United States*, edited by Philip M.

Hamer for the National Historical Publications Commission.[25]
Among the kinds of repositories listed in the *Guide* are archival
institutions, historical societies, libraries, museums, record centers, and others. Over half of the 1,343 holdings described in the
Guide are listed as library holdings.

The methods of arranging and describing manuscripts that
were evolved in libraries were obviously greatly influenced by
library practices in classifying and cataloging publications, and
these practices, it should be noted, relate mainly to the treatment
of individual items.

Volume of Records

A second factor that influenced the development of archival
methodology was the growth in the volume of records. Librarians, it will be recalled from the preceding chapter, devised new
methods of classifying and cataloging only after they had to deal
with a rapidly increasing volume of publications.

In the first half of the last century, the quantity of documentary material found in various repositories of the United
States was small, though its importance can hardly be measured
by its volume. During the centenary of American independence,
an American librarian observed that this event "is calling attention to the history of one hundred years ago, and no fact connected with that history is more striking than the dearth of
materials from which it could be constructed." [26] At the meeting of librarians held in Philadelphia on that occasion, statistics
were presented on manuscript holdings. While incomplete, they
showed that relatively few manuscripts had been accumulated,
since all repositories combined reported having only 1,361
manuscript volumes and 88,771 manuscript items.[27] Of the 46
repositories that reported their holdings, 11 had more than 1,000
manuscript items, 4 had between 500 and 1,000, 13 between 100
and 500, and 18 less than 100.[28]

In the last decades of the nineteenth century, during which, as
we have noted, historical activity was greatly stimulated by the
American Historical Association, a sharp increase in the manuscript holdings occurred. The Massachusetts Historical Society,

for example, which had accumulated about five hundred manuscript volumes by the outbreak of the Civil War, more than doubled its holdings during the next four decades. At the turn of the century, in 1899, Charles Francis Adams (1835–1915), president of the society, predicted what would happen in regard to documentary material during the next century:

The accumulation of historical matter, it is to be remembered, progresses with ever-increasing rapidity. The word is a strong one, but to me the future is in this respect appalling to contemplate. We are to be bankrupted by our possessions. . . . The progression has been, and is, geometric. At the same rate the accumulation of the twentieth century defies computation in advance,—it will altogether defy any nice classification or exhaustive cataloguing.[29]

By 1908, Waldo Gifford Leland, dean of American archivists, said that "one can not fail to be impressed with the strength and resources of American historical societies," after reviewing reports on their holdings.[30]

But the geometric rise in record volume did not occur until the next decade, during World War I. This increase is best reflected in statistics on the volume of federal records at various periods. From them it is evident that the volume created between the establishment of the federal government and the Civil War was about a hundred thousand cubic feet; between the Civil War and World War I, about a million and a half cubic feet; and between World War I and the economic depression, about three and a half million cubic feet. During the decade of the 1930s, when the government was concerned with the economic depression and with the preparation for another world war, ten million more cubic feet were added. During World War II, production reached the rate of two million cubic feet per year. This rate has been exceeded since then.

The problem of mass—of prodigious quantities of documentary material—is essentially the problem of the twentieth-century archivist. It is a problem that confronts him regardless of the type of institution with which he may be associated, whether a library, a historical society, or an archival institution. It is a problem that has become acute for him only recently, about three decades after a similar problem confronted librarians. Just as librarians, in the last half of the nineteenth century, evolved methods to deal with ever-increasing quantities of publications, so archivists, at the present time, are defining and standardizing the methods that will enable them to deal with the problem of mass.

Character of Records

The third factor that influenced the development of archival methodology relates to the character of the records that are being acquired.

Early American historians were primarily interested in political and diplomatic matters, and, for this reason, early collectors acquired mainly papers of important historical personages of the Colonial and Revolutionary periods of American history. Thus, when Jeremy Belknap (1744–98), New Hampshire clergyman, drew up the original plan for the Massachusetts Historical Society in 1790, he urged members to "collect and communicate" manuscripts that might elucidate "the natural and political history of America from the earliest times to the present day." [31] His emphasis on "political" papers is noteworthy.

As historical interests broadened, new kinds of records were acquired. Instead of being concerned primarily with political and diplomatic matters, historians are now interested also in economic, military, cultural, social, religious, and a whole host of other matters. Every aspect of society is now a fit subject of historical inquiry. And scholars in related disciplines—in the fields of economics, sociology, political science, and demography —are making constantly greater use of primary sources. Manuscript curators, for this reason, are now obtaining records needed for investigations that are more comprehensive and more nearly contemporaneous in their subject matter than those undertaken in the formative years of the historical profession. The Massachusetts Historical Society thus accepted, in 1914, records of the Boston Marine Insurance Company, which, its librarian noted, "represent the acquisition of a new type of records . . . literally business records." [32]

Scholarly inquiry, moreover, has not only become more extended in scope; it has been extended forward in time. The Council of the Massachusetts Historical Society, to illustrate, reported as late as 1912 that its manuscript collections for the Colonial and Revolutionary periods "are very strong," but that "as more modern times are reached the number become smaller in number and importance." [33] Three years later the Council noted that recent accessions "have belonged to a great extent to the 19th century, thus marking the advance of the historical period. . . . As each generation comes forward, its predecessors pass into the realm of history." [34] Historical inquiry, which was initially focused on early historical periods, has gradually been extended forward in time, until now "contemporary history"—a phrase that involves a contradiction of terms—has acquired professional respectability.

Recent private papers often have the organic quality of public records.[35] They relate to activities that are generally much more fully documented that those of early Americans. They are often comprised of series pertaining to specific activities or transactions or consisting of specific record types. And recent records produced by economic, religious, cultural, and social institutions and organizations have an archival character. Since material now being acquired is different from that which was the concern of early repositories, different methods are being applied to its management.

III

DEVELOPMENT OF
ARCHIVAL METHODOLOGY

Archival methods that are of concern to us here are those that are similar to the library methods discussed in Chapter I. They are arrangement and description; arrangement being the archival equivalent of library classification, and description of library cataloging.

Arrangement

Archival arrangement principles and techniques are shown in (1) the practices followed in arranging record items and series, (2) the development of classification schemes, (3) the recognition of the principle of provenance, and (4) physical provisions for maintaining records.

ARRANGEMENT PRACTICES

The practices followed in American repositories in arranging records depended somewhat on the quantity of the material that was dealt with. When the holdings of a repository were small in quantity, custodians were not concerned with classing their collections or groups according to any schematic arrangement; they were occupied mainly with the arrangement of items and series within collections or groups.

In arranging record items, manuscript curators, during the nineteenth century, made chronological arrangement the standard practice. The first major collections received by the Massachusetts Historical Society, for example, were arranged chronologically. They were the papers of Jonathan Trumbull, colonial governor of Connecticut, and of Thomas Hutchinson, colonial governor of Massachusetts. The Hutchinson papers, according to the proceedings of the society, were "arranged, as is the usual practice with miscellaneous masses of papers whose only bond of unity is a common source, with no reference to authorship or subject-matter, but . . . in the chronological order of their dates." [1] Practically all manuscript repositories followed the example of Massachusetts in arranging items chronologically.

Chronological arrangement of items also became the standard practice of collectors and historians in dealing with private papers. Jared Sparks arranged the George Washington papers, which came to him in loose bundles, chronologically.[2] Henry Stevens (1819–86), Vermont bibliophile, arranged the Benjamin Franklin papers, found in a Parisian tailor's shop "loosely bundled up," in a chronological order.[3] Historian Albert Bushnell Hart (1854–1943) rearranged chronologically the papers of Chief Justice Salmon P. Chase, consisting of personal letters and financial records, found in an old safe in Washington, D.C.[4]

Public as well as private records have often been arranged chronologically, without regard to their organic origins. The Spanish and Mexican archives of New Mexico and Texas were arranged in this manner by the Library of Congress,[5] the University of Texas,[6] and the Texas State Library;[7] as were also most federal archives acquired by the Library of Congress under the Congressional Act of February 25, 1903.

In recent years, manuscript curators have arranged items within collections in various ways, as is evident from an analysis of the guides produced by the Historical Records Survey conducted under the direction of the Work Projects Administration of the federal government from January, 1936, to June 30, 1942. This analysis reveals that during that period about two thirds of the repositories arranged items chronologically, and about one third by subject, though a combination of methods was employed in many repositories. The Detroit Public Library, for example, arranged most items in the Burton Historical Collection chronologically, but classified some under a modified Dewey decimal system. The Newberry Library arranged me-

dieval and renaissance items both chronologically and geographically, and Oriental and East Asiatic items geographically.
The Huntington Library arranged deed and court rolls
geographically, historical manuscripts chronologically, and literary manuscripts alphabetically by name of writer. The Kansas
State Historical Society arranged private papers chronologically,
and subject material, which included organizational records and
single documents on historical subjects, by subject. The University of Washington Library arranged letters alphabetically
by name of writer, folders and bundles alphabetically by subject, and manuscript volumes alphabetically by title. The California Historical Society placed manuscript volumes among publications in subject classes, and within classes arranged them
alphabetically by name of author; while it boxed single items,
after arranging them alphabetically by name of person or
subject.

In arranging record series, manuscript curators, during the
nineteenth century, followed various practices. When documents within a collection were few in number, they were placed
in a single series; when voluminous, they were grouped into a
number of series.

Practices in grouping items into series are exemplified by the
actions taken by the Massachusetts Historical Society and the
New York State Library in respect to some of the larger collections they received. The papers of Jonathan Trumbull, colonial
governor of Connecticut between 1769 and 1783, which were
given to the Massachusetts Historical Society by the governor's
son, were arranged into series relating to particular activities,
such as military affairs during the Revolution, the Susquehanna
case, and title to the Pequot country, and into series consisting
of specific record types, such as broadsides and newspapers of
the Revolutionary period and letters.[8] The papers of Governor
D. D. Tompkins, which were acquired by the New York State
Library, were "sorted into three groups: drafts of letters and
papers written, 1792–1825; original letters and papers received,
1797–1846; and accounts and memoranda, 1803–24." [9]

Historians grouped private papers into series in the same way as manuscript curators. They usually kept manuscripts from a given source together, for evidence on their source was important to them in citation and interpretation. In establishing series, they took into account such factors as record type and relation to subject or activity. Their practices are exemplified by the work of the two Bancrofts.

George Bancroft arranged the material he acquired for historical writing according to source and chronologically. His papers, when acquired by the Lenox Library, contained series of transcripts from European archives, arranged according to source; several series of documents from the Committee of Correspondence, the Massachusetts Assembly, and Samuel Adams, including the latter's manuscript biography; and a series of newspaper articles, manuscripts, and original letters bearing on historical subjects.[10]

Hubert H. Bancroft arranged manuscripts chronologically under "proper headings" and had them bound and indexed. On acquiring the papers of Mariano Guadalupe Vallejo, Mexican commander of the northern frontier of California, Bancroft put two or three copyists "to work arranging and indexing the documents preparatory to binding."[11] Vallejo, writing to a friend in 1874, stated that his papers were "placed in chronological order, under their proper headings, in order to facilitate the labors" of scholars.[12]

Practices in grouping public records into series are reflected in the activities of Peter Force, Edwin M. Stanton, and Clarence W. Alvord.

Peter Force was asked by the State Department, in 1834, to arrange the loose papers of George Washington, which consisted mainly of official army returns. Force, according to the Secretary of State, classed the army returns "so as to conform as nearly as possible to the various subjects they embrace, keeping each class distinct, and generally in Chronological Order."[13] The classes or series he established were comprised of appointment papers, resignation papers, oaths of allegiance, regimental returns, and other record types.

Edwin M. Stanton, American statesman, who is known

chiefly for having served as Secretary of War in Lincoln's cabinet, was sent to California, in 1858, as a special federal agent to settle land claims. He organized the Spanish and Mexican archives that had been acquired by the federal government into a number of series: land records for Benicia, Sacramento, San Jose, Los Angeles, and Monterey; royal decrees; official orders and correspondence of the Mexican viceroys; official correspondence of the provincial governors; records and correspondence relating to missions, presidios, and pueblos; civil, military, and ecclesiastical records; miscellaneous records; and valuable correspondence relating to navigators of various nations.[14]

Clarence W. Alvord (1868–1928), American historian, arranged the Kaskaskia records, which are archival in character, in two groups: one for the French and the other for the British administration of Illinois. Within these groups he established series that were comprised of specific record types or that related to specific activities, such as auctions, business papers, certificates, church papers, contracts of marriage, and the like. Within the series he grouped records by chronological periods: 1720–29, 1730–39, and so forth.[15]

CLASSIFICATION SCHEMES

In addition to arranging records in chronological sequence and grouping them into series, manuscript curators and archivists, during the nineteenth century, devised classification schemes for large holdings, such as are found in state archival institutions or in a national manuscript repository. The schemes were of four kinds: subject, chronologic-geographic, administrative, and historical.

The subject scheme of classification was first used by James Barlow Felt (1789–1869), Massachusetts clergyman, antiquarian, and librarian. Felt gained his experience in record work with the Massachusetts Historical Society, which employed him in 1835 "to make a catalogue, alphabetical and systematic" of the material in its library.[16] A short time later he was named Public Record Commissioner by the governor of Massachusetts "to classify and arrange large quantities of State papers which were lying in confusion in the Secretary's office." [17] He spent ten years, from 1836 to 1846, classifying state records. Since many of them related to the pre-Revolutionary period, he established a large class for "Colonial" records, and classed the remaining records under 75 additional topical heads. He bound the records into 242 volumes, which he identified by the topics to which they related. While these volumes were described, at his death, as "a memorial of his wise and patient labor," his activity later became "the cause of much criticism on the part of historical students" who had occasion to use the state archives.[18] Unfortunately, Felt's system of classification was continued by James J. Tracy, the first archivist to be appointed by the state of Massachusetts. Tracy added another 84 volumes to the collection, in which records were classified under the same subject heads used by Felt.

Felt's example was followed in the neighboring states of New Hampshire and Connecticut. In New Hampshire, Richard Bartlett (1792–1837), legislator and Secretary of State, looked with favor on the Massachusetts project of classifying state records by subject and binding them into volumes. He predicted "the universal adoption of this practice," and printed a letter of Jared Sparks supporting his views.[19] In Connecticut, the early General Assembly files, now known as the Connecticut Archives, were given a subject arrangement by Sylvester Judd (1813–53), a clergyman from Northampton, Massachusetts.[20]

Though information on early arrangement practices is incomplete, many state archival institutions doubtless classified public records by subject. Among them were the Maryland Historical Society, which arranged the pre-Revolutionary archives, later transferred to the Maryland Hall of Records, in subject classes.

The classification of public records according to subject matter was critically examined by Arnold J. Van Laer (1869–1955), a professionally trained archivist at the New York State Library. Van Laer, according to Melvil Dewey, brought to his work "a rare combination of linguistic ability, professional training, accuracy and enthusiasm." [21] Van Laer said that, by failing to classify records according to their organic relations, "we find the papers of various legislative and judicial bodies and administrative offices combined in such miscellaneous series as 'Colonial manuscripts,' 'Revolutionary papers,' 'Military papers,' 'Land papers,' 'Accounts,' etc., which fail to reflect the functions and activities of each body or office, hide the gaps in the existing files, and make it difficult to ascertain the nature of the papers that are missing." [22]

The chronologic-geographic scheme of classifying records was evolved, late in the nineteenth century, in the Manuscript Division of the Library of Congress. It is quite likely that Dewey's principles of classification were taken into account in developing this scheme, since it follows his method of classifying publications in the field of history. For historical publications, Dewey established subclasses according to geographical area, and within these subclasses divisions according to chronological period.

The "geographic-chronologic" scheme was devised by Herbert Friedenwald (1870–1944), who was given charge of the manuscripts at the Library of Congress early in 1897, and who thought that "the classification of manuscripts permits of development somewhat on the lines of that of books." [23] The scheme was renamed the "chronologic-geographic" by John C. Fitzpatrick (1876–1940), who joined Friedenwald at the library late in 1897. Fitzpatrick described the scheme at length in his book on managing manuscripts, which appeared in 1913. [24]

According to the Friedenwald-Fitzpatrick scheme, all manuscripts, except the "personal papers of great Americans," were arranged in classes. The most important of the classes, from which the scheme derived its name, related to chronological periods and geographical areas. But the scheme included other classes: topics, such as the Army; persons, such as the Presidents of the United States; record types, such as orderly books, journals, and diaries; and to provide for leftovers, i.e., for items that did not fit into any of the above classes, it included a number of classes of miscellany.

While the chronologic-geographic scheme was applied mainly to artificial collections (acquired from collectors) and

small accessions, its application, in the early years of the Manuscript Division, greatly complicated work with manuscripts. It
led to a dispersion of items within collections among many
classes, so that their source or provenance was almost completely
obscured, as is evident from an analysis of the *Handbook of
Manuscripts in the Library of Congress,* published in 1918.[25]
The analysis reveals that items from the Peter Force collection
were dispersed among 64 collections of personal papers, 18
collections of papers pertaining to various states, 6 collections of
particular record types, such as account books and orderly
books, and 12 other collections established on a topical or other
basis. In the course of their dispersion, their source was often
obscured, for 35 entries in the *Handbook* state that items were
"probably" derived from the Force collection, implying that
their source is uncertain. The chronologic-geographic scheme
represents the extreme opposite of the archival principle by
which records are kept according to their provenance, and led to
the practice of tearing manuscript collections apart—a practice
that has immeasurably retarded the development of an effective
control over the documentary resources of the nation.

The scheme gave a wrong direction to manuscript work not
only in the Library of Congress but elsewhere also, for the practice of grouping manuscripts in chronological and geographical
classes was adopted in a number of manuscript repositories. In
the New York Public Library, Victor H. Paltsits (1867–1952),
in 1914, shortly after he was placed in charge of manuscripts,
introduced a scheme in which "the arrangement is by periods
and geographical." [26] Paltsits' assistant was Wilmer R. Leech,
who had worked in the Manuscript Division of the Library of
Congress for eight years. In the Wisconsin Historical Society,
Milo M. Quaife (1880–1959) devised a new classification
scheme in 1916, which he described as "an alphabetical one
based on geographical considerations." [27] In the New York
State Library, Peter Nelson recommended a scheme in 1916 in
which classes were established for chronological periods. Nelson
thought "a broad classification should be adopted for the manuscripts pertaining to the State of New York: 'Governors

(chronologically arranged), Revolution, War of 1812, Civil War. . . .' " [28]

The chronologic-geographic scheme of arrangment was also applied to state and federal archives. When a Department of Public Records was created in Pennsylvania in 1903, the first archivist examined "the methods adopted for the classification, indexing, and general care of manuscripts" at a number of libraries.[29] Among them was the Library of Congress, where C. H. Lincoln (1869–), who joined the Manuscript Division in 1897, suggested "arranging our papers by periods, viz.: Settlement, Colonial, French and Indian War, Revolution, Constitution, 1790–1800, 1800–1820, etc." [30] In addition to grouping records administratively, the Pennsylvania archivist established classes for counties, for the French and Indian War and the Revolutionary War, subdividing the latter class by military units, and "making in all one hundred and twenty-four divisions and sub-divisions, a large number, but unavoidable." [31]

The chronologic-geographic scheme of classification was also applied to the naval records of World War I that were accumulated by the Office of Naval Records and Library for historical purposes. In 1921 Captain Dudley W. Knox, who was in charge of the office, introduced the scheme after consulting with eminent "archivists" in Washington, including Gaillard Hunt (1862–1924), former head of the Manuscript Division of the Library of Congress, who thought it well adapted to the records involved.[32] In the application of the scheme, records of the Navy Department were placed in area and subject classes without regard to their administrative origins. While it thus destroyed evidence on the provenance of records in official activity, the scheme seemingly had the approval of the historical profession and was abandoned only very recently.

An administrative classification scheme was devised by Benjamin F. Shambaugh (1871–1940), Iowa historian. Shambaugh's scheme, which was proposed to the Iowa Historical, Memorial, and Art Department in 1906, was discussed at several meetings of the American Historical Association's Public Archives Commission.[33] The scheme was later greatly elaborated by Cassius

C. Stiles (1867–1941), Iowa archivist, who reproduced it in a manual on *Public Archives* in 1928.[34] Shambaugh based his scheme on a study of the administrative development of the public agencies in Iowa. He established classes for records of the major administrative bodies of the state government, such as the offices of the governor and the secretary of state. Within these classes he established subdivisions on the basis of record type and subject.

Shambaugh also developed a historical classification scheme, according to which series of certain offices were brought together for the territorial period, the period of the first constitution, and the period of the second constitution. This scheme was probably the basis for the proposal of a "uniform method of classification" made by Dunbar Rowland (1864–1937) to the 1910 International Congress of Archivists and Librarians at Brussels. Rowland deplored the lack of "logical classification," and urged the development of a "scientific system" that would, "in its application everywhere, retain a general likeness and uniformity." [35] According to Rowland, "The object to be attained in the arrangement of all government archives is to classify them in such a manner that the documents will tell the story, in an historical way, of the progress and development of the State and its people from the beginning." [36] Rowland's ideas, to which most historically trained archivists were receptive, influenced the classification of the archives of Mississippi and of a number of other states.

During the first decade of this century, archivists thought classification, by which they meant placing public records in predetermined classes, to be the proper practice, as is evident from a 1907 report on the archival situation in various states.[37] Archivists in Alabama, Kansas, Mississippi, North Carolina, Ohio, Pennsylvania, South Carolina, and Virginia all referred to "classifying" activities.

RECOGNITION OF PRINCIPLE OF PROVENANCE

The principle of provenance, which means that records should be arranged according to their origins in an organic body or an organic activity, was formulated at the French National Archives in the third decade of the nineteenth century and became a guiding principle in arranging public records in Europe. It was first given a theoretical justification in a Dutch manual, entitled *Handleiding voor het Ordenen en Beschrijven van Archieven*, written by S. Muller (1848–1922), J. A. Feith (1858–1913), and R. Fruin (1857–1935), and published, in 1898, under the auspices of the Netherlands Association of Archivists. The principle did not become generally known in the United States until the second decade of the present century, and won recognition only very gradually thereafter.

The transition from classification practices to arrangement by provenance is reflected in opinions about the work of Douglas Brymner (1823–1902), archivist of the Dominion of Canada, expressed in meetings of the American Historical Association. Brymner arranged Canadian public records chronologically and then grouped them by subject.[38] In one of the early meetings of the association, in 1889, William F. Poole lauded Brymner's method, stating that it showed "what scientific order can be brought out of a chaos of state papers by well-directed effort." [39] A few years later Poole twitted the Bureau of Rolls and Library at the State Department about its lack of competency in dealing with historical manuscripts, stating that it had "no archivist who understands their management," and comparing it unfavorably with "the excellent department of archives" in Canada, which was "under the charge of a most competent archivist." [40] In the association's meeting as late as 1911, Brymner's work was lauded as establishing "a broad and solid foundation" for the Dominion archives.[41] But a decade later, after the principle of provenance was generally accepted, a Canadian archivist stated that the Dominion archives "can furnish enough horrible examples" of mismanagement "to satisfy any moralist." [42] In regard to the classification of public archives, he stated that in Canada, as elsewhere, "the value of a natural classification according to the principe de la provenance has been apparent at all points. Its disregard by certain officials prior to the last decade has resulted in several awkward series, in numerous amorphous collections, which now, like income taxes and the poor, can not be disregarded, and are ever with us." [43]

The principle of provenance was first made known in the United States by Arnold J. Van Laer, who, in 1898, became head of the Manuscript Division of the New York State Library. Van Laer was trained as an archivist in the Netherlands, where he became acquainted with Dutch archival theory. He applied the principle of provenance to the state archives, changing the method of arranging archives chronologically, and instead arranging them "by Departments, e.g. Executive, Secretary of State, etc., as the old plan was found to be 'too confining.' " [44]

The principle of provenance came to be understood and recognized by American archivists because its meaning and significance were made known during the annual meetings of the Public Archives Commission, organized by the American Historical Association. At the first meeting of the commission, held in New York City on December 30, 1909, Waldo G. Leland read a paper on "American Archival Problems," in which, so far as is known, the principle of provenance was discussed for the first time before American archivists.[45] Leland became thoroughly familiar with French archival thinking during his extended visits to Europe between 1907 and 1927, during which he was in charge of the Carnegie Institution's historical mission to France. While in Europe, he attended the course on "Service des archives" in the Ecole des Chartes; visited archival institutions in Belgium, the Netherlands, and England; and took part in the International Congress of Archivists and Librarians in Brussels in 1910. In his paper before the Public Archives Commission, Leland urged the adoption of "the principle enunciated by the Dutch, and adhered to in most European archives, the 'herkomstbeginsel,' the 'respect des fonds,' or 'principe de la provenance.' "

Van Laer, who participated with Leland in the International Congress at Brussels, reported on its proceedings at the second meeting of the Public Archives Commission in 1910. He discussed the definition given the principle by S. Muller, one of the three Dutch archivists who produced the first manual on archival administration. He stated that, according to Muller's definition, the principle means

a system of arrangement of public archives whereby every document is traced to the governmental body, administrative office or institution by which it was issued or received and to the files of which it last belonged when these files were still in process of natural accretion. In other words, the principle demands that documents shall be classified, not like books, according to their subject matter, but with reference to the organic relations of the papers, the files of each body or office being kept by themselves.

Van Laer stated that there was "practical unanimity among the archivists of continental Europe" as to the importance of adopting the principle, and that the Congress formally had resolved "that the 'principe de la provenance' be adopted for the arrangement and inventorying of archives, with a view to the logical classification of separate documents as well as in the interest of comprehensive historical study." [46]

The principle was again discussed by Leland at the fourth meeting of the Public Archives Commission, held in 1912. The principle, Leland said, is one "which the historian is occasionally inclined to overlook or even ignore"; he also stated that it is "absolutely essential . . . for the classifier to bear constantly in mind the origin of his archives" and that "only by arranging them so that they reflect the processes by which they came into existence can they be made intelligible." [47] Leland also made known his views on the principle of provenance in two articles. The first one was published in 1912, in the *American Historical Review*, and was later reprinted as a Senate document.[48] The second one was a report of recommendations on the management of state archives, made in 1913, to the Illinois State Building Commission.[49]

The principle of provenance was again discussed at the sixth meeting of the Public Archives Commission by Ethel B. Virtue, archivist of Iowa.[50] While they did not formally adopt it, most archivists recognized that the principle should be followed in arranging public records. Paltsits referred to it as the "only sound principle for the classification of the archives"; [51] Virtue, as "the 'summum bonum' to be desired in the classification of archives"; and Charles M. Andrews (1863–1943), American historian, as the "one principle that should govern all the rest." [52] Its meaning, however, was not fully understood by some archivists, who confused a classification showing the historical development of a state with one showing the organic development of a state's government. Dunbar Rowland's scheme of classifying public records to reflect historical developments, which initially resulted in the adoption of a chronological method of classification, was eventually transformed into "a combination of the subject and chronological systems, with the alphabetical arrangement added." [53]

Manuscript curators generally did not recognize that the principle of provenance was applicable to private papers, though most of them now keep documents from a given source together. They no longer classify them, i.e., disperse items from a given collection among various classes. They have generally abandoned the subject and chronologic-geographic schemes of classification. But they use the term "provenance" to designate the place from which private papers were purchased or otherwise acquired, not their organic origins—even in important repositories such as the Library of Congress, the Clements Library, and the Huntington Library.

The principle of provenance is now being applied to series within manuscript collections as well as to series in archival groups. Series, which are units of records arising from organic activities or transactions, are being kept intact by most archivists and manuscript curators.

PHYSICAL ARRANGEMENTS

Manuscript curators of the United States began their work with documentary material by boxing it, then turned to binding it, and finally reverted to boxing it. In 1791, the year of its founding, the Massachusetts Historical Society adopted a rule "that all manuscripts shall be distinctly marked and numbered, and kept in cases of paper, which shall also be numbered and the contents of each registered." [54] This well-conceived procedure, which corresponds to the best modern archival practice, was soon abandoned for the procedure of binding, which became the standard practice among manuscript curators during the nineteenth century. The Massachusetts Historical Society bound the papers of the colonial governors Hutchinson and Trumbull during the 1820s,[55] and by the end of the century had over a thousand volumes of bound material, plus "great masses of unbound letters and manuscripts." [56] Practically all historical societies, during that period, followed the example of Massachusetts, usually pasting, hinging, or mounting documents in scrapbooks, letter books, or other kinds of volumes. Among the societies were the American Antiquarian Society, the New-York Historical Society, the New York State Library, and the Maryland Historical Society—to name but a few. Certain notable institutions continue binding documents to the present day, among which are the Manuscript Division of the Library of Congress and the Clements Library, though they also use archival containers.

The practice of binding also became general among collectors of historical manuscripts: Jared Sparks,[57] Peter Force,[58] Henry Stevens,[59] Lyman C. Draper; [60] and among historians: George Bancroft[61] and Hubert H. Bancroft.[62] Collectors and historians of a more recent period, such as William L. Clements [63] and Clarence W. Alvord,[64] have continued the practice.

During the last century, manuscript curators dealt with small groups of manuscripts or single documents, received as separate accessions, in various ways, usually binding or packaging them, and sometimes neglecting them altogether. The experience of the Massachusetts Historical Society with such material is typical. After binding an accumulation of loose manuscripts in 1838, the society's librarian reported, twenty years later, that there was a "considerable number of small but very valuable manuscripts, that should either be bound, or placed in cases prepared for them." [65] The new accumulation was bound in 1856, but in another thirty-five years the librarian again found parcels of manuscripts "packed away in closets" in such a manner that many of them had "to be displaced and frequently handled in any search." [66] The staff was unable to gain control over the miscellaneous loose material until it began using archival boxes. In the summer of 1950 it began taking the "precious manuscripts out of the careless old dirty bundles of the past, dusting and sorting them, and replacing them safely on the shelves of the stacks." [67] Within a few years it completed the work of placing "unbound manuscripts in approved archival boxes," save for recently acquired papers. [68]

In the latter part of the last century, librarians gave attention to the development of documentary containers. The Library Bureau, the activities of which we have already noted, designed and made available a pamphlet box, which it described in its catalog of 1890 as follows: "Half of one side doubles back on itself, allowing the most convenient possible consultation of contents without removing from the box. The thickness allows the left hand easily to hold the case with the door and flap open, while the right is free to turn the index leaves and select just what is wanted." [69] This type of box was used, as early as 1903, to house the manuscripts of the Astor Library, which became part of the New York Public Library. [70]

The first box intended specifically for archival use was designed by the Iowa State Library. The design of this, and of other early types of archival containers, is discussed in Chapter XIII.

The practice of boxing became fairly widespread about forty years ago, though even now about one fourth of American manuscript repositories maintain some material in bound form, usually oversize material or material that was bound during its current life.

Description

Archival descriptive techniques have evolved rather slowly in the United States. During the last century, manuscript curators produced mainly descriptions of single documents. The technique of describing aggregations of documents—series and collections—was not employed until the present century, when inventories and guides began to appear.

CATALOGS

The first finding aids prepared in American repositories were catalogs of record items. The development of the cataloging technique is reflected in the activities of the Massachusetts Historical Society. Shortly after it was founded, the society adopted a rule that catalogs should be prepared of the manuscripts as well as of the books and museum objects in its custody. This rule was reaffirmed at various intervals, until 1852, when it was superseded by a bylaw—valid for the rest of the century—which prescribed that "exact and perfect catalogues" of manuscripts, as well as of other materials, were to be kept.[71] Initially the society recorded catalog entries in books, but in 1864 it began using paper slips, and, a few years later, cards.[72]

By 1876 a number of other historical societies had produced manuscript catalogs of their holdings. The Connecticut Historical Society and the American Oriental Society reported having a "manuscript card catalogue"; the Essex Institute, "card and box catalogues in manuscript"; the American Antiquarian Society, "manuscript catalogues, full and complete, of the books, pamphlets, manuscripts, relics and curiosities"; the New-York Historical Society, "a manuscript catalogue raisonné"; and the Southern Historical Society of Richmond, a catalog "partially complete in manuscript." [73]

Printed as well as manuscript catalogs soon made their appearance, pertaining initially to publications as well as to documentary material. The first printed catalogs of manuscripts were prepared by Timothy Alden (1781–1839), Massachusetts clergyman, who in 1811 produced a catalog of the library of the Massachusetts Historical Society in which he listed manuscripts,[74] and in 1813 a catalog of the library of the New-York Historical Society in which he listed "names of documents." [75] A printed catalog of library holdings that provided information on manuscripts was produced in 1840 by the New-York Historical Society, followed, in the next three decades, by the catalogs of the Historical Society of Pennsylvania, the New York State Library, the Maryland Historical Society, the Massachusetts Historical Society, the Baptist Historical Society, and the American Baptist Historical Society.[76]

Eventually printed catalogs pertaining exclusively to manuscripts appeared, the first being that produced by the Regents of the University of the State of New York in 1849.[77]

During the nineteenth century, the techniques of cataloging manuscript items received the attention of a number of eminent Americans, including Justin Winsor, Herbert Friedenwald, and Harry M. Lydenberg (1874–1960). Winsor devised the cataloging rules for the Massachusetts Historical Society in 1888, Friedenwald for the Library of Congress in 1897, and Lydenberg for the New York Public Library in 1899.

Though complete information is not available on his cataloging rules, Winsor suggested that a catalog entry, besides identifying the record item, should briefly indicate its subject matter.[78] Friedenwald said a catalog entry should contain the following information about a document: the name of the collection of which it formed a part; the names of its writer and its recipient; the date and place of its production; its size and number of pages; the language in which it was written, if foreign; the character of the material on which it was written; and its type, indicated by the use of abbreviations such as l.s. or a.l.s.[79] Lydenberg listed "eight items as material for identification" in a catalog entry. A typical entry, he said, should have a "form heading," using the term "form" to refer to its type, i.e., letter, diary, etc. The heading should be followed by information on the document pertaining to its author; place and date of production; recipient; contents; authenticity, indicated by the use of abbreviations such as a.l.s. or a.d.s.; and size, shown by giving the number of pages and using the marks of $8°$, $4°$, $f°$.[80]

In recent years, rules for cataloging manuscript items were formulated and published by curators at a number of repositories, notably those at the Manuscript Division of the Library of Congress, the Minnesota Historical Society, the Clements Library, the Detroit Public Library, the Houghton Library of

Harvard University, the Harvard School of Business Administration, and the Cornell University Library.[81]

During the twentieth century, catalogs of individual record items became the standard type of finding aid for manuscripts. While such catalogs were seldom completed, especially in repositories that acquired large quantities of new material, a prodigious number of catalog cards were prepared. The extent of their preparation is reflected in the following statistics derived from the guides produced by the WPA Historical Records Survey:

William L. Clements Library	85,000
Chicago Historical Society	350,000
Detroit Public Library (Burton Collection)	77,000
Duke University Library	40,000
Henry E. Huntington Library	60,000
New York State Library	80,000
North Carolina Historical Commission	80,000
Historical Society of Pennsylvania	182,000
West Virginia University Library	588,000

Even some of the small repositories produced a large number of cards, as witness the following statistics:

Arkansas Historical Commission	20,000
University of Oklahoma (Phillips Collection)	45,000
Oklahoma Historical Society	45,200
Oregon Historical Society	55,000

After the holdings of manuscript repositories became sizable, catalogs were prepared of collections and accessions, as well as of single record items. By the fourth decade of this century, a number of the better-known repositories had produced fairly complete catalogs of such record units, as is evident from an analysis of the WPA Historical Records Survey guides.[82]

CALENDARS

Another type of finding aid that related to single documents, which was prepared extensively by manuscript curators, was the calendar. The calendaring technique originated in England, and probably grew out of the registry practices of English government offices. In such offices, documents are brought together into file units that are registered, i.e., identified by date, by the name of the person initiating a transaction, and by a brief statement on the content of the transaction. The calendaring technique, according to which a brief statement is provided on the content of documents, is essentially similar to the practice of registering current records.

As early as 1825, English archivists began compiling calendars of records in the State Paper Office. In 1838, when the Public Record Office was established, Francis Palgrave (1788–1861), the first Deputy Keeper, began a program of systematically calendaring records as they were identified, sorted, classified, and listed by his staff. From 1841 to 1855 his calendars were printed in appendixes to his annual reports; after 1855 they were issued in a separate series.

The Public Record Office calendars of the colonial series of state papers, compiled over a thirty-year period by W. Noel Sainsbury (1825–95), are of especial interest to American historians. For their production, Sainsbury "has earned a grateful acknowledgement from all students of early American history," said Robert C. Winthrop (1809–94), while president of the Massachusetts Historical Society, for they "inform us not only what is to be found in those venerable British archives, but what is not to be found there, and thus save a world of pains in searching for things which have no existence or no records." [83] As early as 1860, Sainsbury petitioned the United States government to continue the colonial series of calendars, so far as they related to America.[84]

The first calendars prepared in the United States were, in fact, calendars of state papers. Between 1865 and 1868 the New York Secretary of State's office prepared calendars of the Colonial and Revolutionary War records of the state.[85] Between 1875 and 1895 the Virginia state government prepared a *Calendar of Virginia State Papers*.[86] Its title, however, is a misnomer, for it reproduced the full text of documents, and the documents it included constituted "an unsystematized mass of heterogeneous and often worthless items," according to historian Ulrich B. Phillips (1877–1934).[87]

Maryland's historical society was the first to prepare calendars, which it produced after it became custodian of the state archives. In 1883 and 1884 it published calendars of the proceedings and acts of the Maryland General Assembly in the *Archives of Maryland*.[88]

In the federal government, the Bureau of Rolls and Library of the State Department began calendaring its historical manuscripts in 1886. The work was done by Walter Manton and, according to an official estimate, was "prosecuted with an intelligent industry and devotion that runs no risk of being overestimated." [89]

During the next few decades, the papers of a number of important historical figures were calendared. Included among them were the papers of Thomas Jefferson, James Madison, and James Monroe, which were calendared by the State Department before they were transferred to the Library of Congress; the papers of Benjamin Franklin collected by Henry Stevens, certain George Washington papers, and the papers of Franklin Pierce and Martin Van Buren, which were calendared by the Library of Congress; the papers of Benjamin Franklin and certain Revolutionary War officers, by the American Philosophical Society; the papers of Jared Sparks, by Harvard University; and the papers of Sir William Johnson and George Clinton, by the New York State Library.

The calendaring technique has received considerable attention. In 1909 Worthington C. Ford discussed it before the Bibliographical Society of America,[90] and Waldo G. Leland before the Public Archives Commission. Leland thought calendars should be prepared only for important classes of documents, a view that was generally accepted by manuscript curators. In 1921 an Anglo-American Historical Committee formulated rules for calendaring.[91] Late in the 1930s the WPA Historical Records Survey issued instructions for calendaring and sponsored the production of calendars by unemployed persons during the economic depression.[92] The most recent instructions on calendaring are those of Morris L. Radoff, which appeared in the *American Archivist*.[93]

In the United States, the first record indexes that were prepared are found in bound volumes of documentary material. The first institution to prepare them was the Massachusetts Historical Society. In 1822 the society began the practice of indexing the contents of its bound volumes.[94] The first major collections it acquired were thus indexed after they were bound.[95] The Trumbull volumes were "carefully indexed . . . to render them useful to future historians."[96] The rules of the society, adopted in 1849, provided that manuscripts should be "properly arranged, bound, and indexed; and all the indexes of the manuscript volumes of the Society shall be condensed so far as practicable into one."[97]

During the last century, the Massachusetts Historical Society's practice of binding and indexing was followed in most other repositories. In the New York State Library, according to a report on its practices, a "large portion of the manuscripts . . . has been paged and indexed, the latter 'hinged in' at the end of each volume."[98] The Sir William Johnson papers, the first important collection acquired by the library, were bound in 1850, later indexed and calendared, and finally published.[99] Lyman C. Draper (1815–91) assiduously collected material on border heroes and pioneers, which he bound and indexed and later deposited with the Wisconsin Historical Society. In 1851 he wrote that he had "spent the past year in arranging manuscripts for binding into vol—paging & indexing—& the care & minuteness with which I have done it, has made it laborious work."[100]

Modern methods of indexing, as of cataloging, began with the use of cards. While indexes were prepared on cards in France as early as 1775, cards were not used for indexing purposes in the United States until a hundred years later.[101] In the Massachusetts Historical Society, paper slips were used for cataloging, and presumably also for indexing, as early as 1864; cards, like those used during the present day, were introduced in 1878. In 1888 the society used cards to prepare a very extensive index to the papers of Timothy Pickering. The index, which was later published in the society's *Collections*, consists of two parts, one listing subjects and the other names. The subject index gives an abstract of every letter, referring to every important subject in it. The name index, it was thought, would be very "useful to genealogists and biographers." [102]

In the 1880s a number of indexing societies, modeled after those of England, were formed in the United States. These greatly stimulated the production of indexes, as is apparent from a letter to the editor of the Boston *Herald* of February 9, 1883, in which the writer states that recent meetings of librarians and the recent formation of indexing societies "have naturally directed attention to serious defects in our modes of indexing the public records." [103]

In recent years much indexing has been done, especially of genealogical records.

In state archival institutions, probate, land, military service, and court records and vital statistics (information on births, deaths, and marriages) are the most important genealogical series and have often been indexed for genealogical, as well as official, uses. The Maryland Hall of Records has completed indexes to practically all series in its custody that are important for genealogical research. In the Illinois State Archives, the consolidated index to names appearing in state records before 1850, produced under the supervision of Margaret C. Norton, contains over a million references, chiefly to census records.[104] In the Connecticut State Library, a very extensive index was prepared to names appearing in probate records; in the North Carolina Historical Commission and the Mississippi Department of Archives and History, to names appearing in Confederate military records; in the Tennessee State Library, to names appearing on payrolls and muster rolls of the War of 1812 and the Mexican, Seminole, and Cherokee wars; in West Virginia University, to names appearing in county court records; [105] and in the Department of Archives of Louisiana State University, to names appearing in its collections of private papers.[106]

In the National Archives, the indexes that are available were prepared by other government agencies and private genealogists.

INVENTORIES

Inventories of state and local archives were first prepared in the United States under the sponsorship of the Public Archives Commission.[107] Shortly after its establishment, in December, 1899, the commission sent a circular to state officials asking for information on (1) the number of volumes or parcels to be found in various classes of public records, such as committee reports, land office papers, and the like, (2) the "chief contents of miscellaneous collections," and (3) the contents of records, other than purely formal ones, that "appear to have especial historical value."[108] Some of the foremost historians and archivists of the period cooperated in the survey, and the inventories they compiled were published in the *Annual Reports* of the American Historical Association between 1900 and 1917.[109]

The Public Archives Commission also sponsored an inventory of the published archives of the original thirteen states, prepared by Adelaide R. Hasse (1868–1953).[110]

The first inventory of federal archives was made in 1904, by Waldo G. Leland and Claude H. Van Tyne (1869–1930), under the auspices of the Department of Historical Research of the Carnegie Institution.[111]

The technique of preparing inventories was often discussed during the annual meetings of the Public Archives Commission between 1909 and 1919. At the first meeting, in 1909, Waldo G. Leland recommended the French method of describing records in progressively greater detail in a succession of inventories. He discussed three types of finding aids: the first consisting of a mere enumeration of the titles of series, identified in relation to the boxes, volumes, or bundles in which they are contained; the second consisting of a more detailed account of the more important series, in which each volume or box is given brief descriptive notice; and the third consisting of calendars of important classes of documents.[112] In the sixth meeting, held in 1914, Leland named the three types of finding aids he recommended as checklists (*états sommaires*), descriptive catalogs (*inventaires analytiques*), and calendars.[113]

The technique of preparing record inventories was first given extended consideration during the Work Projects Administration's record surveys. Its Historical Records Survey originated in the recommendations of the Committee on Historical Source Materials of the American Historical Association.[114] The WPA "Manual of the Survey of Federal Archives," prepared by the author in 1936, contains instructions on the preparation of inventories of state and local archives.[115] This manual was the model for the one prepared, about a year later, for the WPA Historical Records Survey, which relates to inventories of manuscript collections.[116]

Early in its history the National Archives also established a program of preparing inventories of records that were transferred to its custody. A committee, appointed in 1940 to study the question of preparing finding aids, recommended the preparation of preliminary checklists, preliminary inventories, and final inventories.[117] While its recommendations were officially approved a year later, instructions on the preparation of finding aids were not issued until a decade later, when a circular on the "Preparation of Preliminary Inventories," written by the author, appeared.

In recent years the Manuscript Division of the Library of Congress also began an inventory program. Its procedure, according to Andrew H. Horn, "was frankly borrowed by the Library of Congress from the National Archives" and "was a contribution of the archivist toward the solution of one of the most frustrating problems that had confronted the librarian," i.e., the problem of dealing with large masses of material being produced in the "typewriter age." [118] The procedure for preparing inventories, called registers at the Library of Congress, was devised by Katharine E. Brand.[119] The new technique, according to Dan Lacy, will "provide a far more effective, as well as less expensive, control over the collections." [120]

GUIDES

The first guides in which manuscript collections were listed were prepared by Reuben G. Thwaites (1853–1913) for the Wisconsin Historical Society in 1906 and by Frank H. Severance (1856–1931) for the Buffalo Historical Society in 1910.[121] Thwaites was much interested in descriptive techniques and, in 1891, visited England, where, to quote his own words, he "devoted much time to the libraries and museums—chiefly in the line of technical management." [122] He described his guide, which he called a "descriptive list," as a compromise between calendars and indexes, and he hoped that it "will much lighten the burden of search by giving the student a general survey of our manuscript possession, thereby leading him fairly close to the documents needed in his special work." [123] The first guide to public records was prepared, in 1914, by Dunbar Rowland, and was entitled *Official Guide to the Historical Materials in the Mississippi Department of Archives and History.*

During meetings of the Public Archives Commission, American archivists often stressed the need of producing guides. In 1909 Leland said that "first of all is necessary a general guide to the entire body of archives," which should be followed by more detailed finding aids.[124] This view was supported by Victor Hugo Paltsits, New York archivist and historian, who said that "from the public's point of view, the guide is the first publication that should arrest the attention of the archivist." [125]

Many guides were published in the United States as an outgrowth of the activities of the WPA Historical Records Survey, which issued the only instructions heretofore available on their preparation.[126] Among the more noteworthy guides are those of the historical societies of Minnesota, New York, North Carolina, Pennsylvania, and Wisconsin, and of the universities of North Carolina and Louisiana and Duke University.

Among the important guides that have been issued in recent

years are the comprehensive guide to the holdings of the National Archives; the guides pertaining to special subjects, such as the Civil War, World War II, and Latin America, prepared by the National Archives; the nationwide guide to archives and manuscripts prepared by the National Historical Publications Commission; and the nationwide guide, compiled from entries in its union catalog of manuscript collections, prepared by the Library of Congress.

COOPERATIVE FINDING AID PROJECTS

Cooperative finding aid projects were proposed by manuscript curators, as well as by librarians, during the nineteenth century. The first proposal to create a union catalog of manuscripts was made by Thomas C. Amory, Jr. (1812–99), while librarian of the Massachusetts Historical Society. In 1865, shortly after modern cataloging methods were introduced in the society, Amory stressed the importance of producing "an index or calendar to the large collections of manuscripts" existing in various repositories.[127] The next year he sponsored a motion in the meeting of the society, ordering "that a printed circular be sent to different literary and historical associations, and also to individuals, to request the titles and character of manuscript collections in their possession, with a view of completing a catalogue of the same for the use of historical students." [128]

Many proposals of cooperative projects to produce finding aids were made during meetings of the American Historical Association. Justin Winsor urged the association to call on Congress, in 1887, to institute a system of control on a nationwide basis, in dealing with "what there is still left to use of the historical manuscripts of the country, not in places easily accessible to the student." [129] In 1904 one of the association's committees discussed methods by which state and local history societies should cooperatively produce finding aids. The chief method considered was that proposed by the Wisconsin Historical Society, which involved preparing lists of manuscript collections in repositories in the Mississippi Valley, publishing the lists, and compiling a common index to them.[130] In 1938 the association's

Committee on Historical Source Materials proposed that "a comprehensive guide" to manuscript collections should be compiled from information produced by the WPA Historical Records Survey and available in published sources.[131] This proposal was amplified, a few years later, by Herbert A. Kellar (1887–1955), who was then chairman of the committee. In 1945 Kellar proposed that a national union catalog of manuscript collections should be compiled, and a few years later he submitted detailed plans and procedures for its compilation.[132]

The union catalog project, which is now being administered by the Library of Congress, had its immediate origins in a proposal made by Dan Lacy before the Society of American Archivists. Lacy, who was an employee of the Library of Congress, suggested, in September, 1951, that a national register of manuscript collections should be established; that rules should be formulated for cataloging manuscript collections; that entries on collections, compiled according to the rules, should be prepared by repositories throughout the nation; that catalog cards, produced from copy submitted by the repositories, should be embodied in a national register, or catalog; and that reproductions of the cards should be sold.[133] The cataloging rules were developed by the Library of Congress between 1952 and 1954, and a union catalog of manuscript collections is now being produced. This enterprise marks the high point in cooperative effort in the manuscript field.

In summary, then, the methodology of the archival profession is a compound of the ideas of librarians, historians, and archivists.

The librarians' contributions were the techniques of their own profession, i.e., classification and cataloging. Since they dealt with books, they often bound documents into books. Since they classified publications in relation to subjects, they often arranged documentary material in subject classes, regardless of its origin or organic relations. Since they usually cataloged discrete published items, they often cataloged single manuscript items— individual documents and individual volumes of documents.

Most cataloging rules now being applied to records, including the recent rules of the Library of Congress, arose out of practices followed in cataloging publications.

The historians' contributions to the archival profession were promotional, as well as technical, in character. Historians, more than any other professional class, sponsored the establishment of organizations to preserve and make available for use the historical material of the nation. But they were not primarily concerned with the management of such material, unless actually placed in charge of it. They generally recommended the adoption of methods that facilitated historical use, and for such use they needed to know both the source of records and the subjects to which they pertained. They therefore generally treated records from a given source as an integral group, but within the group they often organized documents into subject classes. They favored chronological arrangement of items within groups and classes. They strongly endorsed, though they did not originate, the calendaring technique by which the contents of individual documents are summarized—a technique that literally constitutes a system of comprehensive note-taking.

The archivists' contributions to their own methodology were the methods of arranging and describing records collectively that are reflected in the arrangement principles formulated and in the descriptive techniques devised.

IV

DEVELOPMENT OF THE
ARCHIVAL PROFESSION

The methodological developments that we have reviewed in the last three chapters show the difference between the status of the library profession on the one hand and that of the archival profession on the other.

The library profession, in the United States at least, has developed into a precise and well-defined discipline. Its techniques of classifying, cataloging, and indexing, which were evolved during the nineteenth century, are systematized and standardized.

The archival profession, in contrast, is in a formative stage. Most of its procedures are still evolving and have not been clearly defined. And very little has been done to standardize the procedures that have been developed, for they vary from repository to repository.

While the archival principle of provenance is generally recognized as valid, its actual meaning is often misunderstood, and it is not fully applied. Even federal records have been classified for archival purposes according to the Dewey decimal system with the tacit approval of the National Archives, and state records are still occasionally arranged topically. And private manuscripts are arranged in various ways. While manuscripts from a given source are generally kept together, this is not always the case. Groups of manuscripts that reflect organic activity are still being merged into chronological series.

Descriptive techniques, too, are so ill-defined that many manuscript curators are unable to provide information about their holdings; programs designed to bring together such information on a nation- or statewide basis have foundered, in the past at least, for lack of knowledge of how to go about describing records. In spite of all the finding aid work, neither the location nor the character of the research resources of the nation have been made known completely to scholars; nor has such work shown what records there are in particular repositories.

The techniques that have been given the most attention are those that relate to the description of individual documents, i.e., cataloging and calendaring techniques. While rules for cataloging manuscripts have been formulated by a number of manuscript curators, they have not been standardized, as were library rules for cataloging publications before the end of the nineteenth century. And while manuscript curators have calendared and cataloged with conspicuous zeal and display of energy, many calendars and catalogs either should not have been produced at all or should have been produced only after comprehensive finding aids to the holdings of repositories were available.

The techniques of collective description, of covering aggregations of documents in single descriptive entries, are not understood fully, and those that have been developed are not accepted or applied generally; yet such techniques must be employed if voluminous modern records are to be described successfully. While the methods of describing series of public records have been defined fairly precisely, those applicable to series of private papers have been given relatively little attention. If series of private papers are described at all, it is in various ways and in various types of documents—registers, inventories, summaries, sketches, data sheets, and others. The methods of describing manuscript collections, too, have been given very little attention. Instructions on how to produce guides to such collections are inadequate, and rules for cataloging them have been formulated in reference to publications and fail to elicit information on the most meaningful record attributes.

There are serious obstacles to the development of a methodology that will be acceptable for the management of all kinds of documentary material. They stem mainly from the way such material was accumulated in the United States. It was accumulated, as we have seen, by all kinds of agencies—historical societies, libraries, and archival institutions. In these agencies it was administered by all kinds of persons—manuscript curators, historians, librarians, archivists, and even museum curators and record managers. These facts account for the great diversity of method that is now found in American documentary repositories. This diversity creates an obstacle that will not be easy to overcome. The distinction that is made between the methods of handling private and public records has deep-seated historical roots. It is likely that archival methods will be considered inapplicable to private records for a very long time. And it is further likely that library methods of cataloging, which have been applied to records for very many years, will survive any criticism that is made of them.

A good program of arrangement and description involves a conscious, methodical application of the best principles and techniques of placing records in order and of making known their content and significance. It thus implies a professional knowledge of principles and techniques. And this knowledge is often lacking. It is not conveniently available in the existing literature of the archival profession. Nor is it being taught in archival training courses.

Under the circumstances, is it possible to develop the archival profession to the degree that the library profession has been developed?

There are two things that must be done to develop the archival profession—the same two things that were essential in the development of the library profession. The first is to define the principles and techniques of the archival profession; the second is to standardize them. For a profession, in the proper sense of the term, is the application of systematized or classified knowledge of principles and techniques to some field of activity. Contributions to the systematization of techniques can be made individually, but their standardization must be effected collaboratively. The definition of techniques should come before their standardization.

Definition of Methods

There are several propositions that should be taken into account in defining the methods of the archival profession, to wit:

Archival principles and techniques that have been developed in the past should be thoroughly and comprehensively analyzed. Archivists have seldom been able to give the same careful consideration to the methods of arranging and describing records that librarians, during the nineteenth century, gave to the methods of classifying and cataloging publications. They were usually preoccupied with rendering service on their holdings. In order to deal with day-to-day situations, they often improvised procedures, and once having adopted them they seldom questioned or revised them. At the present time, many of them are unable to explain why things are done in certain ways, and their reasons for doing them in certain ways are rarely more than *ex post facto* excuses—supports and justifications for methods rather than critical examinations of them.

Practically no training, as we have noted, has been available to archivists to help them develop their methodology. And, unfortunately, the methodological training that has been applied to the development of archival procedures has often been training of the wrong kind—training in dealing with secondary rather than primary material, with books rather than with records; or training in dealing with records that are maintained for current use rather than for research use.

It is obviously desirable to reexamine the methods of arranging and describing documentary material now followed in the United States. These methods should be subjected to the test of free and critical discussion, for the literature on them that now exists is quite inadequate and throws light on but few of the problems that are encountered in archival work. And this light is often dispersed through the lenses of distorted vision.

If they reexamine their present methods, archivists are likely to explain how certain practices arose and what they actually are and, while doing so, are likely to discover ways of improving and clarifying them. For archivists should have the professional probity to investigate new concepts and ideas and, if necessary, to correct past mistakes of method and principle.

The principles and techniques of the archival profession should be constructed out of those that have been evolved at different places and times. These must be brought together, evaluated, and presented in methodical order. Archival principles and rules will provide a reliable guide to practice whenever they are educed from a thorough examination of past and present methods and whenever they are developed with regard for the nature of the material to which they apply. Such principles and rules should contain the distillation of the good sense of the profession about how to do things. Their value depends on their intrinsic excellence and on the efficiency that results from their application.

Archival principles and techniques should be applied to private as well as to public records, though a distinction is often made between work with the two classes of material. This distinction stems, in part, from the establishment, early in the life of the American Historical Association, of the Public Archives Commission, which concerned itself exclusively with federal and state archives, and the Historical Manuscripts Commission, which concerned itself exclusively with personal papers. The existence of separate commissions for public and private records tended to underscore the proposition that different methods should be applied to the two classes of material.

It may be questioned, however, whether this proposition is valid. In what respects are private records actually different from public records, and in what respects are they similar? Are their similarities more important than their differences? In what ways should one deal with them differently? In what ways similarly?

Most recent private records have the organic quality of public records and are therefore archival in character. This is the case with all records produced by corporate bodies, such as businesses, churches, and schools, and all records produced by persons in relation to extended activities. Only small groups of personal papers, and artificial collections brought together from a large number of sources, lack organic characteristics.

Even when they lack such characteristics, private records have all the other qualities of public records. They are primary material, just as public records are, and therefore have the qualities of primary material that are quite distinctive from those of secondary material. They consist of the same types as public records: letters, reports, and the like. They are physically similar to public records. They are far more like public records than they are like publications.

In the development of archival principles and techniques, the nature of records should be taken into account. Records are primary material. They should be distinguished from the secondary publications—books, pamphlets, and periodicals—produced from them. Records contain basic information on the political, social, and economic development of a nation. From them the social scientist obtains facts needed to understand how things of the present came about. They are a means of transmitting the cultural heritage of the past, for they contain the ideas and principles upon which governments are based, the explanation of man's intricate social and economic organization, and the evidence of his material and intellectual growth.

Records are organic material. They are the product of activity, of purposive action. This is true of all records produced by governmental and corporate bodies, and by persons who engaged in extended professional, business, or other kinds of work.

Records fall into three broad classes—pictorial, cartographic, and textual. The pictorial class includes motion pictures and still pictures; the cartographic class, maps and charts; and the textual class, public and private papers.

Records are of many physical types—letters, reports, and forms of all kinds. The types vary in the different classes of records. They are both general and specific in nature.

Records are of varied composition. They may be either loose or bound. They may be brought together into file units of various kinds—folders, dossiers, envelopes, and others. And the file units may be brought together under filing systems of various kinds—alphabetical, numerical, subject, and others.

Records are of various sizes.

They are maintained during their current life in various ways —in filing cases, in letter or pamphlet boxes, in bundles or various kinds of packages, or on shelves.

And they come to a documentary repository in various ways —as single items, as small groups of items, as organized files, or, what is commonest, as disarranged masses of material.

The techniques that are applicable to publications are not applicable, without modification, to records. Though records may occasionally be in published form, they differ from publications, when in their antecedent form, in several important respects.

Records are more complex, from a physical point of view, than are publications. They are more varied in their physical makeup, for they may consist of files arranged according to various systems, or file units of various types. They are more varied in their physical classes and types. They are more varied in size and composition.

Records lack the attributes publications acquire in the course of their manufacture. They usually cannot be identified precisely by author, title, and imprint (place and date of publication), and their subject matter cannot be described from information readily obtainable from a title, table of contents, index, and the like. If the concept of title is applied, it is usually in terms of a devised title, derived from an analysis of their record type and their content.

Records have a collective rather than a unitary significance. All records arising from a particular activity have a cohesive character and are part of one another. They have a meaning as a group rather than as single items. They lose their significance if they are dealt with as single items rather than as collective units. Publications, on the other hand, have a meaning that is not dependent on their relation to other items. Each publication stands alone.

Records are primarily significant in relation to activity, and only secondarily in relation to subject. The opposite is true of publications. Records are created and accumulated to accomplish certain functions, activities, or transactions. If they deal with subjects, it is because the subjects are the object of action. Their subject content is acquired only incidentally to accomplishing an action. This may be illustrated by showing how a government agency deals with records. It does not create and accumulate records in regard to the subject field that is its concern; it does this in regard to activities that relate to the subject field. The Forest Service of the federal government, to illustrate, does not methodically embody in its files records pertaining to all phases of forestry; instead, it places in them only records that relate to its activities. While government offices may occasionally accumulate reference or information files on some subject of special interest to them, such files, taken as a whole, are insignificant as sources of information and often consist merely of printed or processed material that is available in libraries.

Records have a more limited subject-matter range than do publications. Since they relate primarily to subjects that are the object of action, records do not completely cover any field of knowledge; and, in their entirety, they do not cover any but a small segment of all fields of knowledge. All archives of the federal government of the United States, however impressive from the point of view of quantity, pertain only to a limited number of the subjects listed in any library classification scheme. All manuscript collections in the United States combined, I am sure, do not cover the various fields of knowledge as completely as do the contents of a small library.

Records are heterogeneous in content; publications, homogeneous. A single document may relate to diverse matters. Aggregations of documents, such as series, groups, and collections, invariably relate to many matters. A publication, on the other hand, is designed to present organized information about a particular subject or, at most, a few subjects.

Records are unique; publications usually exist in multiple copies. The content of one record repository, for this reason, varies almost completely from that of another; but the content of various libraries is approximately alike.

Records are used differently from publications. They are used less extensively than publications in the sense that fewer persons use them; and more intensively than publications in the sense that the few persons who use them do so for a longer period. They are the source material used in producing publications, which represent the finished product. They are like raw material that must be refined by research.

Archival principles and techniques should be applied to records that are deposited in libraries. Librarians will not find this easy to do, for the differences between archival and library methods are difficult to bridge.

Librarians are accustomed to dealing with discrete items. Their methodology of classification and cataloging relates primarily to the treatment of such items. The extent of their preoccupation with such items becomes apparent when they are required to deal with collective units, such as are found in records of organic bodies.

While archivists may occasionally be concerned with single record items, their units of treatment when dealing with organic records are usually collective ones. An archival unit may consist of all records produced by a particular organism or resulting from a particular activity of an organism. A unit may thus be an archival group or a manuscript collection, or a series within a group or collection.

Librarians, moreover, are accustomed to classifying and cataloging publications by subject; archivists, on the other hand, arrange and describe records organically. Librarians and archivists thus take basically different approaches in dealing with their respective materials.

In order to manage records in their custody properly, librarians must literally change their thinking about methodology. They must learn to deal with collective units that have an organic significance. If they do not do so, they are likely to persist in applying unsuitable techniques to material. Once they recognize and understand the basic differences between the methods of dealing with publications and records, librarians can not only effectively manage documentary material but can also teach courses on its management in their schools. There are several reasons why they should do the latter.

Library schools are the proper places in which to provide archival training, for they reach the most important class of record custodians, i.e., the librarians themselves. Existing archival training courses have influenced only a very small proportion of the librarians of this country, and the training provided in them has usually been too discursive and too theoretical to be meaningful.

Library schools are concerned with methodology. Their curricula include courses on the methods of classifying and cataloging publications; there is no reason why they should not include courses on the methods of arranging and describing records. Such courses should be introduced in a limited number of strategically located schools. They should include, initially, an introductory course, followed by an advanced course that includes laboratory work with records as well as lectures. Many existing library courses are useful to archivists, particularly those relating to reference tools, reference service, and government documents. But courses in library classification and cataloging do not provide proper training for arranging and describing records. "Training in library science," observed Bertha E. Josephson, "is not adequate preparation for historical society work except in the limited capacity of book cataloging; museum objects, archives, manuscripts, and maps offer problems which no Dewey or Cutter could answer to satisfaction." [1] In addition to absorbing the methodological training received in library schools, an archivist should be well grounded in history and should, for the more important positions in his field, hold an advanced degree in the social sciences.

Library schools are the only place in which attention is likely to be given to methodological training. Historians are concerned to a limited degree with method, and then primarily as it relates to the interpretation of historical documentation. Manuscript curators do not provide formal training in the methods of dealing with private records. And, until now, archival training has been largely theoretical rather than practical in nature and has dealt with procedures in a most general way. Some archivists, indeed, object to methodological training of any kind, an objection that stems from the erroneous and presumptuous notion that a neophyte can learn more "by doing," under supervision, than "by studying" archival method. They regard the process of training as one of intellectual osmosis; in their case information will presumably be absorbed from a source that is scornful of it.

There is, however, another important and more intangible reason why library schools should provide archival training. Through the years, librarians have developed an attitude of service to the public of unstintingly making available the material in their custody. In regard to their holdings, they emphasize use, not possession. In their profession they emphasize cooperation, not competition. Their views, if inculcated in training courses, will greatly benefit the archival profession. They will promote cooperative effort in the development of archival methodology, as well as the cooperative use of material in the possession of documentary repositories.

Archival techniques can be defined more precisely than those of the historical profession, but not as precisely as those of the library profession. Historians and librarians, as well as other professional groups, can speak of their work as being professional only when they recognize and follow certain principles and techniques.

The more any given line of work is concerned with the manipulation of physical things as distinct from a concern with purely intellectual matters, the more it is necessary to follow precise methods of doing things. The reverse of this statement is also true. The more purely intellectual an activity, the less it is possible to impose on it anything more than general principles of action.

An archivist's work is more analytical and less technical in character than that of the librarian. Archival material must be analyzed from a substantive point of view to a greater degree than library material, but it cannot be analyzed as precisely from a physical point of view. Consequently, the archivist's methods are less precise than are those of the librarian, for methods relating to technical work can be defined far more precisely than those relating to analytical work. While the procedures of describing various record units can be made fairly precise, they can never become as precise as library cataloging procedures, for the reason that records lack the attributes, which publications acquire in the course of their manufacture, in relation to which precise cataloging rules can be formulated.

An archivist's work is less analytical in character than that of the historian. While arranging and describing records, an archivist admittedly must do a great deal of analytical work, but this relates mainly to finding out how records came into being. It is in the nature of historical work, but it is historical inquiry directed to finding out the source of documents, not their meaning. An archivist's historical inquiries, moreover, are merely incidental to the performance of a physical task. He learns about the origins of records in order to arrange and describe them.

Archival methodology can be defined more clearly than the methodology of the historical profession. The historical profession is concerned with the use of documentary material, not with its physical handling as is the archival profession. One speaks of historical work as being professional because of the principles followed in the interpretation of source material, not because of the techniques employed in accumulating information from it, though these techniques, admittedly, are also important.

Archival techniques should be differentiated from the techniques of managing current records. The distinctions between archival and record management activities are basic, not artificial. Record management activities, taken as a whole, are quite as different from archival techniques as are those of a librarian or museum curator. Techniques relating to file room management, to the design and control of forms, and to the development of an issuance system are completely dissimilar from archival techniques. Even when they relate to activities that parallel those of an archival institution, record management techniques are different, or have a different emphasis. For example, in the field of arrangement, the activity of classifying and filing current records differs fundamentally from the arrangement of archives; and in the descriptive field, the finding media produced for current records differ fundamentally from archival descriptive media. In the field of disposition, the emphasis in respect to current records is on destruction; in respect to archives, on selection and preservation.

While they may work with the same kind of material, archivists and records officers follow quite different techniques and objectives. An archivist must give careful analytical attention to records while arranging, describing, servicing, and disposing of them; a record officer, when concerned with their disposition, must deal with records rapidly and in quantity in order to achieve the economy and efficiency by which he can justify his work. An archivist may, of course, concern himself with the management of current records, especially in a small archival program, just as he may concern himself with the management of books and museum objects. He may, in fact, find a greater interest among agency officials, and greater remuneration, in the record management program than in the archival program. But if he is engaged in both kinds of programs, he should not subordinate one to the other, and he should not apply the techniques of one to the other. The techniques of a record center should not be applied in arranging and describing archives, for if such techniques are employed the quality of archival work will deteriorate.

The future strength of the archival profession lies in collaboration among all persons engaged in preserving and making available records for research use to the public as well as to the government. It does not matter with what kind of organization such persons are identified—whether an archival institution, a record center, a library, or a manuscript repository. What matters is their objective in working with such records and the methodology they employ to achieve their objective.

The use of modern gadgetry cannot supplant the use of

proper techniques and principles. Short cuts to the control of historical source material can be found in mechanical, photographic, or electronic devices only after the material has been organized and interpreted by conventional methods.

Archival principles and techniques should be developed with one basic objective in mind, i.e., to make the archivist more effective in servicing his material. Methodology has a value only if it is useful in making documentary material available. An archivist should not become so engrossed with it that he will lose sight of the end of his activities. Methodology becomes restrictive and stifling of initiative only when it is made an end in itself and is overdeveloped.

Standardization of Methods

While it is perhaps premature to write about the standardization of methods before such methods have been properly defined, their standardization is as important a matter as is their definition. Standardization implies general or, at least, widespread acceptance. Acceptance can come about if procedures that have been evolved are reviewed, refined, and revised through the medium of a professional organization, or if they are introduced in professional training courses. The archival training that has hitherto been available, however, has hardly had a perceptible effect in standardizing methodology in either state archival institutions or historical societies.

There are several objections to a standardization of archival procedures, some of which are valid and others not. A practical objection may be raised against modifying existing procedures to make them conform to standards, particularly if they are reasonably satisfactory. No one will seriously advocate a modification under such circumstances.

More hampering than the practical objections, however, are the personal objections. Some arise from an innate resistance to change, for change always brings with it an intellectual wrench. Some objections arise from a pride of authorship of particular techniques, for archivists, following natural human tendencies, are reluctant to disown procedures they have conceived, no matter how faulty they may be. But objections to standardization are mainly attributable to the mistaken belief among certain archivists that their work is primarily of a scholarly rather than a technical nature, and who for this reason regard techniques either as unimportant or in the nature of a restraint that will stifle scholarly initiative.

To be professional, archival work must be disciplined. In few fields of activity has more nonsense been perpetrated by amateurs, i.e., by enthusiasts who are unwilling to submit to professional discipline, than in the archival field. There can be no profession so long as there is no discipline. To argue at this juncture for complete freedom of action in the archival field is to argue against the development of the archival profession. It is to argue for thoughtless improvisation, for faulty adaptation of the methods of other professions, and, generally, for inefficiency in the management of the research resources of this country. The danger at this stage of the development of archival methodology is not overstandardization but no standardization at all.

Archival terminology should be standardized. The present confusion of terms is simply the outward expression of an inward confusion of methods. Archival terms should be fully understood and consistently used. Specifically, the terms relating to record units, record types, and finding aids need to be defined immediately.

While it is perhaps impossible to achieve a common usage of archival terms because of the belief of some archivists that discipline detracts from their professional independence, it is nonetheless important for the archival profession, as it was for the library profession, to define its terms and to apply them consistently. Unless archivists of a country collaboratively evolve a terminology through the instrumentality of their professional society, there is no other course to follow than that suggested by Hilary Jenkinson (1892–1961), the late English archivist. He observed, while discussing terminology, that "there are now so many of us engaged upon the task of conserving archives—not to mention research in them—that in the general interest it is no longer possible to let everyone make his own rules and follow

his own fancy even in so comparatively small a matter as this." [2]
It is therefore not so much an evidence of presumptuousness as it
is of good sense on his part that he suggests that his terms be
accepted, since he has defined them.

*Archival arrangement principles should be generally under-
stood and should be interpreted in a uniform manner.* Not only
should the principle of provenance be recognized as valid, but
the extent of its application should be fully comprehended. It
should be the guiding principle in arranging federal and state
public records; it should be extended in breadth in the sense that
it should be applied to private as well as to public records; it
should be extended in depth in the sense that it should be applied
to series within manuscript collections and archival groups; and
it should be applied in the description as well as in the arrangement of private and public records.

*Archival descriptive techniques should be standardized to the
fullest extent possible.* They can be standardized readily in respect to mechanical things, such as the order in which descriptive attributes are enumerated in title lines and in descriptive
paragraphs in various types of finding aids; the information provided in descriptive entries on record types and record volume;
and the format of finding aids, e.g., card sizes for indexes and
catalogs, and the form of guides. These mechanical things do not
involve basic questions about descriptive techniques, such as
whether records should be described in relation to subject or to
organic or functional origins.

Curtis W. Garrison, formerly of the Manuscript Division of
the Library of Congress, observed that "possibly it would be a
mistake to try" to reduce the description of manuscript collections "to a technique," but that "some general principles could
be standardized, such as use of terms 'papers,' 'correspondence,'
and others; the biographical data; the elimination of meaningless
continuities which make English sentences but hamper thought;
the proper way of enumerating statistics; the amount of analysis
as opposed to general description; the method of handling dates
and names of writers represented in the collection." [3]

Benefits

A correct methodology, in the first place, *will improve the efficiency of an archivist in arrangement and descriptive work.* Since they are the product of organic bodies and organic activities, modern records can be arranged and described by collective units. By dealing with such units rather than with single items, an archivist can gain control over his holdings that has often been lacking in American respositories. He can produce comprehensive finding aids that will make his records immediately accessible, and specialized finding aids that will make his records fully accessible to the persons likely to use them. If he has a mastery of the methods of arrangement and description, he can adopt those methods that will best enable him to accomplish the objective of preserving and making available the resources entrusted to his care.

A correct methodology, in the second place, *will prevent wasted motion in arrangement and descriptive work.* By employing faulty methods, an archivist will fail to bring the material in his custody under control. While engaged in ineffective work, he will be diverted from constructive work.

Thus, while arranging records, he may involve himself in such unproductive activities as classifying records by subject, or breaking up existing series, or rearranging items within series that are already arranged. In such work he may not only waste his time but actually impair or destroy the value that attaches to his records because of their organic character.

Similarly, while describing records, he may dissipate his energies on attempts to catalog every record item in his holdings, or to show, on a comprehensive basis, the specific subjects to which his holdings relate. If he concentrates his attention on the description of single items, he is likely to fall short of providing research workers with the quality of reference service that is possible if proper procedures are followed. His prepossession with single items, which he may painstakingly catalog or calendar, may result in his repository becoming choked with masses of undigested material to which he has been unable to give any attention.

A correct methodology, in the third place, *will enable an archivist to contribute to a control of the total documentary resources of the nation.* Archivists as a group are the custodians of the primary research material in a country. This material is huge in quantity and highly complicated in nature and, therefore, very difficult to describe and to make available for use. It is, moreover, often widely dispersed even when it has a similar provenance or relates to similar matters. It can be fully and efficiently exploited only if it is properly managed by its custodians. The work archivists do provides a key to it.

This material must be described on a nationwide basis. A description of material in any particular repository is not the exclusive business of the archivists of that repository. It is also the concern of other archivists, for archivists as a whole should be concerned with making the records of a nation available on a cooperative basis.

Repeated efforts have been made to provide comprehensive information on all documentary resources of the United States. Until recently, all of them have foundered for two reasons: one being the lack of descriptive information in various manuscript repositories, and the other, the lack of a standard or generally accepted method of describing records. Both reasons are attributable to methodological inadequacies.

Repositories must first describe their own material before they can make information in regard to it available for a union catalog, and they must describe it according to standardized procedures. The importance of this was recognized by Thomas C. Amory, Jr., librarian of the Massachusetts Historical Society, when he first proposed the production of a union catalog in 1865. Amory believed that his "Society can better take the initiative in requesting the co-operation of similar institutions and individuals in the preparation of a general index to all the manuscript treasures of an historical character in the country" [4] once it had produced a catalog of its own holdings.

A correct methodology will enable archivists to achieve a control not only over the manuscripts in their own repositories but in repositories collectively that is far more intensive than that possible under existing procedures and with far less effort than that now expended in descriptive work. If manuscript collections were identified, as suggested in this book, so as to show their relation to particular geographical areas, broad subject fields, and chronological periods, it would be possible, by means of modern mechanical and electronic devices, to find out, at a moment's notice, which of them relate to fairly specific matters, such as military affairs in Virginia between 1800 and 1830, provided, of course, that the collections were analyzed in relation to the chronological period mentioned; in relation to place, by states; and in relation to subjects, by military affairs. Such a threefold analysis of relationships by place, subject, and time would enable a searcher to learn from descriptive entries in catalogs and guides which of the collections thus identified are germane to his investigation. Once they have defined and standardized their descriptive techniques, archivists will be able to carry out cooperative cataloging projects successfully, just as librarians carried out such projects after they had developed their rules and techniques of cataloging.

In conclusion, then, I wish to answer the question that I put at the beginning: Can the work of the archivist be developed into a profession that is as distinctive, as well defined in its methodology, as that of the librarian? While archival methods of arranging and describing cannot be defined as precisely as library methods of classifying and cataloging, the work of the archivist can be developed into a distinct profession. The principles and methods that govern his work can be made much more precise than they now are, and they can, and will, be standardized. For the reverse of Gresham's law applies to methodology: good principles and techniques will replace the bad and will gain general currency.

V

NATURE OF ARCHIVAL ARRANGEMENT

When applied to documentary material, the term "arrangement" pertains to all activities that must be performed to place records in order in the stacks of a repository. These activities are both intellectual and physical in nature.

The intellectual activities consist largely of analyzing the type, provenance, functional origins, and contents of records. They are difficult and complex in nature to the degree that the records involved are remote in origin, complicated in their administrative structure, or in a disarranged condition.

The physical activities consist largely of packing (or inserting) records in containers or bundling them, labeling the containers or bundles, and depositing them in the stacks. Often the physical work in handling recent records is so onerous that archival arrangement seems to be little more than backbreaking work.

Objectives of Arrangement

Records in a repository should not resemble goods on the shelves of a country store, without order and without control of any kind excepting that in the mind of the storekeeper. They should be arranged so that they can be found and properly described.

Usually records come to a repository in many small accessions. They are generally the leavings of a person or corporate body or government agency that are made available for research use after they have ceased to have a current interest, often after a long period of neglect. Such records, coming from many different sources and often in a disarranged condition, must all be arranged and described. Not only must the components of accessions be placed in order, but the accessions themselves must be placed in the stacks according to plan. If records are not properly arranged, they cannot be found readily, or at all, when needed.

By the way he arranges them, an archivist determines how records may be described. If he arranges them in one way, he can only describe them as discrete items; if he arranges them in another way, he is able to describe them collectively by aggregations of items.

Thus, if he arranges records according to their provenance in particular organic bodies, he is able to describe them in relation to the bodies that created them. He may describe each archival group and each manuscript collection by describing the government agency, corporate body, or person that created it. Information on organizational origins is as important in respect to records as is information on authorship in respect to publications.

Or if he establishes series within an archival group or manuscript collection, an archivist is able to describe records in relation to organic activities or transactions. If they are the product of activity, records have a meaning that is derived from their relation to activity, and they must therefore be grouped by activity in order to be meaningful. There is no information that is more revealing of the content and significance of records than that relating to their functional origins. This information is as important in respect to records as is information on subject matter in respect to publications.

Arrangement thus is largely a process of grouping individual documents into meaningful units and of grouping such units in a meaningful relation to one another. An archivist, continually and instinctively, must bring order and relation to unrelated things by sorting and categorizing—to the end of revealing the content and significance of the records with which he works. He must give meaning to them in order to make them known to others.

The order he is able to impose on his holdings and the finding aids he is able to produce determine his success as an archivist.

Relation to Classification

The nature of archival arrangement can be clarified best by contrasting it with library classification. A librarian is able to classify a publication because it is a discrete physical entity. A thing is classifiable whenever it can be dealt with separately—a point stressed by Thelma Eaton when she said that "a thing as a substance for classification is whatever has separate existence." [1] A librarian classifies a publication by determining the subject class or subclass to which it should be assigned, marking it with symbols to denote its place in the class or subclass, and shelving it.

An archivist should not classify records, whether public or private in origin, in the way publications are classified. The material he deals with does not lend itself to classification. The largest documentary units an archivist handles are either archival groups or manuscript collections, or accessions to such groups or collections. Because they are so large and cumbersome, such units cannot be inserted on shelves, as can books, in such a way that their placement will make apparent their relation to subject. More importantly, such units are discrete neither in a physical nor a substantive sense. They are unitary neither in their physical type, for they may consist of letters, reports, or other record types; nor in their subject matter, for they may relate to various subjects, geographical areas, and chronological periods. Therefore they cannot be grouped into subject, place, or time classes. Their multiple relations can be shown more easily and more usefully in descriptive documents than by their physical placement. This simple fact is important. If it had always been taken into account in the management of manuscript collections, a great deal of useless work would have been avoided, much more information than is now available would be extant, and the evidential value of collections that had an organic character would have been preserved. The problem is not one of classifying such units, for they are ordinarily few in number and for this reason the order in which they are placed in the stacks has little bearing on subject or other relationships.

Nor can units within archival groups and manuscript collections—series and items within series—be classified as are publications. "A *corpus* of manuscript papers, being something more than the sum of its parts, is not susceptible to regimented arrangement without loss of character," observes Lester J. Cappon, director of the Institute of Early American History and Culture.[2] The process of arranging such a corpus, whether public or private in origin, is one of grouping it into units that reflect organic activity. It is a process of identifying or establishing series. For records should be arranged, says Waldo G. Leland, so as to "make clear the processes by which they have come into existence," for they "are the product and record of the performance of its functions by an organic body, and they should faithfully reflect the workings of that organism."[3]

The process of arranging items, too, is not one of classification in the library sense of the term. An archivist should not place items into subject classes or subclasses, for "the average manuscript, unlike the average book, has an individuality that defies neat classification schemes ready for use and adaptable to most libraries of printed works," observes Cappon.[4]

Library classification schemes—such as the Dewey, the Cutter, and the Library of Congress—should not be used for the organization of documentary material. Such schemes are universal in scope in the sense that they cover all human knowledge, as does the Dewey system, or in the sense that they cover publications so numerous that they encompass all human knowledge, as does the Library of Congress scheme. Most classes and subclasses of such schemes are inapplicable to records. Their major classes may, in exceptional circumstances, be used to classify manuscript collections in large repositories; but the subclasses within such schemes, if used, will serve only to complicate the work of an archivist. This fact was emphasized by Van Laer and Leland, in meetings of the Public Archives Commission. While discussing the principle of provenance, Van Laer said that "the principle demands that documents shall be classified, not like books, according to their subject matter, but with reference to the organic relations of the papers, the files of each body or office being kept by themselves." [5] Leland said that "nothing is more disastrous than the application of modern library methods of classification." [6]

The chronologic-geographic scheme, discussed in a previous chapter, should also not be used in the arrangement of documentary material. While chronological and geographical divisions may occasionally exist, most manuscript groups cross chronological and geographical dividing lines to such an extent that these divisions are almost useless as units of classification. Considerations of time and place, in fact, have very little classificatory value when applied to records.

An administrative classification scheme, such as the Iowa scheme discussed earlier, also embodies a wrong approach to the organization of documentary material. Since it was based on a thorough analysis of the organizational structure of the state government, the Iowa scheme is basically sound in respect to its main classes, which were established for the records of the offices of the governor, secretary of state, auditor, and other major organizational units. The main classes in the scheme were subdivided into series. Thus, records of the governor's office were classified into thirteen main series, as follows: commissions, correspondence, elections, extraditions, legislation, petitions, proclamations, reports, vouchers, bonds, executive journals, criminal records, and miscellaneous. The series were further subdivided into subseries. The correspondence of the governor's office, for example, was subdivided into bound and unbound documents, the latter being classified under the following subjects: affairs outside the state, appointments, charities, commissions, counties and towns, etc.

The Iowa scheme suggests some of the problems in developing an organic classification scheme for archives. To what extent should classes be preestablished for archives? Should they be preestablished only for records of major organizational units, such as the offices of the governor, secretary of state, and auditor in the Iowa scheme? Or also for records of subdivisions within major organizational units, such as divisions and branches in a federal bureau? Or should they be preestablished also in relation to record types, such as the commissions, correspondence, reports, etc., in the Iowa scheme?

The question here is how fine a classification scheme should be. It is a question that librarians discussed at length, and often quite heatedly, when the Dewey and other library schemes of classification were evolved. The two types of classification librarians considered were: broad classification, in which publications are simply placed in broad classes, such as history, science, etc.; and close classification, in which publications are placed in specific subject or other kinds of classes. It is important for archivists to know how far they should go in preestablishing classes into which their material should be grouped.

Ordinarily, an archivist should preestablish classes only for records of major organizational units within government agencies or corporate bodies. The exact nature of these classes is discussed in Chapter X.

An archivist should not predesignate classes for series in a classification scheme. Even if based on a thorough analysis of the structure and functioning of an organic body, a scheme cannot be devised that will anticipate all the record series that may exist. Series should be identified or established as records are analyzed, and should normally be placed in the stacks in the order in which they are isolated.

An archivist should not preestablish classes on the basis of factors other than provenance. Whenever such factors—time, place, or subject—are taken into account in establishing classes, records are likely to be arranged in violation of the basic archival principle of provenance.

An archivist, in a word, should not attempt to develop a classification system at all. He should simply establish large units or groups among the material with which he works and arrange such units in the order of their establishment; and he should arrange series and items within series in an order that reflects their provenance and reveals their significance.

Essential Steps

An archivist should analyze the structure and functions of the body that produced the records with which he is working. He must know how records came into being. If he is dealing with the records of an organic body, such as a government agency, he must learn about its structure and functions; if with the records of a person, about his life and activities.

The older records are, the more difficult it is to find out about their origins. Ancient and medieval documents can be interpreted properly only by applying the knowledge gained from the study of the auxiliary sciences of history. If an archivist is dealing with a medieval document, for example, he may discover its source by analyzing its style, which may require a knowledge of medieval modes of writing (paleography and diplomatics) and seals (sphragistics or sigillography), or by analyzing its content, which may require a knowledge of medieval languages (linguistics), place names (toponymics), dates (chronology), etc.

While a modern archivist is concerned predominantly with modern documents produced since the eighteenth century, his problem is essentially the same as that of a medievalist. He must find out how groups or collections produced in modern times arose—what sort of body produced them, and what sort of activities were performed by the body. He has available more information about the provenance of his records than has the medievalist, and his search for information is not so complicated.

If an archivist is dealing with records of a government agency, his analysis of their origins will lead him to a search into the authorizations for its existence, the responsibilities assigned to it, and its functional and structural developments. "The administrative entity must be the starting point and the unit," according to Leland, "and the classifier must have a thorough knowledge of the history and functions of the office whose records he is arranging; he must know what relation the office has borne to other offices, and the relation of each function to every other function." [7] In respect to records of the federal government of the United States, information on such matters is generally available in published form, often conveniently arranged in organizational manuals, agency histories, or agency accomplishment reports. Similar information often exists for state governments.

If an archivist is dealing with records of a private body—personal or corporate—information on its history is a bit more elusive. The *Dictionary of American Biography*, and similar dictionaries, will help him identify persons of national significance; compilations relating to the various states, such as *The Handbook of Texas*,[8] supply information on persons of state significance.

An archivist should also analyze a body of records as a whole, before proceeding to arrange any of its parts. European archivists have been wont to compare the procedures of an archivist in arranging records with those of a paleontologist in arranging the bones of a prehistoric vertebrate. A paleontologist analyzes each bone and fits it, on the basis of his knowledge of its structure and of the functions it served, into its proper place in a skeleton. An archivist proceeds in a somewhat similar manner. He generally deals with skeletal remains of a number of organic bodies. He fits together individual documents and series on the basis of his knowledge of the structure and functioning of the body that produced them.

To understand an archival group or a manuscript collection, an archivist should analyze it carefully in order to know its organization and to distinguish its constituent elements. He should obtain a general knowledge of its meaning or essential nature and its structure before proceeding to deal with its parts. Arrangement, in a word, should proceed from an understanding of the whole group or collection; it should not be started on a piecemeal basis. This fact has been ably stressed by Ellen Jackson: [9]

It is worse than useless—it is extremely dangerous—to try to arrange any portion of a collection without a considerable familiarity with the whole. Even if the papers appear to be completely disordered, breaking up an old file may destroy a clue vital to the nature and original condition of the whole collection. The librarian or assistant who is to handle it can do no better at the start of work than to sit down and begin exploring like an archeologist digging into a prehistoric rubbish heap, not looking for anything in particular, but alert for whatever significant items may meet his eye, always aware that the arrangement of materials may be as significant as the materials themselves.

Whenever feasible, an archivist should identify or establish series within an archival group or manuscript collection. All classification or arrangement work involves a breakdown of a whole into its parts. In the physical sciences a biological specimen is dissected in order to classify it, and a compound chemical substance is separated into its constituents in order to identify it. The very process of analysis is one of separating anything, whether an object of the senses or of the intellect, into its parts. By this process it is possible to distinguish each of the parts separately and to understand their relation to one another and to the whole.

Once he has a general knowledge of a group or collection, an archivist should separate it into its parts so they can be placed in proper relation to one another. If a large group or collection is properly broken down into its constituent parts, it can be described easily and intelligibly. If the constituent parts are identified and properly described, the meaning or essential nature of the group or collection as a whole is elucidated and can be made known to potential users. By the establishment of smaller units within the collection or group in which searching must be done, searches are localized and need not cover an entire group or collection.

When dealing with a large body of material, an archivist should first plan the arrangement of records on paper before proceeding to the physical task of placing them in order and packing and shelving them. He should first number (with crayon or pencil) the containers in which records came to a repository, regardless of their type. He should then analyze the content of the containers, one by one, and prepare notes on each of them, preferably on 5 x 8 paper sheets. On each sheet he should identify the series, or segments of series, found in a particular container, noting carefully how much of a series is found in it. Such sheets should be keyed to the numbers assigned to containers.

After he has analyzed the contents of all containers, he should sort his sheets by series, so that all sheets for each series are together. He may then determine the order in which the original containers should be unpacked and their contents arranged.[10]

In arranging his material, an archivist should follow principles of arrangement that are generally recognized as valid in his profession. These principles will be discussed in the next chapter.

PRINCIPLES OF ARCHIVAL ARRANGEMENT

There are two basic principles of archival arrangement that have been developed through decades of experience. The first, which is known as the principle of provenance, is that records should be kept according to their source. The second, which is known as the principle of original order, is that records should be kept in the order originally imposed on them.

Provenance

The principle of provenance, a European contribution to the American archival profession, stems from the French principle of *respect des fonds*, which provides that records from similar types of institutions should be grouped into *fonds*. The French principle was made more precise and restrictive in application by Prussian archivists, who formulated the *Provenienzprinzip*, the equivalent of the modern principle of provenance. The Prussian principle, which was later embodied in a Dutch manual on archival management, provides that public records should be grouped according to their origin in public administrative bodies. Archivists of the United States obtained their knowledge of the principle from its French and Dutch versions.

The principle of provenance means that records should be arranged so as to show their source in an organic body or an organic activity. It relates to two kinds of record units: archival groups and series.

REASONS FOR APPLICATION

If an archivist follows the principle of provenance, he will do things with records that, on the surface at least, seem to run counter to what his users want him to do, i.e., to arrange and describe records in relation to subject. Historians, as a class of users, almost always want him to arrange and describe records in this manner. If an archivist arranges records by subjects in which historians are particularly interested, they will reward him with their commendations, but he, by doing so, is likely to fall short of making documentary material fully accessible for historical research.

An archivist cannot arrange records by both their source and their subject. He must arrange them either organically or in accordance with some classification scheme. He must choose one of the two methods of arrangement; he cannot follow both.

His job is neither to "systematize" records—to classify them according to a classification scheme—nor to place them in a "rational" order, if by rational order is meant an arrangement by subject. For a "rational" order of this sort is actually irrational; it obscures the rationale of the records, i.e., the reasons why they came into being.

While an archivist should arrange records according to their source, this does not mean that he should fail to make known their relation to subjects, geographical areas, or chronological periods. He should make this relation known in finding aids, not by a physical manipulation of records.

Since his application of the principle of provenance will lead to his work being questioned by those who do not understand it, an archivist should completely understand why the principle of provenance must be followed. He should not accept it simply because it is generally recognized as valid in his profession. He should accept it for the following reasons.

The principle serves to protect the value of evidence in archives. Private papers usually contain expressions of personal views and opinions about events, persons, places, and the like. And human beings cannot express the exact truth about matters, except in cases so exceptionally rare that they only prove the rule. But if, when performing some action, they record information, and are unaware of its historical importance, then such information is more likely to be impersonal and impartial. For this reason, archives—documents created for purposes of action —are further removed from personal bias and are more accurate than are private papers.

The peculiar value of evidence in archives has been stressed for many years. As early as 1632, Baldassare Bonifacio, recognizing this value in his essay *De Archivis*, wrote, "So great is the respect for archives that credence is obviously to be given to instruments produced from a public archives, and they make, as the jurisconsults say, 'full faith.' " [1]

The late English archivist Hilary Jenkinson also stresses the "evidential value" of public records, which, he says, have a quality that is derived from the way they came into being, a quality that makes their evidence on matters to which they pertain unusually valuable.[2] In commenting on Jenkinson's views, Ian Maclean, the Chief Archives Officer of the Commonwealth of Australia, observes that "the archivist's whole methodology is based on the sanctity of his Archives as evidence. Being records of transactions of which they themselves formed a part, Archives are, in a particular sense, authentic and impartial." [3]

The "evidential value" of records—using the term in the Jenkinsonian sense of its meaning—is derived, in part at least, from the way they were arranged when they were created. They were brought together, originally, in relation to activities that resulted in their production. If they are torn apart and rearranged under a subjective or other arbitrary system of arrangement, much of the evidence on their source is obscured or lost. The content of individual documents that are the product of activity can be fully understood only in context with other documents that relate to the same activity. The way they were brought together is therefore significant. According to Jenkinson, "They have . . . a structure, an articulation and a natural relationship between parts, which are essential to their significance. . . . Archive quality only survives unimpaired so long as their natural form and relationship are maintained." [4]

Jenkinson's observation applies also to private papers that have an organic character. A collection of manuscripts, says Lester J. Cappon, is more than "the sum of its parts," [5] so that the mathematical formula "the whole is equal to the sum of its parts," known to every schoolboy, does not apply. The added meaning a manuscript collection has is derived from the arrangement of its parts, the context in which they were kept, and the way in which, generally, the collection was organized during its creation.

The principle correctly takes into account the nature of the material to which it is applied. Records, for the most part, are primary material having an organic origin. Publications, for the most part, are secondary material having a cultural origin. Records are usually produced to accomplish some purpose, some activity; they are not produced, as are publications, to elucidate some subject. While records may pertain to subjects, they ordinarily do so only to the extent that such subjects are the object of action.

Whenever records are brought together originally in relation to action, they should not be rearranged in relation to subject. A subject arrangement is alien to their nature. If they are rearranged by subject, an entirely different order is imposed on them than the one given them in the course of current use.

Before the formulation of the principle of provenance, records were often rearranged in relation to subject. This involved archivists in very complicated, difficult, and often frustrating work, for records cannot easily be organized into subject classes. Such classes cannot be established until a thorough analysis has been made of the records to be reorganized. The classes vary from one record group to another. If classes are established in a faulty manner, records are given a faulty arrangement. And even if they are established very carefully, it is not likely that subject heads will be found in relation to which all records can be classified. Some records will fit equally well into any one of several classes, or will not fit into any particular class.

When archivists adopted the principle of provenance, they stopped the procedure of arranging records according to subject. The principle supplanted a method of arrangement de-

signed for publications, which can be identified by subject, by a
method designed for records, which can be identified by their
organic relations. It thus replaced a completely impractical
method by a practical one.

*The principle enables an archivist to deal with records collec-
tively.* It enables him to treat records from a given organic
source or a given organic activity as a unit; to deal with groups
and series instead of single record items or single record volumes.
For this reason, the principle is as basic to the archival profession
in dealing with large bodies of documentary material as is
Dewey's decimal classification system in dealing with expanding
library holdings. Both the principle of provenance and Dewey's
system provide methods that can be applied to ever-increasing
quantities of material: the former because it applies to collective
record units, and the latter because its classes and subclasses may
be expanded indefinitely.

The principle facilitates the arrangement of records. If the
principle is observed, organic records will be arranged by groups
and series that can be identified on the basis of an analysis of the
organizational structure and functions of the body that produced them. The principle, for this reason, gives definite direction to arrangement work. It leads an archivist to look into the
source of his material—to identify the organic body that produced a group and to identify the specific activities that resulted
in the production of series. It thus provides an objective approach to arrangement work that an archivist is especially well
equipped to take if he has had training in historical methodology, which has taught him to trace the origin, development,
and functioning of human institutions.

The principle facilitates the description of records. In 1910
the International Congress of Archivists and Librarians, meeting
in Brussels, resolved "that the 'principe de la provenance' be
adopted for the arrangement and inventorying of archives." The
applicability of the principle to inventory or descriptive work is
little understood or has been largely overlooked in the United
States. Because records are the product of activity, their most
significant attributes are those relating to their organizational

and functional origins. The attributes of organization and function are the equivalent in records of author and subject in publications. If they are preserved according to provenance, records may be described in terms of attributes derived from their provenance. The principle of provenance thus is a key to effective descriptive work, for it enables an archivist to describe records in meaningful terms.

APPLICATION TO GROUPS AND COLLECTIONS

Several propositions should be taken into account in applying the principle of provenance to archival groups and manuscript collections.

An archivist should observe the principle of provenance in arranging all organic records regardless of their origin. The principle is applicable to all records of public bodies; all records of private corporate bodies, such as businesses, churches, and schools; and many records of persons who engaged in extended activities of one kind or another. It is applicable to a degree even to private records that lack organic qualities, e.g., artificial collections of manuscripts, autographs, and other types of documents.

According to the principle of provenance, *an archivist should keep each group and subgroup intact and treat it as an integral unit.* He should not merge records of one governmental agency with those of another, nor records of one bureau with those of another, nor records of one office with those of another. He should keep them agency by agency, bureau by bureau, and office by office. And he should not merge records from one private source with those of another. He should keep them collection by collection.

According to the principle of provenance, *an archivist should not disperse records, from a particular group or subgroup, among subject or other kinds of classes.* A subjective or other schematic arrangement not only obscures the source of records in organic bodies, it also destroys the order imposed on them originally. It is thus a violation of both the principle of provenance and the principle of original order.

An archivist should not regroup public records into subject, chronological, or geographical classes. He should keep them, in so far as is possible, in the order given them by a government agency in the course of official business. If he must rearrange them, he should be careful not to obscure their organizational origins, for evidence of their source should be preserved in all arrangement work.

Similarly, he should not regroup private records into subject, chronological, or geographical classes. He should not scatter records from a given source. He should not remove record items from a particular collection in order to place them with collections pertaining to historical personages or to notable historical events. Even when a record is in book form, he should normally keep it with the collection to which it belongs. He should not remove an account book, an orderly book, a journal, or a diary to place it in collections of such special types, for such collections should be developed only under special circumstances, which will be considered later.

According to the principle of provenance, *a record officer in a government agency should not obscure the organizational origins of records while rearranging them after they have served their current use.* While the principle is generally observed in arranging public records in an archival institution, it is often violated before records come into archival custody. The War Production Board records of World War II, for example, were rearranged according to a decimal system of classification within the agency.

A record officer should not reorganize records according to a decimal or any other system of classification after they are non-current. He should not reorganize records of various offices into a new file.

When selected for archival retention, records obviously will be given a new arrangement. The retained records will be placed in a different relation to one another than the one they had in their current life. But this does not mean that the retained records should be reorganized. If sound archival principles are followed, the selected records will be kept office by office and activity by activity. There will be no fusion of files from various offices, no creation of new files except by those who do not understand or who have no regard for archival principles.

In governmental agencies, official historians occasionally rearrange records, usually in relation to topics on which they are writing historical accounts. In doing this they seriously impair the quality of the evidence in records on organization and function. If historians fail to preserve the quality of evidence in records, their action may be attributed to an ignorance of the principle of provenance, about which they are expected to know little; for this reason they may be excused. But there is no justification, other than that of professional immaturity or ignorance, for an archivist to sanction or to participate in rearrangement projects that will destroy the evidential value of records. To the extent that he has an influence in regard to them, he should counsel against such projects.

In a nation, public records should neither be alienated nor dispersed among private repositories so that their organizational origins are obscured. The evidential value of public records may be impaired by removing them improperly from public custody. Such records often lose their significance when they are taken from the archival groups or subgroups in which they belong. They lose their organic character, their meaning in relation to activities of a particular office. They should not be removed from archival groups in which they are embodied and scattered among various repositories.

While working with research material, historians may discover organic relations that were destroyed by the dispersal of public records. They may thus find a map, the identity of which was obscured by being buried in a geographic file, that was once one of a series of maps pertaining to the Lewis and Clark Expedition (1803–6). Or they may find a letter embodied in a strictly chronological file that was once a part of the files of a committee of the House of Representatives. While a historian may derive a great deal of satisfaction from fitting together pieces of evidence, it is not the function of an archivist to create a jigsaw puzzle out of the research material of his nation. It is his function to preserve it in such a way and at such places that its significance will be made apparent and the evidence it contains will be preserved.

APPLICATION TO SERIES

Several propositions should be taken into account in applying the principle of provenance to series.

An archivist should observe the principle of provenance in arranging series of records produced as a result of organic activity. Series of public records are created in the course of performing specific kinds of action. An archival group produced by a federal bureau typically includes the following series, all of which relate to classes of action:

A series of general correspondence of the bureau as a whole
A series of the bureau chief's correspondence
Several series of divisional correspondence
Series of questionnaires, reports, and other forms created to perform classes of action
Series of technical and fiscal records

The series consisting of bureau correspondence organized into a central file embodies records resulting from actions of the bureau. The series consisting of records of particular types denotes particular classes of actions—reports for reporting, questionnaires for questioning, and so forth. The series of fiscal and technical records relates to activities of specific kinds.

Series within a manuscript collection are similar in character to those in an archival group. Even a small collection will often include series of legal and business papers. In a large collection, relating to many activities, a number of series are ordinarily distinguishable on the basis of their relation to specific activities or transactions. A collection of a noted writer, for example, may include a separate file pertaining to his literary activities, including manuscripts of his writings, correspondence relating to them, reviews of them, and other types of documents. If he also engaged in politics, he doubtless accumulated an office file, perhaps pertaining to his service in a legislative body, which he probably removed on retiring from office. If he was actively interested in business, he doubtless kept records on his financial transactions, if for no other reason than that of tax accountability. He probably also kept his personal and family papers apart from those relating to his other activities. His collection, in a word, falls into several natural series, each relating to a specific activity.

According to the principle of provenance, *an archivist should keep each series intact and treat it as an integral unit.* Since a series generally reflects action, he should preserve it as a record of a specific action. While the arrangement of record items within a series may not significantly reflect action, the series as a whole does. Each record item in it is thus part of an organic whole. To separate it from the series in which it is embodied will impair its meaning, for the series as a whole has a meaning greater than its parts, i.e., than individual record items.

According to the principle of provenance, *an archivist should not merge record items from several series with one another.* If items on different kinds of action are arbitrarily combined into one file, the record of action will be confused and the evidence will be vitiated that derives from the way records were brought together in the course of action. This fact can be illustrated in respect to the series of a federal bureau. The bureau's central file of general correspondence contains records on all bureau activities and has a significance because it contains such records and no others. Its value as a record of bureau activities will be vitiated if it is merged with the central file of another bureau or, for that matter, if records unrelated to the activities of the bureau are interfiled in it. Similarly, the office file of a bureau chief has significance as a record of his administrative actions, and this significance is obscured the moment the series, as such, is torn apart and the record items within it are merged with another file.

Series in a manuscript collection have a similar value as a record of the activities to which they pertain. This value is lost the moment the series are not kept intact—the moment, for example, various series are merged with each other in a chronological file—and once this value is lost it cannot be regained.

According to the principle of provenance, *an archivist should not disperse record items within series among subject or other kinds of classes.* He should not tear series apart to create new series. When he rearranges items within series by subject, time, or place, he obscures or destroys altogether evidence on their source.

The principle of provenance has no bearing on the placement of series in relation to one another. The way series are arranged in relation to one another is important mainly from the point of view of their usability, not from the point of view of their integrity as evidence of organization and function. The main consideration in preserving the evidential value of records is that series should be kept intact and treated as integral units. But the order in which series within a group or subgroup are placed has little effect on their evidential value. For example, the series within a federal bureau may be placed in any conceivable relation to one another without affecting the integrity of each of them or of the group as a whole. The arrangement, whatever it is, should be one that will contribute to an understanding of the significance of the records and make them intelligible to the user.

Original Order

The second principle of archival arrangement, that records should be kept in the order imposed on them during their current life, is an outgrowth of the *Registraturprinzip* formulated by the Prussian State Archives. The principle states that "official papers are to be maintained in the order and with the designations which they received in the course of the official activity of the agency concerned." [6] This principle, which can be applied whenever records are properly arranged in an agency before their release to the archival institution (as they are in German registry offices), has been the subject of a great deal of discussion among archivists of various countries.

According to the principle of original order, *an archivist should keep items within a series in the order given them originally whenever this reflects organic activity.* The original order may show the sequence of actions; or may reveal administrative processes, such as how a given fiscal or technical operation was performed; or may reflect other organic connections. If it has any value in showing organic activity, the original order should by all means be preserved.

The order imposed on items within a series may also reflect how things were done in an office. Disorder in files is often characteristic of disorder in administration. Logically, therefore, an archivist, to preserve evidence of how things were actually done, should preserve records in the condition of disorder in which they were maintained during their current life. But this is obviously carrying logic too far.

In most modern filing systems, the original order given record items contributes little to an understanding of organic activity, and an archivist should therefore preserve the order only if it is useful. Various filing systems are in current use wherein record items are arranged as they accumulate. The individual record items may be arranged alphabetically, chronologically, numerically, or by subject, or under a combination of these various systems. From an archivist's point of view, most of these systems are notoriously bad, because they do not show how records were accumulated in relation to the activities to which they pertain. A file organized according to the Dewey decimal system of notation, for example, may be broken down into ten main subject classes having little relation to the activities of the government body that produced the file. Nor are the divisions of the main classes likely to bear a relation to activity. While some filing systems are to be preferred to others from an archival point of view, no modern system reflects fully the activities of the body that produced the records organized by it. In a word, the arrangement of the individual record items does not contribute to an understanding of the activity that is reflected in the series as a whole.

Often public records are not filed according to any sort of system; they are simply left in a disorganized state. The basic condition necessary in order to apply the original order principle of the German and Dutch archivists is too often lacking in public records of the United States. Records are not organized as well in American file rooms as they are in European registry offices. The reconstruction of the original order, therefore, is often very difficult and occasionally undesirable. The original order—to use the words of the director of the Prussian State Archives in describing older registries—is "without system, foolish, and impractical." [7] In such cases, the arrangement to be given records in the archival institution should be determined by the archivist.

Methods of filing are unimportant to an archivist, except from the point of view of their utility in making records accessible. They may show personal idiosyncrasies in filing, but these are important only if the person who did the filing is important. Thomas Jefferson, for example, who was accustomed to cataloging his library systematically, placed William Wirt's biography of Patrick Henry under the head of fiction. This was important because it revealed Jefferson's estimate of the merits of the biography.[8] But the idiosyncrasies of a file clerk in filing papers are seldom important. Bad filing is more often attributable to a lack of understanding of filing techniques and classification principles than to personal idiosyncrasies.

Usually the order given items in an archival series does not reveal any significant facts about activity, administrative processes, and the like. It does not, ordinarily, show how an activity was begun, the manner in which it was carried out, or the results obtained from it. Such facts are revealed because the series as such was kept intact, not because of the order given items within it.

Normally an archivist should preserve the order given records originally, rather than substitute one of his own. He should work to understand the order and should change it only if it is unusable. If it does not contribute to an understanding of organic activity, he should, however, have no compunction about changing it, so as to make the records intelligible and serviceable.

An archivist need not observe the principle of original order in arranging items within archival series that are preserved solely for their informational value. Here emphasis is on record series that contain essential information on matters with which an organic body dealt—the "research" records, which contain information useful for studies in a variety of subject fields—in contrast to records on the dealings themselves. In the National Archives, such series include population census schedules, passenger lists, military service records, and other personal records, which are preserved solely for their information on persons (not for their evidence of government functioning). An archivist should arrange items in such series solely with a view to their accessibility, though he should normally keep series intact to show their source in an organic activity.

The manner in which Weather Bureau climatological reports were dealt with in the National Archives illustrates how items were rearranged within series that were preserved solely for their informational value. It was impossible to ascertain what reports existed for a given place under their original arrangement. The volumes containing the reports were therefore unbound, and individual reports within them were rearranged by places (states and localities) and thereunder in chronological sequence. This was done for the reports within each of several series—the series of the Surgeon General's Office, the Smithsonian Institution, the Signal Office, the Weather Bureau, and so forth. The series created by each of the agencies were kept intact.

An archivist should apply the principle of original order to manuscript series that have an organic character. The order given items in a manuscript collection is important to the degree that it reflects organic activity. Many manuscript collections, even early ones, come to a repository complete and undisturbed in respect to the arrangement of their series. Recent collections, having passed through fewer hands, are often received in their original order. The more a collection is the product of organic or extended activity, the more significant is its original order, and the more applicable is the archival principle that items within it should be preserved in the order given them by their creators.

If the order given items in a manuscript collection does not reflect organic activity, it has no presumptive value but must be judged strictly on its merits. It is important only to the extent that it makes a collection usable. The single items derive no added meaning from their position among other items, though a good arrangement may make their meaning more apparent. The items stand by themselves and can be treated in a repository individually. An archivist should therefore have no compunction about grouping items within such collections into series.

An archivist need not observe the principle of original order in arranging private papers in artificial collections. An artificial collection of manuscripts consists of items that were "collected," i.e., gathered from many sources. An archivist should arrange items within such collections in whatever way will make them accessible.

The order imposed on items in an artificial collection is not a result of the activity in which the items had their origin, as is often the case in regard to archives; it is the result merely of a collecting activity. The single items, therefore, derive no added meaning from their position among other items, though a good arrangement may make their meaning more apparent. The items stand by themselves and can be treated individually in a repository, without reference to the collection of which they form a part. In this respect, it is to be noted, they differ fundamentally from archives, in which each single item torn from its context is likely to lose some of its meaning. An archivist or manuscript curator should have no compunction about rearranging items within an artificial collection, though while doing so he should preserve evidence on their source and the place at which they were acquired. Such a rearrangement, however, even if organic in character, has no presumptive value and should be judged strictly on its merits.

In recapitulation, then, there are two principles of archival arrangement to be observed. While the principle of provenance is basic and inflexible and relates to a matter of the highest importance to the archival profession, the principle relating to the original order of records involves mainly matters of convenience or use.

The principle of provenance relates to the integrity of archives—the preservation of values that inhere in them because of their organic character. In the arrangement of records there are two things which will seriously affect the evidential values of the records: doing anything which will obscure the origin of the records in a particular body and doing anything which will obscure their origin in a particular activity.

The principle of original order relates mainly to use or convenience. Normally an archivist should preserve the order given record items within series during their current life, if it is one that enables him to find records when they are wanted and to describe records effectively. But if it does not, he should have no compunction about disturbing the original order. The test here is a very practical one, that of usability.

VII

CHARACTER OF A
DESCRIPTIVE PROGRAM

When applied to documentary material, the term "description" covers all activities that must be performed in preparing finding aids. "Description," according to its dictionary definition, means an enumeration of the essential qualities of a thing. This definition applies to records as well as to other things.

Record description involves two actions: the first is to identify the record unit that is to be described, and the second is to enumerate its essential qualities or attributes.

As we have seen in previous chapters, there are three kinds of record units: the large, consisting of groups of public records or collections of private papers; the intermediate, consisting of series within groups and collections; and the small, consisting of individual record items within series.

The largest and the smallest of these units are easily identifiable. The largest units are generally cohesive bodies of material received from particular sources. The smallest units are separate physical entities, such as bound volumes, binders or folders, or single documents or pieces.

Archival descriptive techniques devised in the United States relate mainly to the large and small record units, i.e., to groups and collections and to single items, although less attention has been given to the techniques that apply to the former than to those that apply to the latter. The literature on the description of private papers is concerned almost exclusively with cataloging and calendaring single items. Many articles may be found in American archival and library journals that relate to such techniques. Relatively little attention, on the other hand, has been paid to the description of series. To these intermediate units an archivist must give special attention if he wishes to carry out a well-balanced descriptive program.

Qualities or attributes by which records may be described are both substantive and physical in nature. Records may be described substantively in relation to the government agency, corporate body, or person that produced them, the functions that resulted in their production, and their subject content. They may be described structurally in relation to their physical type, composition, volume, and other physical characteristics. These attributes will be discussed fully in the next chapter.

Records may be described either as single documents or collectively as units that contain a number of documents. The descriptive information about each unit may be either general or detailed, i.e., all or only a few of its qualities may be enumerated. The descriptions may pertain to all units or only to particular units within a repository.

Finding aids may thus be of various types: comprehensive or limited in their coverage, general or detailed in their descriptive data, and pertaining to record units of various sizes. They may consist of guides, inventories, calendars, catalogs, lists, indexes, and the like.

The terms used to designate various types of finding aids are not well defined. During the formative years of the American archival profession, the term "catalog" was used in a generic sense to cover all types of finding aids. During the conferences of archivists held between 1909 and 1919, Waldo G. Leland, Victor H. Paltsits, and other archivists used the term to refer to guides and inventories, as well as to calendars. Since the meaning of the term "catalog" is generally understood because of library usage, it is now often used in a generic sense to explain to laymen the nature of finding aid work in an archival institution. It is so used by the National Archives in budgetary documents.

The term "finding aid" should be used as the generic term to cover all types of archival descriptive documents.

The term "catalog" should be used to refer to archival descriptive documents that appear in card form. While catalogs can obviously be produced in page form, archival descriptive documents produced in that form can usually be designated more accurately as guides, inventories, or lists. The units of description in a catalog may be manuscript collections or items.

The term "inventory" should be used in the dictionary sense of its meaning when applied to goods. It is a stocktaking of record series in an archival group or manuscript accession.

The term "list" should be used to refer to a detailed descriptive document in which record items are identified and described; the term "calendar," to refer to a chronological list of record items with a brief summary of the contents of each.

The term "index" should be used to refer to a finding aid, in card form, that shows where information on specific matters may be found in record units. An index should merely identify the record units, not describe them.

Objectives

The object of descriptive work is to make records in the custody of an archival institution accessible for use. Finding aids serve a twofold purpose: to make records known to potential users and to facilitate the archivist in searching for them.

It is the duty of an archivist to open up the research treasures that are entrusted to his care, not to hoard them and keep them from others. He should not only accumulate and preserve documentary material; he should also make it accessible to others. A possessive or secretive attitude is inexcusable. In order to make records accessible, he should prepare finding aids to them.

Descriptive work involves an element of self-abnegation for an archivist, in that it makes available to others his own knowledge about documents. As his work progresses, he makes himself increasingly unnecessary in the use of his material. He may, occasionally, be tempted to make himself indispensable to his institution by keeping this knowledge to himself. It is understandable if he should mistakenly yield to this temptation, for the dependence of the institution on him in rendering service gives him a sort of job security that may be destroyed by work that will make his personal mediation less necessary.

An archivist should not fear that he will harm himself by recording his knowledge about records. His personal knowledge will increase as he creates finding aids, and this knowledge, obviously, can never be completely supplanted by finding aids. No matter how well finding aids are prepared, they cannot impart all the knowledge that is in the head of a well-informed archivist. Nor are they intended to supplant his help. They are "aids," in the true sense of the word, being designed simply to help him and the searcher in finding the material needed. An archivist's knowledge is still necessary to help find records more easily and more abundantly, a fact that has been stressed by a number of scholars. For instance, Frontis W. Johnston, an American historian, wrote that "a good inventory is the first requirement of effective control" but that there must be "interviews with the people who service the material. The researcher must lean on the learning and professional competence of the experts who serve him." [1] Boyd Shafer, executive secretary of the American Historical Association, echoed this view: "Perhaps . . . the historians need to know that there is no real substitute for personal relationships between themselves and the custodian of the relevant and particular records, that no written pamphlet of instructions can take the place of a few good questions addressed to the man who handles the documents day in and day out." [2]

Whether dealing with material of public or private origin, archivists almost always fail to keep abreast of descriptive work. "Manuscripts are received here faster than they can be supplied with checklists and calendars," reported W. Edwin Hemphill while at the University of Virginia Library. [3]

The failure to keep abreast of finding aid work is due to a number of reasons, the chief of which is that projects are begun that are difficult to complete. When Reuben Thwaites produced his guide to manuscripts in the Wisconsin Historical Society in 1906, he pointed out in its preface that it was but a temporary expedient designed to "lighten the burden of search" and that it would be superseded by calendars. [4] These have not yet appeared. In the State Museum of New Orleans, the calendaring, cataloging, and indexing of French and Spanish colonial records was begun early in the present century and was continued for several decades, though twice interrupted for lack of funds. Initially, a subject index to individual items was prepared, but as indexing progressed it was thought necessary to include "a succinct statement of the contents of each record." [5] This, obviously, is an interminable undertaking.

Calendaring projects, in particular, are never-ending, as are also cataloging projects when they relate to single items. Victor Hugo Paltsits, working in the New York Public Library in 1915, referred to "thousands of uncatalogued manuscripts" in his custody.[6] When the WPA Historical Records Survey undertook to produce a series of *Guides to Depositories of Manuscript Collections in the United States,* between 1936 and 1942, it requested information on the status of cataloging work in various repositories.[7] Information was provided on two types of catalogs: accessions catalogs and item catalogs. The following statistics indicate the percentage of material for which catalogs had been prepared in representative repositories:

Repository	Item catalogs (percentage)	Accessions catalogs (percentage)
Detroit Public Library (Burton Collection)	35	98
Duke University Library	10	
California Historical Society	5	90
Clements Library	50	100
Illinois State Archives	10	
Indiana State Library	25	60
Minnesota Historical Society	20	80
North Carolina University		70
North Carolina Historical Commission		60
Pennsylvania State Archives	25	8
Wisconsin Historical Society	10	100

Another reason for the failure to keep abreast of finding aid work is that archival institutions find themselves preoccupied, in the course of time, with reference service work. The National Archives initiated a finding aid program in 1941 that envisaged the production of preliminary checklists, preliminary inventories, and final inventories.[8] Twenty years later, only half of the preliminary inventories had been completed, mainly because of the constantly increasing demands for reference service.

Archivists occasionally fall heir to an accumulation of work left undone by their predecessors. When Dr. Ruth Nuermberger was appointed to the Duke University Library, she found "a mass of unaccessioned and uncataloged manuscripts."[9] When Charles Shetler was appointed to the West Virginia University Library, he "inherited," to use his own words, "a large and rich but almost completely unorganized mass of manuscripts and records."[10]

It is obvious, then, that an archivist should develop a program for the description of his holdings. He should plan his program carefully, so that he will make known the content and significance of his holdings as soon as possible, so that he will progressively increase the knowledge about them as resources are available for descriptive work, and so that he will meet the particular needs of his clientele. He should determine the kind of finding aids needed for each group in his custody, establishing an order of priority for their production on the basis of the use and research significance of various record groups.

An archivist may, as was observed in Chapter IV, dissipate his energies on unproductive projects if he does not develop a descriptive program or if he develops an improper one. If this occurs, he will fail to provide the information that is needed or will provide information in excess of that needed on records in his custody.

Essentials

A descriptive program should be designed to provide information on all records in a repository. When he first comes to an archival institution, a searcher wants to know something about its entire holdings. He wants to know what is available, so that he may determine if specific bodies of material pertain to his subject of inquiry. While archival finding aids cannot help a searcher find specific items to the extent that library catalogs can, such aids should enable him to obtain immediately a general knowledge of the holdings in a repository and to proceed from such a general knowledge to descriptions that provide specific information about particular groups that may interest him. To meet a searcher's needs, then, the thing to do is to provide a general perspective of the holdings and to show the most pertinent facts about each group or collection.

An archivist should thus describe his entire holdings immediately in summary finding aids consisting of (1) guides and catalogs in which concise descriptions are provided of all groups and collections and (2) inventories in which descriptions are provided of record series within large or significant groups and collections. He should definitely forego the detailed description of individual record items until he has provided a comprehensive description of his holdings.

When dealing with the large masses of recent documentary material, it is especially necessary to adopt a technique whereby records are described collectively by series and groups. Few repositories "can afford either to set up piece-by-piece arrangements, or to prepare piece-by-piece indexes or calendars," noted Katharine E. Brand while with the Manuscripts Division of the Library of Congress.[11]

In recent years, many large repositories of the United States have discontinued cataloging single pieces. Among them are the Manuscript Division of the Library of Congress and the Henry E. Huntington Library. The curator of the latter library frankly admits that its holdings are "so large that elaborate cataloging is impossible." [12] Library manuscript repositories have "despaired of piece-by-piece cataloging and calendaring in the face of the size of collections accumulated in the 'typewriter age,' " according to Andrew H. Horn.[13] The *Ad Hoc* Committee on Manuscripts, established by the American Historical Association in 1948, observed that, while older manuscripts "are undoubtedly well suited to . . . individual indexing, cataloging, or calendaring," the mass of modern manuscripts cannot be dealt with in that way. It recommended "that, in the case of large groups of recent materials, indexing of individual manuscript items, however ideally desirable, be considered for practical purposes the exception rather than the rule," and that there be substituted therefor other kinds of finding aids, such as guides and inventories.[14]

The technique of collective description provides a short cut to attaining a control over the holdings of a repository. No archivist is fully trained in his profession until he understands it and knows how to apply it. And having learned the technique, he should first describe records collectively by groups and series, and thereafter, only if their character and value justify individual treatment, by single items. If he does not learn the technique, he is likely to founder among innumerable individual items that are found in every repository, however small it may be.

A descriptive program should be designed to provide the special information about records that is needed. The emphasis here is on selectivity in the type of finding aid to be prepared.

Different groups of records have different values and, consequently, different uses. Some are useful mainly to the genealogist, some mainly to the antiquarian, and some have predominantly a scholarly interest and contain little information on either persons or places.

Different types of finding aids are needed by different classes of searchers. If a finding aid is to serve the needs of a genealogist effectively, it should contain information on persons; if it is to serve the needs of an antiquarian, it should contain information on places or things; and if it is to serve the needs of a scholar, it should contain information that will make known the significance and content of various groups. For groups that are chiefly of genealogical or antiquarian interest, indexes to names of persons and places will usually suffice. For groups that have a general research interest, the scholar will want to have information on their relation to chronological periods, geographical areas, and broad subject fields. Generally, summary descriptions in guides, catalogs, or inventories will meet his needs.

An archivist, then, should decide what kinds of finding aids should be prepared for various record groups. He should adapt his descriptive program to facilitate the special uses to which particular record groups may be put. While such a program should be designed to serve the needs of all kinds of users—scholars as well as genealogists and antiquarians—it should serve especially well the needs of the principal users.

An archivist should not develop a descriptive program that calls for completely uniform treatment of every group in his custody. His program should be flexible. Unfortunately, for the sake of consistency, archivists have often produced certain kinds of finding aids—indexes, catalogs, and the like—regardless of whether or not they are needed or usable. Archivists concerned chiefly with genealogical inquiries have prepared indexes to personal names, often comprising case after case of index cards. Others, to serve the same need, have prepared extensive biographical sketches of persons important in a state or community. Some, concerned with inquiries about places, have prepared indexes to names of places. Others still, have custody of correspondence or other early records important to the history of an area, have laboriously prepared calendars. Many, following library practices, have heaped catalogs on catalogs. A few, not knowing what kind of finding aids to prepare, have prepared none at all.

One thing is certain: every repository, regardless of the degree to which it is intended to serve a specialized clientele, should make its holdings generally accessible for scholarly research. Because of the lack of a considered program for developing finding aids, archivists are often able to serve only the bare needs of genealogists and antiquarians. Scholars are often given short shrift. Repositories established by religious groups, local historical societies, or genealogical organizations should serve not only their special interests but also the interests of scholarly research, for their holdings usually include material that has a general research interest broader than that of the institutions that established them.

A descriptive program should be designed to provide specific information about particular records. The emphasis here is on selectivity in the degree of detail in finding aids.

A descriptive program should provide constantly more information about the holdings of a repository as resources are available for their description. It should be one that involves the production of a series of finding aids in which the sequence is from the general to the particular, the descriptions becoming progressively more detailed as descriptive work proceeds. Such a program was recommended by Waldo G. Leland in the formative years of the American archival profession. He thought that the initial finding aids should be similar to the French numerical inventory, that a numerical inventory should be followed by an analytical inventory, and that the inventories should be followed by calendars, prepared selectively for items in highly important record series.[15] The program adopted by the National Archives, in its early years, involved a sequence from a preliminary checklist, to a preliminary inventory, to a final inventory.[16] The purpose in providing progressively more intensive descriptive information is to improve the quality of reference service.

A descriptive program for private papers, in my opinion, should result in the production of a preliminary finding aid to each large accession in the form of an inventory, followed by a catalog of each collection, and that by a guide to the holdings of a repository. Thereafter, special finding aids should be produced to meet specific needs. These should be in the form of indexes, or catalogs and lists of record items.

A descriptive program for public papers should differ somewhat from that for private papers. An inventory of public papers, which should also be preliminary in character, should cover an archival group, instead of an accession. It should be followed by a guide, instead of a catalog. Thereafter, special finding aids should be produced to meet specific needs.

A descriptive program should be designed to produce finding aids in a form that will best make known the content and significance and best facilitate the use of records. The emphasis here is on selectivity in the form of the finding aids. There are two forms to be considered: the card form and the page form.

The card form is obviously suited to library finding aids. Library collections are growing collections. Materials need constantly to be inserted in various places in a collection, and cards, which can be inserted at any point in a card file, are best suited to the description of the discrete items in a library collection. In the last two decades of the nineteenth century, card systems of cataloging were so generally adopted in libraries that everyone now regards a card catalog as the only type of finding aid suited to library material.

As scholars are accustomed to using card catalogs in regard to books, they expect to find them also for documentary material. Many of them, in fact, are so used to scanning cards to find a book on a particular subject that they expect to scan cards to find original source material on a particular subject. Their preference for finding aids in card form is largely attributable to habit.

The card form is suited to archival finding aids whenever the record unit to be described is a discrete entity and whenever it is desirable to indicate where information on specific subjects is to be found in records. Cards are thus suited to the production of catalogs of collections and groups, catalogs of discrete textual record items, and catalogs of pictorial and cartographic record items that need to be described singly. Cards are also suited to the production of indexes of all kinds.

Information in regard to certain kinds of documentary material, however, can be made more rapidly apparent and can be more completely presented in page form. The card form is not suited to the description of record series that have an organic or other relation to one another. Descriptions of series within collections or groups should normally appear on pages, instead of on cards. The page form is desirable for two reasons:

The first is the lack of space on cards. The provenance of the series often cannot be indicated in a few words. Similarly, the content, arrangement, and significance of particular series often cannot be indicated in a few words since such series may consist of many physical types and may relate to diverse subjects or activities.

The second reason is the lack of continuity of information on cards. Each card usually contains information that is unrelated to that on other cards. The intricate relation of various series to one another cannot be readily made apparent on cards without resorting to elaborate cross-references. In contrast, the organic and subject relations of various series can be easily made apparent on pages by the way the series entries are grouped and arranged.

Finding aids produced in a descriptive program should be readily accessible to the user. Information about record holdings may be made available in three ways: by properly organizing finding aids for the use of searchers, by publishing finding aids, and by participating in cooperative cataloging projects that will serve to make known the documentary resources of many repositories.

Finding aids should be presented in an accessible form and place and be properly organized in card file drawers or in looseleaf binders, so that their content and organization is readily apparent. They should be neatly arranged and not encumbered with documents, such as drafts of agency finding aids, that are difficult to understand or that are useful only to the archivist for his own work. They should be placed in the search room in a conspicuous and convenient location and be as accessible as are the catalogs in a library.

Finding aids that are worth publishing should be reproduced and distributed among research repositories. Their merit for publication is determined by the importance of the information they convey and the importance of the records to which they relate. It is more desirable to publish a finding aid that is comprehensive than one that is limited in its descriptive coverage of the holdings of a repository, and to publish a finding aid that provides full rather than limited information about record units. A finding aid that pertains to highly important records should be published as soon as it is completed, no matter how sketchy its descriptive information may be. Often, archivists dealing with important manuscript collections provide very little information about them, other than their titles and dates. A notable example of a useful guide that is very sketchy in its information is the *Handbook of the Massachusetts Historical Society, 1791–1948,* produced by the society in 1949.

A nation's documentary resources can be exploited effectively by scholars only if they are made known through finding aids produced by the repositories that hold them. Archivists have successfully collaborated in obtaining copies of documents, specifically of documents in the archives of Europe, and they can also successfully collaborate in describing documents, once the essential preliminary step has been taken.

When the cataloging techniques of the archival profession have been fully developed, card catalogs of manuscript collections will largely replace printed finding aids. Projects for the cooperative cataloging of manuscript material may be developed either on a national, regional, or state basis, or on the basis of research interests in particular fields of human activity, such as the economic, religious, military, or diplomatic fields. Such projects will result in the distribution of descriptive information produced by individual repositories among institutions that have need of it.

VIII

RECORD ATTRIBUTES

Before analyzing the distinctive attributes by which records should be described, it is well to consider briefly certain general factors that affect record description.

The accuracy of any description depends on the extent to which the nature of the thing that is being described is taken into account. Records cannot be described accurately by taking into account the nature of other things—such as books. They have characteristics, as we noted in Chapter III, that are quite different from those of publications. It is as foolish to describe primary and secondary material in the same way as it is to describe raw material in the same way as the goods that are made from it. The descriptive techniques of the archival profession should be developed in relation to the nature of records, not borrowed from library cataloging techniques that have been evolved in relation to things that are quite different from records in their physical and substantive attributes.

Before discussing record attributes, it is perhaps well to recall the differences between documentary and library material.

The first basic difference between the two classes of material is that records are source or primary material rather than secondary in character. This difference largely accounts for the physical variations between the two classes of material. Since records are primary in character, they have attributes they received when they were first created, varying in type, size, and composition. They lack the attributes publications acquire in the course of their manufacture.

The second basic difference is that records are organic material, which largely accounts for the substantive variations between them and publications. Unlike publications, they have a collective significance, a significance primarily in relation to activity and only secondarily in relation to subject. And if analyzed from the point of view of their subject content, they are heterogeneous, instead of being homogeneous in subject matter as are publications.

Physical differences make it impossible to describe records in respect to the same attributes in reference to which publications are cataloged, i.e., their acquired attributes relating to title, authorship, imprint, and the like.

Substantive differences make it impossible to describe records by the physical units by which publications are cataloged and by the subjects in reference to which publications are cataloged. Organic material must be described collectively and in relation to function; library material, individually and in relation to subject. There are thus two basically divergent approaches in the descriptive techniques of the library and archival professions, one being a functional approach, the other a subject approach.

A description of a record unit involves essentially nothing more than an enumeration of its attributes. Record attributes are identified in general terms in the accompanying chart. These attributes may be ascertained by analyzing the provenance of a unit, the time and place of its production, its functional origins, the subjects to which it relates, its types, and its composition. These are matters about which an archivist can obtain information if he knows what he is looking for and how to look for it. While information on some of the matters is not easy to obtain, record description is not an indefinable process—so esoteric and so difficult that an archivist must throw up his hands in hopeless despair when confronted with a complicated archival series or manuscript collection.

The substantive and physical attributes, which I will discuss in this chapter, should be taken into account in preparing all kinds of finding aids. The main difference in the kinds of finding aids is the order in which attributes are enumerated and the extent to which information is provided about them.

What, then, are the distinctive qualities or attributes by which

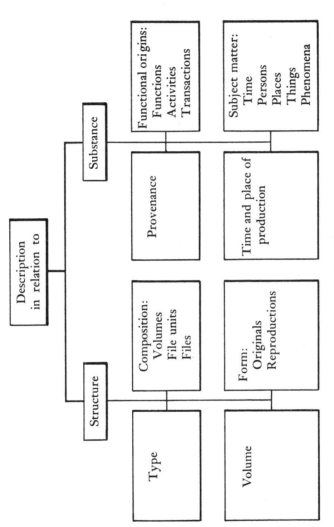

Record Attributes

a record unit should be described? What distinguishes one unit from another?

Physical Attributes

While physical attributes are not as significant as are substantive attributes in the description of records, it is nonetheless necessary to understand them. Physical attributes relate to (1) the type, (2) the composition, (3) the volume, and (4) the form of records.

TYPE

In describing a textual record unit, it is important to identify its type. The term "type" refers to the kind of records. Record types may be either general or specific.

General types

In describing manuscript collections in recent American guides, archivists have used several terms interchangeably to denote general types. Some archivists have attempted to define and to standardize the use of such terms. William R. Hogan, for example, devised a system of titling manuscript collections for the Louisiana State University guide that he hoped would be a step "toward remedying the prevailing lack of uniformity in usage of the terms 'papers,' 'collections,' 'manuscripts,' and other designations." [1] Alice E. Smith, in her 1944 guide to the manuscripts in the Wisconsin Historical Society, used the term "papers" as a general and comprehensive term to designate more than one type of manuscript material and terms such as "correspondence," "diaries," "minutes," and "reminiscences" to designate specific types.[2] In reviewing the Smith guide, Curtis W. Garrison observed that descriptive practices can be standardized to some degree in various ways, and specifically in the use of terms such as "papers," "collections," and "correspondence." [3]

While it is highly desirable to bring about a common understanding of the meaning of these collective terms, and even more important to bring about a common usage of them, this result will not be achieved until the archival profession is more fully developed. The terms most often used are "papers" and "records," the former to refer to material of a personal origin and the latter to material of a corporate origin. The term "manuscripts," when used to refer to historical source material, has usually been modified by the adjective "historical" to distinguish between historical and literary manuscripts.

Each collective term may be given a specialized meaning for archival descriptive purposes. The descriptions of source material in guides and other finding aids will obviously be more precise and accurate if specialized meanings are generally accepted.

The term "records," for example, should be used to refer to material produced by corporate bodies or government agencies. This is in line with the recommendations of the Library of Congress rules for the descriptive cataloging of manuscripts.[4]

The term "papers" should be used to refer to material produced by persons. This is also in line with the Library of Congress rules.

The term "manuscripts" should be used to refer to compositions that are normally published, whether produced by a person, a corporate body, or a government agency. Thus a manuscript, using the term in this restricted sense, is the unprinted version of a book or an extended writing, such as a memoir, autobiography, essay, sermon, oration, or the like.

The term "collection" should not be used for descriptive purposes. It refers to matters other than record type. It is similar to the term "files," which is generally avoided in describing documentary material.

Specific record types

General types are divisible into a number of specific types, which can be easily identified by answering the question: *What kind?* Are they letters, reports, memoranda, diaries, or some other kind of documents?

In the description of textual records, the term "type" often refers to more than just physical characteristics; it also refers to a kind of action. Thus the term "correspondence" shows that a type was produced as a result of letter writing; the term "questionnaire," as a result of asking questions; and the term "accounts," as a result of keeping accounts. By showing the kind of action that resulted in the production of records, an archivist provides information on type that often reveals the substance as well as the physical structure of a record unit. Record types in the pictorial record class, in contrast, reveal only the method by which they were produced, not the kind of action that resulted in their production.

To describe textual records, no matter what their age may be, an archivist should, first, ascertain their type and, secondly, use precise and accurate terms to designate their type. In regard to a medieval document, he should try to determine, on the basis of internal evidence and information provided in formularies, if it is an act, diploma, treaty, contract, or some other type. Many definitions now being formulated in Europe by the committee on terminology of the International Council on Archives are designed to facilitate the description of medieval record types.

The terms used for modern record types are not clearly defined. Special terms are used to designate types that result from specialized activities of private corporate bodies and public agencies. A given term may have a different meaning from one period to another. Or it may refer to record types resulting from different kinds of activity. The term "warrants," for example, has one meaning when referring to records resulting from military activities, another when referring to those resulting from legal activities, and still another when referring to those resulting from fiscal activities. A given term, moreover, may have several meanings. The terms "journal" and "daybook" thus refer either to a narrative account of happenings or to a fiscal account. Or several terms, often used interchangeably, may be employed to designate a given record type.

In order to choose terms that will properly identify modern record types, an archivist should understand the specialized activities that resulted in their production and the specialized meaning that terms have acquired in various periods and in various activities. If a term has several meanings, he should not use it unless its specialized meaning is apparent from the context in which it appears. He should thus use the term "journal" to describe fiscal records only when it is apparent that the descriptive entry in which it occurs relates to fiscal records. He should not use obsolete terms. If several terms exist for a given record type, he should use the term that is most generally understood.

Modern record types are very numerous. For purposes of discussion, they may be divided into those pertaining to personal, corporate, and governmental activities. Such a division is not absolute, for there are many types that pertain to all kinds of activity. These may be designated as "common record types." Such types, which result chiefly from the communication of information from one person to another, include the following:

Correspondence	Memoranda	Notes
Letters	Messages	Reports
Letter books	Minutes	Telegrams

The term "correspondence" should be used to designate both incoming and outgoing letters; the term "letters," to designate either incoming or outgoing letters.

Many *personal record types* are difficult to identify precisely. In his bibliography of American diaries, William Matthews says that the terms "journals" and "diaries" are often misused; that religious journals are generally autobiographies; and that travel journals are often travel narratives.[5] In recent American guides to manuscript collections, the following terms are often used interchangeably to denote the same type:

Diaries, journals, daybooks, and commonplace books
Genealogies, family trees, and pedigree charts
Memoirs and reminiscences
Scrapbooks, memory books, and commonplace books

The term "commonplace book," Matthews says, denotes a book of clippings and quotations. The term "diary" denotes a contemporaneous narrative account, which, Matthews says, "is written for personal reasons." The term "journal" denotes a contemporaneous narrative account, which, according to Matthews, "is kept as part of a job." The terms "memoirs" and "reminiscences" denote narrative accounts written in retrospect.

While there are very many personal record types, the following are some of the commoner ones:

Autobiographies	Family histories	Orations
Biographies	Family trees	Piece books (poetry)
Clippings	Genealogical notes,	Poems
Commonplace books	papers, or sketches	Reminiscences
(obsolete and con-	Genealogies	Scrapbooks
fusing)	Journals	Sermons
Daybooks (confusing)	Memoirs	Speeches
Essays	Obituaries	
Example books		

Corporate record types are developed in business, educational, and other kinds of institutional activity. In the course of a legal process, for example, several special types are produced, such as bills, decrees, depositions, examinations, judgments, pleas, pleadings, proofs, and verdicts. Or in shipping activities, special types include a ship's certificate of registry, her manifest, license, passport, muster roll, logbook, invoices, articles, bills of lading, and other types.

Corporate record types relating to fiscal activities are especially difficult to identify. The term "account books" is often used as a collective term to cover a number of types of accounting records. Professor Lewis E. Atherton points out that the term is rather meaningless to an economic historian and that a number of specific terms should be used in preference to it.[6] These are defined in dictionaries of business terms, of which the following are useful: *Crowell's Dictionary of Business and Finance*,[7] Donald T. Clark's *Dictionary of Business and Finance*,[8] Harold Lazarus' *American Business Dictionary*,[9] and the Schwartz *Dictionary of Business and Industry*.[10] Legal record types are defined in *Bouvier's Law Dictionary*,[11] which has been issued in several editions, the most notable of which is the three-volume edition of 1914.

For descriptive purposes, account books may be divided into two classes: books of first entry and books into which are posted data taken from books of first entry.

Among the books of first entry, the most important is the "journal." The terms formerly applied to it were "daybook," "wastebook," and "blotter." For many years it represented the only book of first entry, and it is all that is now used in many small businesses. In modern bookkeeping it is split up into numerous books of first entry, among which the following are noteworthy:

Cash journals, formerly called cashbooks
Purchase journals, also called invoice books, invoice registers, voucher books, or voucher registers
Sales journals, also called sales books

Among the books to which information is posted, the "ledger" is the most important. In modern bookkeeping it is split up into a number of subsidiary books, among which the following are noteworthy:

General ledgers
Private ledgers
Purchase ledgers, better known in modern accounting as accounts payable ledgers, and formerly known as bills payable books
Sales ledgers, better known in modern accounting as accounts receivable ledgers, and formerly known as bills receivable books

The following are some of the commoner corporate record types:

Abstracts of title	Briefs	Inventories
Accounts	Certificates (of)	Invoices
Affidavits	deposit	Judgments
Agreements	incorporation	Leases
Appeals	land	Letters testamentary
Articles (of)	purchases	Licenses
agreement	registry	Lists (of)
incorporation	stock	cargo
partnership	Checks	freight
Awards	Claims	passengers
Bids	Contracts	prices
Bills (of)	Conveyances	stock
exchange	Debentures	taxes
indictment	Decisions	Logbooks
lading	Deeds	Manifests
sale	Depositions	Mortgages
Bonds	Insurance policies	Opinions

Payrolls	warehouse	Titles
Pleadings	Requisitions	Vouchers
Pleas	Securities	Warrants
Proceedings	Specifications	Waybills
Receipts (of)	Statements	Wills
sales	Summonses	
taxes	Testaments	

Governmental record types are those that emanate from public authority—federal, state, and local. The corporate record types enumerated above occur also in governmental agencies.

Governmental types are difficult to identify, mainly because of their complexity, which they derive not only from the specialized activities that resulted in their production but also from changes in their character from one period to another. It is especially important for an archivist to know how such types came into being and to identify them accurately. To obtain this knowledge, he may have to make a careful study of governmental processes, both past and present.

The following are some of the record types created mainly in relation to governmental activity:

Announcements	Land grants	Petitions
Applications	Land patents	Questionnaires
Appointments	Land warrants	Ration books
Authorizations	Laws	Recommendations
Charters	Letters patent	Regulations
Circulars	Memorials	Releases
Commissions	Muster rolls	Resolutions
Decrees	Notices	Returns
Directives	Notifications	Rolls
Discharges	Orderly books (same as	Rosters
Dispatches	order books)	Rules
Endorsements	Orders	Schedules
Franchises	Ordinances	Statutes
Grants	Passports	Surveys
Instructions	Patents	Tables
Interpretations	Pension certificates	Tabulations

Distinctive characteristics of types.

Almost every record type, whether general or specific in nature, has characteristics that distinguish it from other types.

These distinctive characteristics are acquired as records are produced and relate to the producer or creator or records, the activities or transactions that resulted in the production of records, and the objects (persons, places, things, or phenomena) that are involved in such activities or transactions.

General record types—records, papers, and manuscripts—may thus be identified more precisely and accurately by noting their distinctive characteristics. This may be done by specifying, either in general or specific terms, the kind of activity that resulted in their production, as in the following examples:

> PERSONAL PAPERS
> SCIENTIFIC PAPERS
> BANKING RECORDS
> PHILIPPINE INSURRECTION RECORDS

Specific record types—whether personal, corporate, or governmental in origin—may also be identified more precisely and accurately by noting their distinctive characteristics.

Account books, for example, may have been produced by a baker, banker, or candlestick maker; or may consist of specific types of journals or ledgers; or may relate to a specific action, such as the settlement of an estate.

Histories may be administrative, political, economic, or social in nature; or may be general or detailed in their treatment of a subject. An administrative history may relate to various sizes of organizational units: an agency, a bureau within the agency, a division within the bureau, etc.

Letters may be official, business, or personal in nature. They may, moreover, relate to a specific kind of action: endorsements, inquiries, recommendations, or the like.

Lists may pertain to cargoes, freight, passengers, prices, stocks, taxes, and the like.

Manuals may be governmental or private in origin and may relate to various matters, such as procedures, filing, correspondence, and the like.

Reports may relate to inspections, surveys, or the progress of specific activities; or may be narrative or statistical in nature; or may have been produced at annual, monthly, or daily intervals.

In identifying a record type, an archivist should indicate its distinctive characteristics, as in the following examples:

FARMER'S ACCOUNT BOOK

PASSENGER LIST

NATIONAL ARCHIVES PROCEDURE MANUAL

ANNUAL NARRATIVE PROGRESS REPORT

COMPOSITION

Information on the composition of a record unit is important in its description only in special circumstances.

The term "composition" is here used to refer to the way records were brought together when they were originally created or accumulated. They may have been brought together into volumes, file units, and files.

An archivist may clearly show the composition of a record unit by answering the following questions:

If a bound volume, what kind?
Account book?
Ledger?
Letter book?
Press-copy book?
Wage book? etc.
If a file unit, what kind?
Folder?
Binder?
Docket?
Dossier? etc.
If an aggregation of file units, in what arrangement?
Alphabetical?
Numerical?
Subject?
Subject-numeric?
Dewey decimal? etc.

Volumes are simply accumulations of records in bound form. Certain types of business and financial information—such as information on sales, expenditures, wages, orders, income, and the like—often are recorded in blank volumes, and hence one finds account books, sales books, wage books, order books, ledgers, and a whole host of other similar types. Certain types of volumes, such as letter books, press-copy books, and correspondence registers, are produced while following certain office practices; scrapbooks and other types are the result of a collecting activity.

Information showing that records were bound is not especially significant. It merely reveals that certain volumes contain records of a particular type, such as letters, accounts, or orders; or that records were produced by letterpress or some other process.

Information showing the kind of file units into which records were assembled is ordinarily also not significant. File units, which are segments of organized files, may consist of folders, binders, dossiers, dockets, and the like. Certain types of file units reveal, to a small extent, the character of the documents they contain. Thus, a dossier contains documents relating to a particular person or matter of business; a case file, which is similar to a dossier, contains documents relating to a particular transaction.

Information showing the kind of filing system by which records were organized may not be significant to a searcher but is often quite important to an archivist in that it tells him how to approach a given file to find specific records in it. Files are accumulations of file units. They may be arranged according to various systems, of which the two main ones are the registry system and the modern filing system. Filing systems range from simple numerical, alphabetical, and subject systems to highly complex subject-numeric, duplex-numeric, Dewey decimal, and other systems.

Information on the system of arrangement may also occasionally throw light on the nature of a file. Thus, information showing that letters were organized into a reading file or a chronological file indicates their nature (at least when dealing with records of the federal government of the United States).

VOLUME

An archivist should always show the volume of a record unit. This has been done in various ways in guides recently produced in the United States: by giving the number of physical entities of which a record unit is comprised, such as boxes, containers, bundles, volumes, items, pieces, folders, pages, and leaves; by giving the measurements of the space occupied by records or by their containers, in terms of linear inches and feet.

Quantity should be indicated in terms of the number of pieces contained in each record unit, according to the Historical Records Survey manual on the preparation of guides to manuscripts, issued in 1937; [12] and in terms of the number of items or linear feet, according to the Library of Congress rules for the descriptive cataloging of manuscripts, issued in 1954.[13]

It is desirable to standardize the method of reporting quantity in the United States, to the extent that this is feasible. Standard units of measurement should be of a type that can be employed anywhere. Containers or bundles do not constitute suitable units of measurement, since they are not standard in size. Units that are standard and can be employed anywhere are items, provided that the meaning of the term is properly defined and understood; linear feet and inches; and volumes.

In order to show the quantity of material in a repository, it is desirable to describe each record unit in terms of linear feet and inches and to provide additional information on quantity in terms of the number of items or volumes, whenever this is necessary.

An archivist should indicate volume by answering the following questions:

If loose, how many papers are there? In terms of linear feet and inches, if more than 3 inches (when dealing with public archives); in terms of number of items or pieces, if less than 3 inches (when dealing with historical manuscripts).

If in bound form, how many volumes are there?

If in microfilm form, how many feet of film if less than one reel, how many reels if more than one?

An archivist should indicate the kind of copy, if material does not consist of original records. The reproductions may have been made either manually or photographically. If made manually, the copy should be designated as a transcript, regardless of whether it was made by typewriter or by hand. If the copy is made photographically, two forms of photographic reproductions should be distinguished, photoprints and microfilms. No attempt should be made to differentiate the various types of photographic prints and films.

Substantive Attributes

The course to follow in order to show the content, or substance, of a record unit is to adduce all the facts that show how it came into being. A record unit should be described substantively by (1) identifying its producer or creator, (2) enumerating the activities or transactions that resulted in its production, (3) indicating the time at which it was produced, (4) indicating the place at which it was produced, and (5) ascertaining the objects (persons, places, things, and phenomena) to which the activities or transactions relate. This procedure will almost always yield information that is adequate to describe the content of the record unit.

Description thus consists largely of analyzing precisely how records came into being. While the topical relations of manuscript collections are often shown more fully in recent American guides than are their relations to the activities that resulted in their production, the subject matter of records can actually be revealed much more clearly by taking a functional, rather than a subject, approach in analyzing their content.

PROVENANCE

In the description of a record unit, a very important attribute, which an archivist should take into account, relates to its provenance. The term "provenance" has a distinctive meaning in the archival profession. It refers, as we have seen, to a principle of arrangement that is as basic to the archival profession as the Dewey decimal system of classification is to the library profession. Its meaning should be differentiated sharply from the meaning given it in the library profession. In the broad sense in which the term is used in the archival profession, it refers to how documentary material came into being, and particularly to its source in some organic body. In a library sense, the term is used to refer to matters that are far less important, specifically when used in reference to manuscripts. It refers, in such cases, to the person from whom manuscripts were obtained by purchase or gift, not necessarily to their producer or creator.

An archivist may clearly identify the provenance of a record unit by answering the question: *Who?* Which person, corporate body, or government agency produced the unit?

A certain amount of meaningful information can be provided about public records simply by identifying the government agency that produced them. The more precise the information on their producer, the more precise is the information on their content. If records were produced by a government agency, a mere identification of the agency will reveal, to a degree at least, their content or nature. Thus, records produced by the United States Department of Agriculture obviously relate to agricultural matters; those of the Forest Service within the department, to forestry; and those of the Division of Forest Disease Research, to forest diseases.

Similarly, information on source is helpful in describing private records. Reviewers of finding aids generally recognize the importance of identifying the kind of personal or corporate body that produced a manuscript collection. But it is not yet generally recognized that it is as important to provide such an identification about the body that produced a manuscript collection as it is to provide data about the administrative status of a public body that produced an archival group. In reviewing the Smith guide to the Wisconsin Historical Society manuscripts, Curtis W. Garrison pointed out that it has a "minimum of biographical detail," and that this is "true of practically every guide" except that of the Clements Library. Garrison added that "a sketch of the subject should be the skeletal organization [of the description] of each important collection." [14] In reviewing the guide to the University of Missouri manuscript collection, Marguerite J. Pease pointed out that information contained in biographical sketches "is very helpful to searchers." [15] In reviewing the Withington catalog of manuscripts of Western Americana in the Yale University Library, Henry P. Beers observed that its usefulness "has been greatly enhanced by the inclusion of biographical information." [16]

An archivist should specify, when dealing with business records, what kind of a business produced them—whether a manufacturing, marketing, or transportation business. Or when dealing with institutional records, whether they were produced by an educational, religious, or charitable institution.

When describing personal records, an archivist should similarly provide information about the person's occupation, profession, business, or positions held. Was the person a lawyer, farmer, businessman, Congressman, or was he noteworthy for having been associated with a particular organization or institution? Biographical reference works will help provide this kind of information. Merely by indicating a person's occupation or profession, a great deal is made known about his papers. Thus, if it is made known that Roy Bedichek is a Texas naturalist, educator, and author, the general nature of his papers is made known. Information about a person's career may be indicated briefly in the manner used in biographical dictionaries, e.g.: John Doe (Congressman, lumberman, farmer).

FUNCTIONAL ORIGINS

Information on the functional origins of a record unit is very important in its description.

An archivist can clearly identify the functional origins of a record unit by answering the question: *How?* How did the record unit come into being? What organic function resulted in its production?

The term "function" is here used in a broad generic sense to cover all actions taken by a government agency, corporate body, or person to accomplish some project or purpose. In the case of a government agency, this may be the major program for which it was established. The term may be broken down into more specific terms. Thus, the term "activity" may be used, in a more specific sense than "function," to signify a class of actions that are taken in carrying out a specific function. The term "transaction" is yet more specific than the term "activity" and may be used to refer to specific actions.

The meaning of the terms "functions," "activities," and "transactions" may be illustrated by referring to the work of the National Archives. Its functions are to appraise, accession, repair, maintain, arrange, describe, publish, and service valuable records of the federal government. For administrative purposes, these functions have been grouped under the following heads: Disposition, Preservation and Arrangement, Description and Publication, and Reference Service. Under the function designated as Disposition, two activities occur: the *disposal activity*, which involves primarily the appraisal of records proposed for disposal by other government agencies, and the *accessioning activity*, which involves the appraisal and movement of records offered for transfer to the National Archives by other government agencies. In the performance of each of these activities, a number of specific transactions occur. In the disposal activity, the handling of a specific proposal to destroy records results in a *disposal transaction;* in the accessioning activity, the handling of a specific offer of records results in an *accessioning transaction.*

Functions of a private corporate body, or even of a person, may be similarly broken down into activities and transactions. In the case of a business, for example, it is important to know what it did. Its main function may have been to make, sell, or transport a specific kind of product. In carrying out its function, it performed a number of kinds of activities. In every business there is the activity of keeping accounts—of recording debits and credits of all kinds. This activity merely reflects, in monetary terms, actions of all kinds: buying, selling, and delivering products; buying and maintaining equipment and buildings; hiring and paying workers, and the like.

A person, in a similar way, may have been engaged in various kinds of activities—professional, legal, diplomatic, religious, cultural, or other kinds. Within these classes of activities, he may have been associated with particular transactions, such as the establishment of a school, the construction of a railroad, or the management of a bank.

The more precise the information about functional origins, the more descriptive it is of the content of records. Thus, the content of records of a government agency can be shown quite precisely merely by showing what activities and transactions resulted in their production. To illustrate: certain records of the National Archives may be described in general terms by showing that they relate to the disposition function; they may be described more precisely by showing that they relate to either disposal activities or accessioning activities; and they may be described with complete precision by showing that they relate to either a specific disposal or a specific accessioning transaction.

An archivist thus should determine what specific activities and transactions are reflected in the records he is describing. Records can be described more effectively in relation to their functional origins than to any other attribute. For the significance, character, and content of records are revealed by showing what actions resulted in their creation. Their content, in fact, is often shown both in relation to the actions that resulted in their creation and in relation to the subjects—persons, places, things—that were involved in the actions.

TIME OF PRODUCTION

In describing a record unit, an archivist should ask himself, *when* was it produced? Between which dates? If most of the papers or unusually significant papers were produced between particular dates, an archivist may give such dates in parentheses between the first and the last dates. He may also show important gaps and inexact dates.

PLACE OF PRODUCTION

In describing a record unit, an archivist should always show *where* it was produced.

Information on place is quite important to a searcher in determining if a given unit is germane to his inquiry. In the Duke University Library guide by Tilley and Goodwin, place is indicated by giving the names of cities and towns and, in some cases, counties.[17] For cities and large towns, counties are not indicated; for small towns, the county names are indicated in parentheses after the names of the towns, thus: Summerfield (Guilford County), N.C. If a place cannot be shown by giving the name of a town or village, the name of the county is given. A similar practice is followed in the Ohio Archaeological and Historical Society guide by Biggert, in which the county name is indicated in parentheses after the town and village name, if the town or village has less than five thousand people according to the 1940 census.[18] In the guide to the archives and manuscripts of the United States, produced by the National Historical Publications Commission, place is indicated by showing the state within the United States in which the records were produced, thus: Tutwiler, Julia Strudwick (Ala.).[19]

Place may thus be indicated by referring to countries, states, regions, cities, towns, or counties. The kind of place to be indicated depends on the nature of the holdings that are being described. The holdings of a national repository should be identified in terms of states; those of a state repository, in terms of cities, towns, or counties.

SUBJECT MATTER

An archivist should indicate the subject matter of a record unit in both general and specific terms.

While public records should be described under organizational and functional heads, private records should be identified, in catalogs and guides, in reference to major heads that relate to three elements: place, time, and subjects reflecting broad fields of human activity. The geographical and chronological heads, the nature of which is obvious, should be derived from the place and time at which records were produced. Functional heads, in contrast, should be derived from an analysis of the major fields of activity that resulted in the production of records. The concept of functional (or activity) heads is somewhat alien to the thinking of persons working with source materials. Usually such persons select subject heads from library classification schemes and cataloging lists. While existing bibliographic categorizations are suggestive in compiling a list of subject heads for records, the subject heads used in respect to publications are likely to be inapplicable, if not misleading, because they are keyed to classes of human knowledge, not to classes of human activity.

Since source material—historical manuscripts and public archives—is always the result of function, and is usually arranged according to function, it should be analyzed in relation to function. The broad subject heads, in relation to which records are identified, should be consciously chosen to reflect human activities or functions. While it is difficult to select the major classes of activities that result in the production of records, the following are some of the more important ones: agricultural, business, diplomatic, educational, governmental, military, political, religious, scientific, and social activities. These activities, expressed in their nominative form, indicate the broad subject heads that should be used in catalogs and guides. When combined with geographical and chronological heads, they will provide a threefold analysis of records by subject, time, and place; and this analysis ordinarily will enable a searcher to use a catalog or guide effectively in that it will help him determine which record units are likely to pertain to his subject of inquiry.

Specific subjects to which records relate should be identified by analyzing the content of records, not by analyzing subject lists used for library classification and cataloging purposes. No matter how well conceived for library work, such lists have only a limited usefulness in describing the subject content of records.

To find out the specific subjects to which records relate, an archivist should try consciously to discover the objects of the various activities and transactions that led to the creation of records. Such objects are the subjects in relation to which records should be described, using the term "object" in the sense in which it is defined in Webster's *New International Dictionary* as "that on which the purposes are fixed as the end of action or effort." Specific subjects, then, should be ascertained deductively from an analysis of the objects of activities and transactions.

The specific subjects are of four kinds: persons, places, things, and phenomena. These kinds may be analyzed as follows:

Persons:
Individuals
Corporate bodies:
Private—businesses, churches, universities, and organizations and institutions of all kinds.
Public—government agencies and instrumentalities of all kinds: federal, state, and local

Places:
Geographical areas: countries, states, regions, counties, cities, and towns

Things:
Artificial (man-made):
Structures—buildings, bridges, and the like
Machines—automobiles, trains, and the like
Goods—commodities, merchandise, and wares
Natural:
Land (with its topographical features, such as mountains, rivers, lakes, and the like)
Minerals
Vegetables
Animals

Phenomena:
Generic classes of phenomena, such as agricultural, business, and military classes
Specific phenomena, such as particular events, episodes, transactions, conditions, or problems

It is easy to determine if records relate to certain of the specific subjects mentioned above, that is to say, if they relate to persons, places, and things. Such subjects are clearly distinguishable in records and, fortunately, are the subjects that are the most important from the point of view of the use that is made of records. If he has information on them, a searcher usually can tell if a given record unit has information on his subject of inquiry.

The term "persons," as we have noted, includes both personal and corporate bodies and refers to bodies mentioned in a record unit or contributing to its production. Practices vary in recording names of persons in finding aids. In the Clements Library guide by Peckham, all names are listed—to the annoyance of some reviewers; [20] in the Huntington Library guide by Cuthbert, the names of persons who wrote several (two or more) documents are listed; [21] in the Oneida Historical Society catalog, the names of the principal or most important writers are listed.[22] In most guides, names of writers are simply listed by happenstance. A reviewer criticized the Wisconsin Historical Society guide by Smith because names are "selected at random from some collections." [23] This criticism, whether valid or not, may be leveled with equal justification at most American guides. Information on persons is especially useful in genealogical and biographical studies, but is also valuable for historical research, whether this is focused on national, state, or local matters.

The term "place" refers to geographical location. Information on the places mentioned in a record unit, or to which a record unit pertains, is also useful in all kinds of researches. In the Duke University Library guide by Tilley and Goodwin, such information is provided in the italicized lines:

THOMAS WHITE JR., PAPERS, 1860–61. 15 items. (Enfield, N.C.)
Correspondence and papers of Thomas White, Jr. . . . Included are . . . descriptions of various resorts, including *White Sulphur Springs, Virginia, and Jones Springs, Virginia, and Shocco Springs, North Carolina.*

The term "things" may include a great variety of man-made and natural objects. While such objects are more difficult to identify than persons and places, an archivist usually can determine which particular things, or classes of things, should be mentioned in the description of a record unit.

The term "phenomena" relates to what happens to either persons or things—to conditions, problems, activities, programs, events, episodes, and the like. The phenomena that are identified as specific subjects in records should be distinguished from the activities that resulted in the production of records, for these are also phenomena. For example, land entry papers are the result of the activity of the General Land Office in opening the public domain for private ownership of land. This is the activity that resulted in their production. They relate, however, to such phenomena as the settlement of the West, the frontier movement, and land utilization. Or, to cite another example, population census schedules are the result of the census-taking activity of the Census Bureau, but relate to such phenomena as population growth and movements, as well as urban and rural developments. Phenomena are even more difficult to identify as specific subjects than are things, for they are infinitely varied, are often indefinite and intangible, and are both general and specific in character.

An archivist may identify the specific subjects to which a record unit relates by answering the following questions:

Who? To which person or corporate body does the record unit relate?

What? To what things does the record unit relate?

How? How are either persons or things dealt with in the record unit? What phenomenon is recorded in it?

Where? Where did the phenomenon occur to which the record unit relates?

Under the procedure outlined above, an archivist, while describing the consular correspondence of the State Department relating to foreign trade relations, for example, should note what objects are being promoted for trade. Are they agricultural commodities, manufactured goods, or minerals? And if so, what specific kind? These are the objects of the activity of promoting trade relations, and they are also the subjects to which the correspondence relates. Or in describing correspondence that relates to persons, an archivist should note who they are. Or if it relates to classes of persons, what are the classes? Here the persons or classes of persons are the subjects of the correspondence. Or if he is describing correspondence that relates to episodes, events, places or some other matters, what are they? Here the phenomena or the places are the subjects of the correspondence.

IX

NOTATIONAL SYSTEMS

One of the few works in the annals of literature in which an archivist plays a major role is Anatole France's *The Revolt of the Angels*. In this fictional account of the descent of a number of angels from Heaven in search of truth about religion, the archivist and paleographer Julien Sariette stands guard over an extensive private collection of manuscript and library material. He is described as poor and retiring, seated at his desk and cataloging, and casting a Medusa-like look at anyone who enters his sacred precinct wishing to use his holdings.

Monsieur Sariette, we are told, assigned symbols to all items of his vast holdings, which may serve as a point of departure for discussing the purpose and use of notation generally.

The system he invented and put into practice was so complicated, the labels he put on the books were made up of so many capital letters and small letters, both Latin and Greek, so many Arabic and Roman numerals, asterisks, double asterisks, triple asterisks, and those signs which in arithmetic express powers and roots, that the mere study of it would have involved more time and labor than would have been required for the complete mastery of algebra, and as no one could be found who would give the hours, that might be more profitably employed in discovering the law of numbers, to the solving of these cryptic symbols, Monsieur Sariette remained the only one capable of finding his way among the intricacies of his system.[1]

A notational system should not consist of long and cabalistic marks, understood only by the archivist who devises them. Almost every purpose can be served by using a simple combination of letters and numbers. Symbols may be either pure, i.e., numbers only or letters only, or mixed, i.e., letters and numbers combined. Numbers, ordinarily, should be of only one kind, i.e., Arabic, for little purpose is served by also using Roman numerals, which are, generally, difficult to understand. The letters, also, need be of only one kind, not both Latin and Greek.

A notational system may become excessively complex because too much is attempted by its use. It may be intended to show too many things about records: their subject matter, provenance, and type, as well as their location in the stacks. And being designed to show too many things, the symbols may become long and involved, as did those of Monsieur Sariette. A notational system loses its usefulness to the degree that it becomes complex; the simpler the system, the better.

A notational system is as important in the management of records as it is in the classification and cataloging of publications. For archival uses, symbols should be assigned to three objects: (1) record units, i.e., collections, groups, series, and, occasionally, individual items; (2) stacks, i.e., areas, rows, compartments, and, occasionally, shelves; and (3) containers. Symbols assigned to such objects should not be combined into a single set of notations, for each set of them has a fairly distinctive use. Once a well-conceived notational system has been adopted, symbols should not be changed.

Notation for Record Units

Manuscript curators have given relatively little attention to the development of notational systems. However, the Manuscript Division of the Library of Congress, in the early years of its activities, devised a system in which symbols were used to designate the geographical classes into which it organized its miscellaneous manuscripts. For example, material relating to Mexico was designated by the symbol "Mx," or, if relating to Sonora, by "Mxs." Number symbols were applied to manuscripts in the sequence in which they were assigned to classes, thus: "Mx37" referred to the 37th item relating to Mexico as a whole, and "Mxs38" to the 38th item relating to Sonora.[2]

In 1916 Worthington C. Ford sent a questionnaire to a number of manuscript repositories to obtain information about their arrangement practices and notational systems. Ford recognized four types of record units to be dealt with: personal collections, artificial collections, individual record items, and manuscript volumes.[3]

While returns to Ford's questionnaire are unavailable, annual reports of a few historical societies refer to the questionnaire. The 1916 report of the New York State Library, which was then under the direction of Peter Nelson, reveals that personal collections were regarded as separate series and were assigned mnemonic letter symbols, such as "J" to the Johnson papers and "C" to the Clinton papers; artificial collections were classified into series, each of which was comprised of papers that related to "general topics that cover the whole State, such as Revolutionary War, War of 1812 and Civil War" and each of the series thus constituted was assigned a letter symbol; individual items were classified into one or the other of the above constituted series and were assigned letter symbols; and manuscript volumes were treated as single items and were assigned letter symbols.[4]

The Wisconsin Historical Society also responded to Ford's questionnaire. The society divided the Draper Collection, which initially constituted the major part of its holdings, "into fifty groups or series, the first twenty-five being given each a single letter of the alphabet (the letter I being skipped because of its similarity to J) and the second twenty-five each a double letter (i.e., AA, BB, CC, and so forth) of the alphabet." In 1916 the society adopted a new classification scheme that was described by Milo M. Quaife, its director, as one in which manuscript collections are grouped according to the state to which they chiefly pertain, and series within each group are designated by letters of the alphabet. If series in a group are so numerous that they exhaust the twenty-five letters (omitting I), double letters are used, i.e., AA, AB, AC, etc.[5]

The Minnesota Historical Society, at the present time, uses symbols to designate its main classes as follows: A for personal papers; B for corporate papers; C for catchall papers, i.e., those that belong to neither A nor B; D for documents from other repositories; and E for internal documents.[6] The Minnesota system was introduced to the Historical Society of Western Pennsylvania by Solon J. Buck (1884–1962) when he became director of the Western Pennsylvania Historical Survey; it was later adopted, with some modification, by other historical societies.

The Department of Archives of the Louisiana State University uses the following symbols to designate its collections: B for bound volumes, UB for unbound volumes, and M for miscellaneous items.[7]

TYPES OF RECORD UNITS

The types of record units to which symbols should be assigned are manuscript collections, archival groups, series, and items.

In the assignment of symbols to manuscript collections, the following procedure should be followed:

In a manuscript repository in which all collections, whether large or small, are maintained in a single series, a sequence of simple numbers, i.e., 1, 2, 3, 4, is satisfactory.

In a manuscript repository in which collections are organized into classes and within classes are arranged in a numerical sequence, symbols should be assigned that will denote both the class and the order in which collections are received within each class. A letter symbol should be prefixed to the number symbol for each collection, the letter referring to the class and the number to the sequence in which the collection within the class was received, thus: A-1, A-2, A-3, etc.; B-1, B-2, B-3, etc.

If accretions, or additions of material, are received that are added to existing collections, the accession number of each accretion should be composed of two figures, the first being the one assigned to the collection on its receipt, and the second, after the decimal point, being the one assigned to each new accretion, thus: 1.1, 1.2, 1.3 or 4.2, 4.3, 4.4, etc.; A-1.1, A-2.1, A-3.1 or A-4.2, A-4.3, etc.

If small lots of items are embodied in a collection of miscellany, each lot within it should be assigned a number as it is received. To distinguish the lots of miscellany from other collections, a letter symbol should be prefixed to the number symbol for each lot, thus: M-1, M-2, M-3, etc.

If bound material is embodied in a collection of miscellany, each volume within it should be assigned a number as it is received. To distinguish the collection of miscellaneous bound material from a collection of miscellaneous loose material, an additional letter symbol should be prefixed to the symbol for each volume, thus: MV-1, MV-2, MV-3, etc.

If collections of volumes of particular record types are maintained, a double letter should be assigned to each volume, the first denoting that it belongs to a collection of miscellany, and the second denoting its record type, e.g., A for account books, D for diaries, L for letter books, etc. The complete symbol should thus be: MA-1, MD-1, ML-1, etc.

In the assignment of symbols to archival groups, the procedures are slightly different from those followed with respect to manuscript collections. Symbols, which may be either numbers or letters, are usually assigned to such groups in the order of their establishment, not in the order of their receipt.

In the National Archives, numbers are used. The numbers assigned to the groups created by the U.S. Department of Agriculture, for example, are 7, 8, 16, 17, 33, 83, etc. Since they were assigned in the order in which such groups were established, they do not reflect administrative relationships.

In the Public Record Office, letters are used to identify groups, of which there are seventy-eight. Often they consist of abbreviations of the titles of the governmental offices that produced archival groups. Examples of such symbols are: C.O. for Colonial Office, F.O. for Foreign Office, and Adm. for Admiralty. Such symbols reflect the organic origins of the archival groups to which they are assigned. This is quite important, for the origin of the groups that are often used by scholars is quickly made apparent by the symbols they bear. "The system," according to Hilary Jenkinson, "did not attain full utility until a method of abbreviation had been worked out." [8] It is obviously very difficult to devise symbols for a large number of archival groups, each of which will reflect the title of the office that produced a group. This difficulty is apparent, also, in the notational system of the Public Record Office, which only partially serves to reveal the organic origins of its archival groups.[9]

In the assignment of symbols to series, the practices are determined by the degree to which items within series have been arranged. In the National Archives, descriptive entries for series in preliminary inventories are numbered, but the series themselves have not been numbered, since many of them have not been given their final arrangement. In the Public Record Office, archival groups are divided into classes, of which there were 3,250 in 1949. Since arrangement work has proceeded further in that institution than in the National Archives, classes, which are the British equivalent of American series, have been assigned numbers. Thus, class 2 of the Admiralty group is identified as "Adm.2."

In the assignment of symbols to items, various practices are followed. In the National Archives, items within series have not been numbered, because the series produced by the federal government are too numerous and too varied in their physical makeup to allow them to be numbered. But in the French National Archives and in the British Public Record Office record items are numbered. In the latter institution, classes (or series) are composed of "pieces"—volumes, rolls, bundles, and the like —of which there were estimated to be 680,000 in 1949. The first piece within the second class of the Admiralty group is identified as "Adm. 2/1," and the first document within this piece as "Adm. 2/1/1."

Manuscript repositories will generally find it practicable to number items in small collections, and should always number items in highly important collections.

MAIN USES OF SYMBOLS

Symbols assigned to records provide a shorthand system of identification for an archivist. They facilitate reference to record units in internal administrative documents; descriptive documents, particularly lists, catalogs, and indexes; and reference service documents. They also facilitate citation by the user.

The two types of administrative documents that involve the use of symbols are accessions registers and location registers, which are discussed in Chapter XIII. In a location register, the position of record units is indicated by means of stack symbols and container numbers; the record units themselves are identified by symbols, as well as by title.

In descriptive documents, symbols assigned to records should be used only if the notational system is simple in character; expansive, in the sense that it may be applied progressively to new accessions; and stable, in the sense that it will not be changed once it has been adopted.

When listing, cataloging, and indexing record items, it is obviously necessary to identify the collection or group to which each item belongs. The collection or group, in a word, must be identified before an item within it can be dealt with. If this must be done by giving the title of the record unit to which each item belongs, as well as the title of the item itself, listing, cataloging, and indexing become very tedious tasks.

Symbols provide a means of quickly and easily identifying collections. They reduce the tedious work of showing the identity of record items and permit the archivist to concentrate on the analysis of the items themselves. The collection in which a particular item may be found can be identified simply by the symbol assigned to it, e.g., 1, 2, or A-1, A-2, etc.

When discrete items are listed, the collections should be identified thus:

Request for indemnity, Sister St. Etienne Vassas, Columbia, S.C., to French minister, Dec. 11, 1865, for losses incurred during the burning of the city by General Sherman's army, Feb. 17, 1865.
(56-4)
Personal diary, John Doe (Knoxville, Tenn., Confederate soldier), 1861 (1863–67) 1878, 24 pages.   (B-12)

When items of a given record type are listed, the collections should be identified thus:

ACCOUNT BOOKS
    Ames, Ezra (Albany, N.Y.; artist), 1790–1826   (18)
    Arthur & Deall (N.Y.C.; merchants), 1783–85   (22)

When items in a collection of miscellaneous account books are listed, the collection in which they are found should be identified thus:

ACCOUNT BOOKS:
    Canova Brothers, Inc. (N.Y.C., builders), 1819–30   (MA-17)
    Potomac Farm Market (Washington, D.C.; produce merchants), 1821–41   (MA-41)

When discrete items or items of a given record type are cataloged, the symbols that identify the collections in which they are found should be placed in the upper left-hand side of the catalog cards, thus:

B-12
Doe, John (Knoxville, Tenn.; Confederate soldier), Personal diary, 1861(1863–67)1878, 24 pages.

or if the particular item has been numbered, thus:

54-45
Doe, John (Lubbock, Texas; farmer), Personal letter to Richard Roe, Feb. 24, 1914, about land speculation in Texas.

When items in a collection of miscellany are cataloged, the folders in which they are found should be identified thus:

M-13
Doe, John (Newton, Kansas; miller), Personal letter to Richard Roe, Oct. 1, 1901, about the introduction of Turkey Red seed wheat from Russia.

Symbols are especially useful in preparing indexes, which, as we have seen, are a means of indicating which collections contain information on particular subjects. The collections in which information is found must obviously be precisely identified in an index, and symbols are an easy and quick means of identifying them. The work of preparing copy for an index can be reduced to a routine if the subjects (that are being indexed) are written out and if the record units (that contain information on the subjects) are identified only by symbol. In an index to personal names, to illustrate, the collections should be identified on index cards in the following manner:

A-15	Hall, Albert
B-5	Hall, Carl
A-1	Hall, Ethel
C-4	Hall, Francis
B-17	Hall, George

Symbols are also quite useful in servicing records. They facilitate citation of particular record units in outcards, service requests, loan receipts, and other documents used in rendering reference service. They are useful in restoring the order of records, if it has been disturbed in use. They are also a means of accounting for records while they are in use, enabling an archivist to check quickly and easily if all items have been returned.

Symbols also make it easier for the user of records to cite them in footnotes and bibliographies. The problem of citation is an especially difficult one in a documentary repository.

In the British Public Record Office, in which the problem of citation has been solved in an almost ideal fashion, the notational system refers to three elements: the first is the "group," the second is the "class," and the third is the "piece."

A citation to documents in the Public Record Office refers to the above three elements as follows: C.O. (Colonial Office); 5 (class 5, which relates to America and the West Indies); 1 (piece 1, which is volume 1 covering the years 1689–97); or, in short, C.O./5/1. If a piece consists of loose papers, the citation is carried one step further, for the loose papers within a piece are also numbered. Thus C.O./5/2/1 may refer to the first loose paper in a bundle, identified as piece 2.

In the National Archives, the method of citation is far more cumbersome than in the Public Record Office. At the present time, searchers are enjoined to "identify the particular document, the series to which it belongs, and the agency among whose records it is found. . . . The record group number assigned by the National Archives to the body of records involved may facilitate finding the document but it is not an essential part of citation." [10] Eventually, when the arrangement of series within archival groups has been perfected, it may be possible to develop the equivalent of the British notational system in the National Archives, using archival group numbers and series numbers as symbols for purposes of citation.

SUBSIDIARY USES OF SYMBOLS

Symbols have possible subsidiary values in showing record attributes. They have often been used to show the provenance, record type, and subject relations of record units. The advantages of using symbols for such purposes, however, are largely illusory, for usually symbols become so complex, if used in this way, that their very complexity defeats the purposes for which they are used.

Symbols that are used to show the provenance of record units may be of two kinds: those devised quite arbitrarily without regard for the titles of offices, and those derived from abbreviations of titles of offices. The latter kind, obviously, has a mnemonic value that the former lacks.

When dealing with record bodies that have organic relations, an archivist is tempted to use symbols to show such relations. In its very early years, the National Archives attempted to classify records produced by particular government agencies in very much the same way that books are classified in a library. In fact, a Division of Classification was established, the function of which was to develop schemes for the classification (or arrangement) of the components of various archival groups. The classification schemes, of course, had symbols or notations embodied in them. These symbols were keyed to organizational units, as well as to record units.

The classification scheme for the records of the United States Food Administration, for the period 1917–20, illustrates the method of using symbols. The symbols consist of numbers combined with letters, as follows:

1H   Office of the United States Food Administrator
2H   Appointment Division
3H   Mailing Division
4H   Filing Division
5H   Home Conservation Division
            5HA General Office
            5HB Speakers' Bureau
            5HC Office of the Pledge Card Campaign
6H   States Administration Division
etc.

The series created by each organizational unit within the Food Administration were given additional symbols by the Division of Classification, as follows: A1, A2, A3, A4, B1, B2, B3. The symbols assigned to series were combined with those assigned to organizational units, as follows: 1H-A1, 1H-A2, 1H-A3, 1H-A4, 1H-B1, etc.

According to the author of the notational system devised by the Classification Division, a symbol for a given record unit is "made up of three elements."

The first element identifies the archival group as such, e.g., FA for Food Administration.

The second, called the "organizational element of the symbol," identifies the organizational unit within the agency that produced the archival group. It consists "of the number of the division, or other parts of the administration to which, in cases where the divisions had sections, a letter is added to the divisional designation." In the symbol 8HA, 8H refers to the Cereal Division, and A to the Coarse Grain Section within it.

The third, called the "record element" of the symbol, "comprises, first, a letter to designate each group of records found within the division or section, and this, in turn, is followed by a number which indicates the unit." In the symbol B1, B refers to group B, and 1 to item one within it.

A complete symbol for the record unit is thus: FA 8HA-B1.

While one may agree with the author of the notational system described above, that "adequate symbols must be provided which will permit shelving on the basis of relative location," it may be observed that the system he devised shows more than relative location: it shows the relation of record units to the large body that created them and to organizational units within it. It is not possible to avoid "cumbersome symbols," as the author enjoins us to do, if the symbols are to show administrative origins in the detail he suggests.[11]

Symbols cannot ordinarily be used effectively to show organic relations within groups or collections. Even if symbols can be devised to reflect the organic structure of records or, rather, the structure of the office that created them, this structure is characteristically so complex that it would require extremely complex symbols, and the complexity of the symbols will diminish their usefulness. They are not useful for mnemonic purposes because they are far too complex to remember.

Symbols may also be used to designate record type, and for this purpose they may be applied to single items or to series.

Symbols have often been used to denote the record type of single items in calendars, catalogs, and lists. A fairly elaborate set of symbols has been devised for this purpose, the most common of which are the following:

L	A letter or writing in the form of a communication
L.S.	A letter signed
A.L.S.	An autograph letter signed
D	A document other than a letter
D.S.	A document signed
A.D.S.	An autograph document signed

One of the earliest statements in the United States in regard to their use is found in an article written by H. M. Lydenberg in 1899 on the cataloging of manuscripts at the New York Public Library. Lydenberg stated that symbols should be used in cataloging to provide information on the authenticity of items being cataloged.[12] In recent years, many additional symbols have been devised to denote additional record types, but, no matter how many may be added, their number will never be adequate to designate the innumerable types one encounters in modern records. And if symbols are devised to designate the multiplicity of modern types, they will become so complicated that they will become meaningless. At the present time, type symbols are useful primarily to manuscript dealers.

Symbols have occasionally been used to denote the record type of series in inventories and guides. They can be used for this purpose only when a series consists exclusively of a particular record type. This means that they have a rather limited application, for many series are established on the basis of a consideration of factors other than record type. The factors of arrangement and relation to activity are also important in establishing series, as I have emphasized earlier. Symbols for record type cannot be made part of a general system of notation.

Symbols can be used to advantage, however, to single out for attention specific record types, because of the importance of the information they contain or for other reasons. This practice is followed in the Baker Library of Harvard University in respect to account books, which are given a distinctive symbol because of their importance for studies of prices, costs, profits, losses, and the like. Symbols are used in a similar way in certain National Archives lists.

Symbols may be used, to a limited extent, to show subject relations. Since library classifications schemes are designed to cover all human knowledge, many symbols of such schemes relate to classes and subclasses for which no records exist. When such symbols are applied to records, the most that can be done is to use only those symbols that pertain to subject classes for which there are records. If the holdings of a repository are classified by major subjects, symbols can thus be used to show that a particular manuscript collection is found in a particular subject class, such as the military or business class of collections. Or if the holdings of a repository are specialized, consisting, for example, of business records, and have been classified by major subjects, symbols can be used to show that a particular collection is found in a particular subject class. This is done at the Baker Library at Harvard University.[13] This library classifies its collections (except large ones) by industry and assigns symbols to each class that show its relation to a particular industry. Symbols devised by William P. Cutter, noted librarian, are used to designate the various industries. Collections on cotton manufacturing are assigned number .442; those on canal transportation, number .731, etc. The same purpose could have been accomplished more easily, without reference to the notation of a library classification scheme, simply by using a letter or number to denote each industry class.

Symbols should not be used to interpret the resources of a repository to a searcher by showing their relation to subject. They will obviously fail to do this, for their meaning will be understood only by the person who mistakenly applied them for such a purpose.

Notation for Stacks

American librarians, as we noted in Chapter I, began with "fixed-location" schemes. Their initial classification schemes were based on the idea that symbols should be assigned to fixed points in the stacks, as well as to publications. The following table indicates how this scheme was applied in several important libraries.

| | FIXED LOCATION | | | |
Library	Alcove	Range	Case	Shelf
Boston Public Library	x	x		x
Library of Congress				x
Brooklyn Public Library		x	x	x
Chicago Public Library			x	x
Harvard University Library		x	x	x

Librarians got away from such schemes largely as a result of the work of Dewey. The Dewey and Cutter classification schemes, which replaced the earlier schemes, use notational systems that omit the element that refers to fixed locations. In the Dewey system, notation refers to the relative position of each publication within a class or subclass. In the Cutter system, the symbols, as Cutter explains, "consist of two parts (a) the class-mark, which shows in what class the book belongs; and (b) the book-mark, which distinguishes that book from other works in the same class." [14]

The early notational systems were satisfactory before the rapid expansion of library holdings, when books remained in a fairly fixed position. Since records, once they have been properly arranged, should be kept in place in the stacks, notations that designate fixed points in the stacks are useful to archivists. They facilitate showing the location of records.

Archivists, therefore, should use symbols in the way they were used by American librarians during the formative years of the library profession. They should plan to maintain record units in fixed positions and should assign symbols to such positions in the stacks. These symbols should be distinctive. If numbers are used, a particular number should be used for one position, and one position only. No matter how complicated the stacks may be, it will be possible to devise a numbering system under which each position is assigned a number that distinguishes it from all other positions. The number should refer to the following elements: the stack area, the row within the stack area, and the compartment within the row.

Notation for Containers

Containers should be numbered in the sequence in which records are arranged within a manuscript collection or an archival series.

Symbols assigned to stacks will help show the fixed positions at which record units are shelved; those assigned to containers will show the position of particular units among other units on shelves.

Symbols assigned to stacks and containers should normally not be embodied in descriptive entries of finding aids, for, as records are shifted from one location to another, they will be misleading. They can be recorded on office copies of finding aids, as a means of quickly locating the record units described in such aids during the period when they remain at a fixed position.

Symbols assigned to stacks and containers should be keyed to symbols assigned to record units in a location register, which should be maintained in every sizable repository.

Part II

APPLICATION OF PRINCIPLES
AND TECHNIQUES

To accumulate was our special function in the nineteenth century;
our function in the twentieth will be to make all accumulations
available.

Charles Francis Adams, April 13, 1899

X

ARRANGEMENT OF
ARCHIVAL GROUPS

In arranging archives—records that are the product of purposive action—an archivist should ordinarily do two things: establish or identify record units and place such units in proper order in the stacks of a repository.

The record units to which he will have to give professional attention are of two kinds: units that have their origin in administrative bodies and units that have their origin in functions or activities. The term "group" will be used to refer to units established on the basis of their *organizational* origins; the term "series," to refer to units established on the basis of their *functional* origins.

The first section of this chapter is devoted to a discussion of how archival groups and subgroups should be established and arranged; the second, of how archival series should be established and arranged.

Archival Groups and Subgroups

ESTABLISHMENT

In order to deal effectively with the voluminous records created by a national or state government, a large business, or a large professional or ecclesiastical institution or organization, an archivist should determine the major groups into which such records may be divided. Such groups are of three kinds: (*a*) archival groups established strictly according to their provenance in some major organizational unit of a governmental or corporate body, (*b*) general archival groups established for records that relate to a governmental or corporate body as a whole, not only to one of its organizational units, and (*c*) collective archival groups established for records of a given class of corporate bodies or agencies.

Archival groups for major organizational units

An archival group established on the basis of its origins in a major organizational unit should be produced by an administrative entity that has distinctive programs with exclusive jurisdiction over them. This fact was stressed by Hilary Jenkinson, who defined an "archive group" as comprising all records "resulting from the work of an Administration which was an organic whole, complete in itself, capable of dealing independently, without added or external authority, with every side of any business which could normally be presented to it." [1] The entity, in short, should be of such a character that the records it produces are clearly separable from others, so that they can be dealt with as a distinct record unit.

In a highly complex government, such as the federal government of the United States, no governmental unit completely meets Jenkinson's requirements, for all units are interrelated and few are completely independent in their dealing with the business that is their main concern. Jenkinson's requirements, therefore, have to be tempered somewhat if they are to be applied to the federal archives of the United States. The National Archives established archival groups for administrative units that lack the quality of completeness and independence emphasized by Jenkinson, and considered quantity, as well as provenance, in establishing them.[2] It defined the term "archival group" as meaning "a major archival unit established somewhat arbitrarily with due regard to the principle of provenance and to the desirability of making the unit of convenient size and character for the work of arrangement and description and for the publication of inventories." [3]

In a state archival institution, archival groups may be established for records of major offices, such as the offices of the governor, secretary of state, or auditor. In an ecclesiastical archival institution, such groups may be found for the central governing body and for specific and well-defined organizational units, such as those concerned with publishing, education, or missionary activities.

General archival groups

An archivist, normally, should establish a general archival group for each organic body, as well as groups for its major organizational units. Such a general archival group should include all records that relate to the organic body as a whole, not only to one of its organizational units.

In the federal government, a general archival group may be comprised of the records of the central staff offices of an agency, as well as records pertaining to the agency as a whole. For example, the records produced by the staff offices of the Department of Agriculture are considered a general record group in the National Archives. To this group may be added records that relate to the entire Department of Agriculture, such as a master set of its organizational charts and directories; a master set of its formal policy and procedural issuances; authoritative documents that affect or define its functions, such as laws and executive orders; annual narrative and statistical reports on its accomplishments, and the like.

In an ecclesiastical archival institution, a general archival group may be established for records of the central governing body of the church organization, to which may be added any documents that relate to the entire organization, not only to any particular unit within it. Such documents may include annual reports, minutes of conferences, budgetary records, and the like.

In a university archival institution, a general archival group may be established for records of the president's office, to which may be added any documents that relate to the entire university, not only to one of its departments or offices.

Collective archival groups

The archival groups that were established in accordance with the French principle of *respect des fonds* were defined rather loosely. The French *fonds* are comprised of records from similar types of institutions—governmental, ecclesiastical, educational, etc. They are "collective archival groups," which may be defined as groups that are comprised of records of a number of agencies that have common characteristics. The records may have a similarity because they emanate from a like kind of person or corporate body, or because they are of the same record type.

The purpose of establishing a collective archival group is to bring together similar records that are received from many different sources.

Thus, the National Archives established collective archival groups for records of Congressional committees and commissions and other small agencies that have common characteristics. In an ecclesiastical archival institution, a collective group may be comprised of records of individual churches or records of individual missions. In a university archival institution, such groups may include records produced by a class of offices or a class of persons, such as the personal papers of individual faculty members.

Archival subgroups

An archivist should establish archival subgroups when dealing with records of very large organic bodies. A large organic body for which an archival group has been established may be divisible into a number of small administrative units. A bureau of an executive department of the federal government usually has "divisions," "branches," or "sections." The records created by such units may be considered as subgroups of an archival group.

If a bureau passed through many organizational changes, the records produced by superseded or discontinued units may also be considered as subgroups.

If a bureau has field offices, the records of field offices may be considered as subgroups.

In a collective archival group, consisting of records of a given class of organizations, records of each organization may be considered as a subgroup.

ARRANGEMENT

An archivist should arrange archival groups according to the following principles:

He should maintain each archival group, established on an administrative basis, as an integral unit. The logic that underlies the creation of such groups requires that records in each group should be kept together without intermingling them with records of other groups. An archivist should deviate from this rule only when parts of an archival group require special equipment or are security classified so that they cannot be kept with the group to which they belong.

An archivist will find it difficult, however, to maintain groups as integral units if he receives many new records, for he will find it easier to place new accessions where there is space for them than where they belong from an organic point of view. The more he attempts to bring new accessions into a completely organic relation to records already accessioned, the more he will have to shift records from one place to another in the stacks. If records are moved, he will find that each change of position is followed by a chain reaction of other changes.

An archivist may therefore properly question how far he should go to maintain a completely organic arrangement. In England, archivists believe that the objectives of an archival institution can be accomplished simply by bringing accessions together by archival groups; a completely organic arrangement is not attempted. In Germany, by way of contrast, archivists attempt to fit new accessions into the series to which they belong.

Normally, an archivist should keep his records in a fixed position, not constantly shift records to accommodate insertions. He should, however, attempt to place new accessions with the groups to which they belong. He should also attempt to integrate new accessions with the series to which they belong, if this is not so difficult as to be impracticable. But it is likely that he will not be able to avoid periodic "fruit-basket upset" operations, in which new accessions are brought into a proper relation to one another during a major rearrangement of the stack contents.

An archivist should arrange archival groups in an organizational or functional relation to one another. Whenever possible, he should arrange groups so that their arrangement reflects the organizational structure of the organism that created them. In the federal government, he should arrange groups for bureaus and offices in conformity with the hierarchical structure of the executive department in which they are located. He should first place the archival group that represents the central staff offices, and then follow with the groups representing bureau or line offices. In the National Archives, this plan of arrangement is illustrated by the placement of records of the Department of Agriculture, which are divided into a number of groups. The group established for the general records of the department, consisting of records of the Office of the Secretary and certain staff offices, is placed in first position, while groups established for records of bureaus are arranged alphabetically by name.

If an archivist is dealing with archival groups of a succession of agencies or offices that were concerned with a specific function, he should arrange them in the chronological order of their creation, the group of a predecessor agency or office preceding that of the successor agency or office.

If an archivist is dealing with archival groups created by independent agencies, he should place those that relate to common or similar functions near one another.

An archivist may also take into account considerations of accessibility in arranging archival groups in stacks. A particular group may be so active as to justify placing it out of its normal position in order to bring it closer to a search room. An archivist may also find that the size of a group may make it desirable to modify a strictly organizational or functional pattern of arrangement.

An archivist should arrange archival subgroups in an organizational relation to one another. Whenever possible, he should arrange subgroups so that their arrangement reflects the organizational structure of the organism that produced the archival group of which they are a part. He should place subgroups representing the highest administrative office first, followed by subgroups of subordinate line or operating offices arranged in descending order of authority. If the administrative units that created subgroups are coordinate in authority, e.g., "divisions" within a "bureau," he should arrange them in an alphabetical order.

An archivist should also take the hierarchical approach in arranging subgroups within an archival group that contains both central and field office records. He should place subgroups representing the central office first, followed by subgroups of field offices. The latter he may arrange in any one of several ways. If field offices are numbered, he may arrange the subgroups they created numerically; or he may arrange them alphabetically by the name of the offices that created them; or he may arrange them geographically.

An archivist may also arrange subgroups so that their order reflects the historical development of the organism that created the archival group of which they are a part. He may find a strictly hierarchical arrangement of subgroups difficult to maintain when units that created them passed through successive organizational changes. He should, in such a case, allow the chronological sequence of the creation of the units, rather than their administrative status, to determine the placement of the subgroups. He should arrange subgroups created by each of the successive organizational units in an order of time. Thus, subgroups of a predecessor unit should be placed before those of its successor.

Archival Series

The term "series" refers to a unit of records that has its origin in an activity or transaction. Such a unit is organic in character. It may consist of records of a particular type, such as reports or questionnaires, that are maintained separately. Or it may consist of records of various types that are organized according to an integrated file system. Or it may even include an aggregation of records brought together without perceptible order, whose only bond of coherence is their common relation to a specific activity. This extended use of the term belies the dictionary definition: "a number of things . . . standing or succeeding in order, and connected by a like relation."

The term "series" has been adopted in the United States, for

want of a better term. Any other term, short of a highly artificial one such as "archimon," which was proposed in the early
years of the National Archives, would have done as well.[4] English archivists use the term "class," but the meaning of this term
is not very clear, since the factors on the basis of which classes of
records are established in the Public Record Office are not apparent from an analysis of its finding aids.

The term "series" is defined differently in the United States
than in Europe or other parts of the world. In Europe, the
record unit that is the equivalent of an American series consists
of registered files of a particular record type, such as a series of
personnel files or a series of reports. These are called *Rei-
henakten* in Germany, *liasse* in France, and *Bundel* in the Netherlands. They are to be distinguished from file units that contain
a variety of documents pertaining to specific subjects, which in
Germany are called *Sachakten,* in France and the Netherlands,
dossiers.

ESTABLISHMENT

In the National Archives, series of records are established
chiefly on the basis of the following factors: (*a*) their arrangement, (*b*) their record type, and (*c*) their relation to activity.

Factor of arrangement

In breaking down an archival group into its constituent elements, an archivist should first take into account the arrangement given records within it. If a group was created by a bureau
of an executive department of the federal government, it will
consist typically of a central file, an office file in the chief's
office, office files in divisional offices, sets of authoritative issuances and reports, and distinct lots of fiscal and technical records. Each of the files organized according to a particular filing
system should be treated as a record unit. Here the deciding
factor in determining the bounds or limits of a record unit is
arrangement. It does not matter what filing system is followed
—whether an alphabetical, a numerical, a subject, a classified, or

some other—the important consideration is that all records organized according to an integrated filing system should be regarded as one unit. Nor does the quantity of records matter, for a series may be large or small.

Factor of record type

The second factor an archivist should take into account in establishing series is record type. In most American archival groups, records fall into three major physical classes that may be broken down into record types. In the pictorial class are found photographs and original and press productions; in the cartographic class, maps and charts. Here we are concerned with the class of textual records; this class can be broken into very many record types, as we noted in Chapter VIII. In a government office, the commonest of these are letters, reports, and directives. Forms are also created to accomplish routine actions or for some other specific purpose. Thus are created "applications," "contracts," "payrolls," "requisitions," "questionnaires," "schedules," and other record types. If he cannot form series within an archival group on the basis of arrangement, an archivist should form them on the basis of type.

Factor of relation to activity

The third factor an archivist should take into account in establishing series is the relation of records to activity. He should consider this factor only if he cannot establish archival series on the basis of other factors. If he cannot divide records into series on the basis of their arrangement or type, he may arbitrarily designate a lot of them as a series on the ground of their relation to a specific transaction or matter of business.

If he cannot group them in this manner, he may describe the entire lot of records as a series of miscellany.

ARRANGEMENT

While he may place series in any conceivable order without adversely affecting their organic quality, an archivist should arrange them logically within an archival group. He should arrange them in a manner that will show clearly their character, significance, and relationship, using one or a combination of the following schemes: an organizational, a functional, a chronological, or a geographical scheme, or one according to the type of records.

An archivist, normally, should arrange series in an administrative relation to one another. Such an arrangement will reflect the hierarchical levels within an agency, such as the bureaus, divisions, and sections, and the hierarchical relations between central and field offices. Series created by staff offices should precede those produced by subordinate administrative subdivisions; series of the larger administrative units, those of the smaller; series of headquarters offices, those of field offices; and series of antecedent offices, those of the offices that assumed their functions.

If he cannot arrange them organizationally, an archivist should arrange series functionally. Such an arrangement will bring together series that relate to a particular function. Series of a general character, relating to more than one activity under the function, should precede those that are specific and relate to single activities. Or the sequence of the series should reflect the order in which a function was performed. Or it may reflect the chronological growth of records around a given function, as when the first series represents the earliest record accumulation and later series subsequent accumulations.

If he cannot arrange them organizationally or functionally, an archivist may arrange series in other ways. He may arrange them by type, if they are type series; or by place, if they relate to geographical areas; or by time, if they relate to chronological periods.

If he arranges them by record type, he should take note of the content of various types, placing types whose contents are general, such as correspondence, before types of specific content, such as contracts. Since a series of general correspondence or a central file ordinarily does not reflect either organizational or functional patterns, but relates to all activities of the administrative unit it covers, he should place it before all other series of such a unit.

He should place indexes before the series to which they relate.

He should place series of miscellany and isolated pieces of uncertain provenance at the end of the archival group until their proper attribution can be determined.

XI

ARRANGEMENT OF MANUSCRIPT COLLECTIONS

In arranging historical manuscripts, an archivist should proceed in somewhat the same way as he does when arranging archives. He should ordinarily determine how he will define or establish collections, how he will arrange collections in the stacks of a repository, how he will create series within collections, and how he will arrange items within series.

The first section of this chapter relates to the establishment and arrangement of manuscript collections; the second, to the creation of series within collections. The arrangement of record items will be discussed in the next chapter.

Manuscript Collections

Worthington C. Ford was, perhaps, the first manuscript curator to concern himself with the nature of collections received by manuscript repositories. When writing in 1904, for Charles A. Cutter's *Rules for a Dictionary Catalog*, he divided manuscripts into three classes, as follows: "1. Separate volumes of distinct material, such as orderly books, journals of exploration, or a formal report of government. 2. A collection of the correspondence of a public character, or of a public office. 3. Loose papers which have no connection with one another and are occasional in nature." [1] In 1916 Ford again alluded to the matter in a questionnaire on arrangement and notational systems which he sent to a number of manuscript repositories. In the questionnaire he recognized four types of record units to be dealt with:

personal collections, artificial collections, individual record items, and manuscript volumes.[2]

The term "collection" has been applied to documentary material in two ways: to refer to the entire holdings of a repository, e.g., the New-York Historical Society Collection, or to refer to particular groups within such holdings. The term "holdings" is preferable to the term "collection" if used in the first sense.

The term "collection" is used by some manuscript curators to refer to material brought together by collectors, a restricted meaning that should not be accepted.

ESTABLISHMENT

Collections of private papers fall into three types that may be distinguished from one another by the way they came into being. The main kind of collection consists of papers created by particular bodies, either personal or corporate. Other kinds of collections consist of record items brought together from various sources. If brought together by collectors, they should be called artificial collections; if by manuscript curators, collections of miscellany. There are thus three kinds of collections: (*a*) organic collections, (*b*) artificial collections, and (*c*) collections of miscellany.

Definitions of the term "collection" now in vogue usually fail to make a distinction among collections on the basis of source. They ordinarily encompass all kinds of collections. The term, for example, has been defined, for purposes of the National Union Catalog of Manuscript Collections, as a "group of papers . . . usually having a common source, and formed by or around an individual, a family, a corporate entity, or devoted to a single theme." [3] It has been defined by the Duke University Library as "any body of manuscripts constituting a unit by reason of its centering about one person, one family, an institution, or a society." [4]

The Huntington Library distinguishes between homogeneous and heterogeneous collections. It defines a homogeneous collection as letters of one person, one family, or an allied family group which have a relationship or continuity, or as the office correspondence of an individual, corporation, government, or the like. It also recognizes that papers on a given subject, event, or locality may have homogeneity.[5]

Organic collections

The term "organic collections" should be used to refer to material created by a particular person, or by a particular religious, educational, business, or other corporate body. It should be applied to all manuscript collections that come from a particular organic source, regardless of whether such collections are so small that they lack organic characteristics. Such collections may include all classes of material, pictorial and cartographic as well as textual. The material may be in the form of originals or copies, and the copies may consist of transcripts, photoprints, or microfilms.

An organic collection may be large or small, depending upon the extent of the activity of the body that created it. If it is the product of extended activity, such a collection may have archival characteristics. Usually large collections of corporate origin have such characteristics, and may be treated as archival groups.

Artificial collections

The Huntington Library uses the term "heterogeneous collection," instead of the term "artificial collection," to denote an assortment of papers and volumes that "bear no kinship to one another, are without continuity, and have no common origin." [6]

The term "artificial collection" may be applied to papers that are brought together after the actions to which they relate have occurred, not concurrently, and that are derived from many sources, not a single source. An artificial collection is, in fact, a true collection in the sense that its various pieces were "collected," i.e., brought together. The collecting was usually done by bibliophiles, historians, or dealers for commercial purposes.

Collections of miscellany

A collection of miscellany is composed of single record items or small groups of record items, acquired from various sources, that are formed into a collection in a manuscript repository. Many repositories in the United States develop collections of miscellany consisting of either loose items or bound volumes. MISCELLANIES OF LOOSE MATERIAL. Single documents, or very small groups of documents, present special problems of management. The extent to which small accessions are received by manuscript repositories is revealed in an analysis of the guides produced by Duke University, the Minnesota Historical Society, the University of North Carolina, the North Carolina Historical Commission, West Virginia University, and the Wisconsin Historical Society.[7] This analysis shows that 33.6 percent of the entries in the guides pertain to collections of fewer than 10 items and 52.5 percent to collections of fewer than 100 items. The accompanying table shows the percentages for the various repositories.

NUMBER OF ITEMS

Repository	1–10 No.	%	11–20 No.	%	21–40 No.	%	41–60 No.	%	61–80 No.	%	81–100 No.	%	Total entries in guides
Duke University	587	31	173	9	123	6	63	3	35	2	29	2	1,895
Minnesota Historical Society	136	30	52	11	45	10	24	5	11	2	4	1	455
University of North Carolina	258	32	40	5	55	7	31	4	18	2	15	2	809
North Carolina Historical Commission	423	52	37	5	25	3	14		5	1	1		815
West Virginia University	191	27	23	3	19	3	16	2	13	2	4	1	715
Wisconsin Historical Society	209	30	60	9	36	5	13	2	9	1	3		702
Average percentage		33.6		7		5.7		2.7		2		1.5	Total 52.5%

Should single documents be organized into a collection of miscellany? How numerous should documents be to justify treating them as a separate collection? Or, conversely, when should a small group of documents be embodied in a collection of miscellany?

The number of documents required to constitute a separate collection varies in different manuscript repositories. In the Duke University Library, any lot of material that has two or more documents is regarded as a collection; [8] in the Minnesota Historical Society, the number is three or more documents; [9] and in the Huntington Library, forty or more documents.[10] In the Manuscript Division of the Library of Congress, a collection of "personal miscellany" was established that consisted of one to six manuscripts for each person.[11] In the Louisiana State University Library, a group of manuscripts of more than one loose item is titled "papers." If the group has (1) 1 unbound item and 1 bound item, (2) more than 1 unbound item and 1 bound item, (3) 1 unbound item and more than 1 bound item, or (4) no unbound items and more than 1 bound item, it is designated as a "collection." [12]

Whether a manuscript group should be regarded as a separate collection depends on the number of documents in it and on the size of the containers used in a repository. If the documents fill a container of the smallest size, they should be treated as a separate collection; if they fail to do this, they should be embodied in a collection of miscellany.

MISCELLANIES OF BOUND MATERIAL. Should volumes be organized into a collection of miscellany, regardless of their type? Or should they be organized into special collections of miscellany, according to the type of record they contain? Should there be special collections of account books, diaries, journals, letter books, and orderly books?

In a small repository, each volume may be regarded as a separate collection and shelved among unbound collections; or it may be embodied in a collection of miscellaneous volumes, containing all bound records regardless of their type.

In a large repository, separate collections of miscellany may be needed for special types of bound records, such as account books and diaries, for there is no objection to building up collections of volumes of special types.

But bound records should be placed in collections of miscellany only if they are the sole records from a given source. If both bound and loose records are received from a given source, they should be kept together as a collection. Collections of miscellany should never be developed by separating volumes from related loose papers. It is in this regard that archivists have often erred, for it is as bad to tear apart a collection in order to organize items by form as it is to tear it apart in order to organize them by subject. Once the process of tearing collections apart is begun, for whatever reason, it is not likely to end.

ARRANGEMENT

An archivist should arrange collections of private papers, whether organic or artificial, according to the following principles:

As a general rule, *he should maintain each collection as a separate and integral unit,* just as he should treat an archival group originating in a particular agency as an integral unit. While manuscript collections are now generally kept intact, older manuscript repositories of the United States have many collections that contain records from various sources. Since each collection is an entity in itself, an archivist should treat it as such. He should keep it intact.

Most manuscript collections are received in single accessions, and for this reason a collection is generally the equivalent of an accession. The need of bringing together separate accessions from a given source is determined by the degree to which documents in them have organic relations. Parts of an artificial collection, i.e., those brought together from various sources, have no organic relations; and the parts, if brought into a repository separately, may each be treated as separate collections. But parts of an organic collection that are accessioned separately should be brought together even at the expense of considerable labor in shifting other collections. The actions to be taken with respect to such accessions should be dictated by considerations of convenience. If it is easy to embody them in a collection that has already been established, this should be done. If it is very difficult, for physical reasons, to do this, they should be formed into a new collection.

An archivist should not remove record items that relate to important historical persons, places, or events from a collection in order to form a new collection. He should make known the location of such items in finding aids, not by their physical placement. Nor should he remove bound items when accompanied by loose papers, as has already been noted.

He may, however, remove pictorial and cartographic items from a collection to facilitate their handling. Nontextual records are removed, in most archival institutions, from the collections in which they are embodied and are placed with like items.

He may also remove textual record items from a collection if they present special storage problems because of their physical characteristics—size, bulk, or form—in order to place them in stack equipment in which they can be accommodated. But whenever possible, he should keep textual items from a given source together, even if by so doing he sacrifices neatness and space in the stacks.

He should remove printed items from a collection only if he maintains separate pamphlet, imprint, and newspaper clipping collections in which they may be embodied; otherwise he should leave them with the collection in which they are found.

If he removes items from a collection, he should make a record of their relation to the collection from which they have been removed.

When dealing with both manuscript collections and archival groups, an archivist should place the two types of material in separate parts of the stacks, for the intermingling of private and public papers is inexcusable.

An archivist should normally place collections in the stacks in the order in which they are accessioned. Neal Harlow says that any scheme of arrangement "should be simple, capable of expansion, and easy to handle by informed staff members." [13] The simplest and most practicable scheme, which should be followed in all but very large repositories, is to register new accessions, assign numbers to them consecutively, and place them in the stacks in a numerical sequence. The accession numbers will show the position of accessions in the stacks, facilitate reference to them in descriptive and other internal documents, and facilitate citation of them by the user. This scheme of arrangement, which has been followed with conspicuous success in the Alderman

Library of the University of Virginia,[14] will result in a progressive utilization of stack space, permitting the addition of new accessions without disturbing the relation of those already acquired, and thus obviating the honeycombing of the stacks with empty cells.

An archivist should not arrange collections in the alphabetical order of their titles. An alphabetical arrangement is employed by the Massachusetts Historical Society, which originally arranged its collections on shelves "according to the most significant period covered by the manuscripts" and which introduced an alphabetical arrangement in the 1920s; [15] and by the Manuscript Division of the Library of Congress, which arranges its collections of personal papers alphabetically by title. Such an arrangement has all the disadvantages, without any of the merits, of a completely classified scheme of arrangement, for it results in a classification of collections into twenty-six meaningless classes.

An archivist should group collections into classes only in exceptional circumstances. Obviously, private manuscript collections should be kept apart from public archival groups; and textual records, from cartographic and pictorial records. Single documents, or small groups of documents, should be embodied in a collection of miscellany and thus kept separate from large manuscript collections. And bound records, under certain circumstances, should be kept separate from unbound records. But should other kinds of classes be established?

In the United States, collections of private papers have been classified according to their relation to place (a geographical arrangement), their relation to time (a chronological arrangement), their relation to subject, their provenance, their size, the type of records involved, the alphabetical sequence of their titles, and a combination of subjects, places, time periods, and other factors. Neal Harlow, who in 1948 made a survey of the practices in handling manuscript material in a number of university and research libraries, found that "in one library, collections are divided between Eastern and Western hemispheres; in another by linguistic and geographic areas, plus a few subject specializations; still another into government archives, private papers, and subject specialties; in a fourth, literary manuscripts, historical material in its special field, and all others; and a business library, which is in itself a subject collection, classifies by 'industry,' interestingly enough abandoning the scheme for large collections." [16]

The practice of establishing classes and subclasses for manuscript collections in relation to *time* and *place* is best exemplified in the "chronologic-geographic" scheme of the Library of Congress, the development and defects of which were discussed in Chapter III.

Considerations of *subject*, as well as other factors, are taken into account in the following method of classifying collections at the Huntington Library: [17]

> Maps and plans
> Religion (bibles, psalters, breviaries, *horae*, etc.)
> General medieval history and literature
> Music and art
> Drama
> English and European history
> Literature
> California and Mexican history
> United States history
> Archives (Ellesmere, Hastings, Stowe, Battle Abbey)

The arrangement of collections into classes according to subject is practicable only in large repositories in which several stack areas are available where collections relating to particular subjects may be placed. Ordinarily, classes should not be established beyond those that can be conveniently maintained in separate physical facilities, and the classes should be mutually exclusive, not overlapping. A grouping of collections into subject classes may be justified on the ground that the work of the repository can thereby be departmentalized, thus developing a specialization or subject-matter expertise in the staff. This principle of administration was once followed in the National Archives, in allocating record groups pertaining to broad subject fields to particular organizational units.

Considerations of *provenance* are taken into account in

arranging the collections of the Minnesota Historical Society, which are divided mainly into personal and organizational papers, though provision is also made for miscellaneous source material, transcripts and photostatic copies, finding aids, and other types.[18] The Minnesota scheme was adopted, with slight modification, by the Historical Society of Western Pennsylvania [19] and by the Archives Department of the University of Wyoming.[20] At Wyoming, the factor of *size* is also taken into account in establishing classes, as it is in many other places, for there collections are arranged into the following classes: papers of organizations, large collections, small collections, and miscellaneous items.

A separation of organizational from personal papers may be justified on the ground that the former, which are more likely to be organic in character than personal papers, should be handled differently from the latter. The difference between the two kinds of papers, however, does not always exist. In the Minnesota Historical Society, where such a separation is made, an investigator found that corporate papers cannot clearly be separated from personal papers, many of which contain "a considerable volume of business records and papers of business men," particularly those of "petty capitalists (merchants, lumbermen, fur traders, etc.)." [21]

A plan for classifying collections, no matter what its kind, is likely to waste space. New collections have to be fitted into the classes preestablished for them, with the result that the stacks are likely to be honeycombed with empty cells. Because records are more widely dispersed under them, classified schemes may also defeat the very object of arrangement, which is to facilitate searching.

No plan for classifying collections, moreover, can be devised that can be applied generally. Collections vary in subject matter from one repository to another. There are few repositories in the United States that attempt to accumulate collections relating to the whole of United States history. The Manuscript Division of the Library of Congress is one of the few that does. Most state repositories are interested mainly in the manuscript resources that pertain to their states, though a few acquire material relating to entire regions. Some repositories are primarily interested in documents of a specialized character, such as those relating to industry, to religious institutions, or to other special organizations. The arrangement of collections should thus be different in each repository, for no two repositories have collections that relate, to any marked degree, to similar matters. A scheme that will suit one repository will not suit another.

Manuscript Series

During the nineteenth century, as we have seen in Chapter III, a number of large manuscript collections were divided into series. Manuscript curators of that period, however, never recorded their thinking about the factors that should be taken into account in establishing series; and the factors that they considered varied from collection to collection. The very idea of dividing a collection into a number of constituent elements on the basis of record type or relation to activity seemed to be alien to the thinking of those who wrote about practices in regard to manuscripts. Worthington C. Ford, who was the first to express himself in regard to the arrangement and description of manuscripts, did not recognize that series exist, except in a most general way, in his article on "Manuscripts" in Cutter's *Rules for a Dictionary Catalog* (1904).[22] John C. Fitzpatrick recognized only single manuscripts or single manuscript volumes as appropriate units for cataloging, in his *Notes on the Care, Cataloguing, Calendaring, and Arranging of Manuscripts*.[23] Even now, the practice of establishing manuscript series is regarded as a questionable undertaking by some curators.

But series should be the concern of curators of recent private papers. Their establishment is an essential preliminary to the effective management of collections of such papers. Unless series are established, it is necessary to deal with such collections on an item-by-item basis. Recent papers must be described collectively if they are to be described at all, and they can be described collectively by aggregations of items only if units of collective description, i.e., series, are established. And if such papers are to be serviced effectively, collections must be broken down into their constituent parts, so that searches can be localized in series, instead of being spread over entire collections.

ESTABLISHMENT

An archivist should establish manuscript series in relation to the same factors that are taken into account in establishing archival series, to wit: (*a*) the arrangement of records, (*b*) their record type, and (*c*) their origin in an activity.

He can establish them quite easily in collections of papers produced by corporate bodies—such as churches, businesses, and schools. Ordinarily, he can divide such collections into their constituent parts in the same way as he does archival groups, and he must follow the same processes in doing so: he must analyze the organizational structure and functions of the body that produced them, he must identify the record units that resulted from organization and function, and he must ascertain their arrangement, type, and origin in an activity.

He will find it a bit more difficult to establish series in collections of personal papers than in archival groups, because personal papers are usually arranged badly. And he should establish them only in large collections of personal papers. He should keep small collections of loose papers—regardless of their record type or provenance—in a single series, because this is the easiest thing to do with them.

If series have not been established in an artificial collection of miscellaneous items from various sources, he should keep all items in such a collection as a single series.

Factor of arrangement

The factor of record arrangement is occasionally the basis for establishing series in collections produced by corporate bodies. Such bodies, for reasons of efficiency, probably imposed some order on their records. Since corporate collections are generally of recent origin, they may come to a repository in some semblance of order. More often, however, they are in a state of disorder because they were not properly organized while they were accumulated, or were disarranged as they were relegated to the out-of-the-way places to which obsolete records are usually consigned. An archivist should maintain series as distinct and integral units whenever he finds them in collections of corporate papers.

Factor of record type

Manuscript collections, like archival groups, are composed of various types of records, though ordinarily these are not so numerous as they are in an archival group. The commonest types are account books, diaries, and letters.

In recent years, record type has been taken into account in arranging collections of private papers. In her article on "Manuscript Collections in the General Library," Ellen Jackson illustrated how to arrange a manuscript collection by showing that it would be typically grouped into the following series: [24]

JONES, HORACE, PAPERS.
1. Diaries. 3v. 1856–61 (Personal)
2. Ledgers. 6v. 1860–72 (Of firm of Horace Jones and company, general merchants)
3. Correspondence. 5 bundles. 1860?–71? (Disordered. Includes both personal and business matters, not in distinct series. All incoming)
4. Correspondence. 3v. 1863–66 (letterpress books, copies of outgoing correspondence. Both personal and business matters)

Here the main factor considered in establishing series is record type. Neal Harlow suggested that within large collections there may be "sub-groupings by form, such as personal correspondence, business papers, diaries, speeches, etc., by subject or organizational divisions, or by period or place." [25] Robert B. Downs indicated that the collections of the University of North Carolina Library fall into the following types: diaries, reminiscences, letters, plantation records, and ledgers.[26] R. B. Haselden indicated that large collections in the Huntington Library are "carefully sorted out and arranged in broad categories, such as Accounts and financial papers, Correspondence, Land papers, etc." [27]

The first factor that an archivist should consider in establishing series in a large manuscript collection is record type, and letters are the first type he should normally identify. He can usually also distinguish other types, such as account books, diaries, and journals, and assemble them into series. He need not, however, establish series for every record type found in a collection; ordinarily he will find that series need be established only for the main types.

Factor of relation to activity

If series cannot be established on the basis of record type, an archivist should group into series records that have their origin in a particular activity or transaction.

A collection of corporate papers is essentially similar in its structure to an archival group and can often be divided into series on the basis of the origin of records in an activity. The corporate body, whether a business, church, or school, may have produced a number of series relating to distinct activities. If it was a business, it may have produced separate lots of records relating to buying, selling, and delivering products, to buying and maintaining equipment and buildings, or to hiring and paying workers. If it was a particular church, it may have produced series relating to ministerial, educational, missionary, or administrative activities.

A large collection of personal papers also has some of the characteristics of an archival group. For an individual who creates a large collection must carry on many activities to create many papers—professional, legal, diplomatic, religious, cultural, personal, or other kinds. And these activities are the basis on which his papers were probably grouped and organized during his lifetime.

A collection of personal papers, even if quite small, is usually divisible into at least two groups: one relating to purely personal or family affairs; and the other to the activity for which the person whose papers are being preserved became noteworthy. These groups may be regarded as series.

In establishing series in personal manuscript collections, an archivist should consciously try to determine what specific activities and transactions resulted in their production. These may be activities of an occupational or professional nature, such as farming, teaching, mining, or medical or journalistic activities; activities conducted in carrying out specific enterprises, such as the establishment of a business, the development of an invention, or the production of a book; or specific transactions, such as the settlement of an estate, the litigation of a dispute, and the like.

In a manuscript collection of an educator, historian, writer, or other professional person, an archivist will usually find the following papers:

> Memorabilia, such as clippings, certificates, and diplomas
> Family papers, such as letters from his wife and children
> Professional correspondence of a general nature, not originating in specific activities
> Professional correspondence originating in specific activities
> Professional correspondence relating to publications
> Papers relating to educational and financial matters

Such a collection is divisible into a number of series: the memorabilia, according to record type; the family papers, according to their source in particular persons; the professional correspondence on activities, according to its source in specific activities; the professional correspondence on publications, according to its relation to specific publications; and the educational and financial papers, according to their relation to specific matters. Some of the larger series, such as those relating to specific professional activities or specific publications, may consist of many record types: letters, minutes, clippings, reviews, and others, each of which should be separately organized into a subseries.

Some of the series described above seem to overlap. The general professional correspondence, and even the personal letters to a wife, may refer to specific professional activities. Papers that are the product of various activities may sometimes relate to the same matter, e.g., papers produced in the course of both professional and business activities. In order to determine in which series a given document should be placed, an archivist should ask himself: how did it originate? A document may relate to an activity, but it may not be the product of the activity. If he groups documents strictly according to their source in activity, an archivist will ordinarily be able to determine in which series they belong.

While difficulties may occasionally arise in defining the limits of series, it is possible to group practically all organic collections into a number of mutually exclusive series, so that individual items will fit into only one of them. Establishing series requires an exercise of judgment; it cannot be reduced to a routine, as can work in arranging items chronologically or alphabetically. But series can be established if there is a knowledge of the technique and the will to do so.

An example of a collection that was organized into series largely in relation to activities is that of James Buchanan, fifteenth President of the United States.[28] This collection, which is deposited in the Historical Society of Pennsylvania, consists of about 25,000 items in 114 boxes, arranged as follows:

> Autograph letters and drafts, 1813–68, 3 boxes
> Letters, reports, and documents of Buchanan's ministry to Russia, 1832–33, 1 box
> Letters, reports, and documents of Buchanan's ministry to England, 1854–56, 4 boxes
> Correspondence while Secretary of State, 1845–49, 2 boxes
> Papers and correspondence relating to the growing differences between the North and the South before the Civil War, 1857–61, 1 box
> Notes and articles written by Buchanan concerning his administration and other topics, 1860, 1 box
> Correspondence from miscellaneous persons, 1783–1868, 79 boxes
> Legal correspondence, 1775–1855, 2 boxes, etc.

When dealing with organic collections, an archivist should not establish series on the basis of the relation of records to time or place. An example of series established in relation to such factors is found in the arrangement of the McCormick family papers, which comprise about 100,000 items ranging in time from 1779 to the present date. These papers were grouped into separate series for each year by Herbert A. Kellar. Within each series the papers were arranged alphabetically by individuals, and for any given individual they were arranged chronologically. The incoming letters of the McCormick company (as distinct from the family) were first grouped in relation to geographical areas before they were grouped into separate series by years. There are groups for foreign countries and states. Within states, Kellar even considered establishing further subdivisions, "according to county, city and town." [29]

Kellar seemingly induced the *Ad Hoc* Committee on Manuscripts established by the American Historical Association in December, 1948, of which he was chairman, to endorse his procedure of grouping manuscript collections into series on the basis of time. The committee recommended that "papers covering relatively short time periods (months, years, groups of years, depending on individual circumstances) be treated as subgroups, and within these groups be alphabetically arranged." [30]

Kellar's method represents the sort of "systematization" that should be scrupulously avoided when dealing with organic collections. It stems from his mistaken belief that the principle of provenance "is of doubtful advantage" when dealing with large collections of institutional and business papers.[31] If his method is followed, papers are not arranged in relation to the activities that resulted in their production but are arbitrarily divided into innumerable small units on a chronological or geographical basis. The activities in relation to which organic records should be arranged, however, are far more significant in their description and are a far more "important consideration" in making them "easily available"—to quote Kellar's words in justification of his mistaken method—than are time or place.[32]

ARRANGEMENT

An archivist should arrange manuscript series in relation to one another so as best to reveal the character and significance of the collection of which they are a part. He may arrange them just as he would archival series, on an organizational, functional, chronological, or any other logical basis. And he should determine how he will arrange series in each collection on an *ad hoc* basis.

XII

ARRANGEMENT OF
RECORD ITEMS

The term "record item" refers to a distinct physical record unit. An item may be either a single document or many documents that were brought together, usually in the course of their current use, into volumes, binders, folders, or other containers. Though a volume, binder, or folder may contain many documents, it should be regarded as a single record item because it is a distinct physical unit.

The term "piece" is often used in the United States to refer to a single document. In the WPA Historical Records Survey, the term "item" was used to designate both a bound lot of documents and an unbound document, and the term "piece" to designate a single sheet of paper. In England, the term "piece" is used in the same sense in which the term "record item" has been defined above, as any document or lot of documents fastened together so that it is possible to treat it as a unit. The term "piece" is used in the English sense in the United States, also, for the Duke University Library defined "piece," for purposes of counting, "as a single unit, whether that was a one-page letter, a ten-page sermon, or a huge ledger." [1]

The character of most record items is determined by their creators. As records are made, those that use them decide how they should be brought together, i.e., whether into binders, folders, volumes, or envelopes.

An archivist himself may occasionally create record items. He does this when he binds a lot of documents—as manuscript curators often did in the early American historical societies—and thereafter the bound volume is considered as a record item. Or he may bring material together into a bundle or container, and thereafter deal with the bundle or container as a record item. While American archivists do not use the term "item" to denote a bundle or container, this is the practice among continental European archivists. In Germany, files from registry offices are usually placed in bundles, each of which is appropriately labeled and listed in repertories or inventories. In France, files and loose papers are often brought together in cartons, and these are the units of arrangement and description.

Regardless of how they may be created, record items are physical entities that may be handled as units. They are the smallest units with which an archivist must deal.

Arrangement of Items within Series

SERIES ESTABLISHED ON THE BASIS OF ARRANGEMENT

An archivist should normally keep record items, in a series established on the basis of arrangement, in their original order.

If record items are arranged by a creating agency in an intelligible or usable way, an archivist should preserve the order in which he receives them, whether this be alphabetical, numerical, chronological, or some other order. He should rearrange such items only when the original order has been disturbed, or has been lost, or is unintelligible, or is one that makes reference service very difficult. In such instances, he should attempt to restore the order given records while they were in current use, or impose one of his own. In restoring the original order, he should refer to the filing scheme, if such exists, or to indexes, subject captions, folder labels, file notations, and the like. If the records were organized under a subject system, he should assemble folders under appropriate subject heads and place the heads in the order prescribed by the filing system that governs their arrangement.

SERIES ESTABLISHED ON THE BASIS OF RECORD TYPE

Manuscript series, as was noted in the preceding chapter, may consist of items of a given record type. The commonest type of items are letters, but various other types are found in recent manuscript collections.

Correspondence series

There are several methods of arranging letters: a straight chronological order, an alphabetical order, an alphabetical-chronological order, and a topical order.

The first, and the commonest method of arranging letters, is the chronological one. Chronological arrangement has the sanction of long usage. During the last century, practically all manuscript curators, collectors, and historians arranged letters chronologically. Worthington C. Ford recommended chronological arrangement in his section on "Manuscripts" in Cutter's *Rules for a Dictionary Catalog*, which became a standard reference work that governed library practices in regard to manuscripts for many years. He discussed both alphabetical and chronological arrangement, and concluded that for historical purposes "chronological arrangement offers more distinct advantages" and should be applied to all large collections that "possess a greater historical than personal interest." [2]

Most present-day manuscript curators arrange letters and other loose papers, within a series or collection, in chronological order. Robert B. Downs, while at the University of North Carolina Library, stated that "chronological arrangement has certain defects but on the whole it is the most practical and useful plan." [3] Lester J. Cappon, while at the University of Virginia Library, stated that "chronological arrangement is generally preferred, modified sometimes, however, by certain predetermining factors in relation to the original scheme of arrangement or to the evolution of an organic body of papers." [4] Ruth K. Nuermberger, while at the Duke University Library, stated that "the first and unvarying essential is strict chronological arrangement within each collection. So essential is it that the inexperienced curator must get it firmly fixed in his thinking so that no amount of argument from those investigators who want material arranged by names of writers will swerve him from the chronological system." [5]

An archivist should, without doubt, arrange a small series or collection of letters, both incoming and outgoing, in a straight chronological order. He should place the earliest item first, followed by those that were produced later. This order is the opposite of that followed in arranging items within folders for current use in government and business offices, where the latest item is the action document that must be brought to the attention of the officer first.

A straight chronological arrangement places letters in the order in which they are used in historical inquiry, for they must be read in the sequence in which they were produced to understand the development of events, ideas, relationships, and the like. Such an arrangement is most meaningful to the historian, who is the chief user of personal letters.

The second method of arranging letters is an alphabetical one. Some series of letters in a large collection should first be grouped alphabetically by name of writer and then arranged chronologically. This is true with regard to family letters and purely personal letters that are distinct from letters relating to professional or other kinds of activities. Such series possess a greater personal than historical interest, and Ford observes that "for personal information the alphabetical arrangement is the simpler." [6]

The third method of arrangement is the alphabetical-chronological one, in which outgoing letters are arranged chronologically, and incoming letters alphabetically by name of writer.

Letter writing and filing practices have, in part, determined whether two series of letters should be maintained. After the Civil War, copies of outgoing letters were often made into letterpress books in the chronological sequence in which they were written, and incoming letters were arranged alphabetically in letter boxes especially designed for alphabetical filing by Dewey's Library Bureau. Thus, letters often came to a repository in two series: outgoing and incoming. With the invention of the typewriter and the development of carbon paper, new methods were introduced in writing and filing letters, with the result that both incoming and outgoing letters are now filed together in vertical files.

The Committee on Public Records of the National Association of State Libraries, in 1914, questioned if separate series should be made for outgoing and incoming letters. The consensus of the archivists who replied was that the two should be kept together. "Separate series," observed H. J. Eckenrode (1881–1952), while in charge of the archives and manuscripts at the Virginia State Library, "are confusing and simplicity in arrangement is a great virtue." [7]

The most recent discussion of the advantages in creating two series of letters, when dealing with a large collection, is that of Richard C. Berner, Curator of Manuscripts at the University of Washington Libraries, in his article in the *American Archivist*. [8] Berner stated that an alphabetical arrangement of incoming letters provides a key to the names of writers who produced a collection; that it results in a grouping of letters of important persons (who are often the subject of inquiry), thus making their letters readily accessible; and that it permits the alphabetical series of incoming letters to be used in conjunction with the chronological series of outgoing letters, for the names of writers on incoming letters can easily be related to dates on outgoing letters.

The alphabetical-chronological method of arrangement is employed at the Bancroft Library of the University of California and at the Libraries of the University of Washington, as well as at other repositories.

While letters of important persons are admittedly often the subject of inquiry, and for this reason have even been brought together and published separately, [9] it is doubtful if they should be arranged by persons to make known their relation to persons.

Such a relation can be shown more easily, and more completely, by indexing letters than by placing them in an alphabetical sequence.

There are also difficulties in arranging a series of incoming letters so that all names of correspondents will be revealed. Often only one or two letters will exist for a given correspondent, which will be grouped with small lots of letters from other correspondents in a single folder. Separate folders for a particular correspondent will be prepared, ordinarily, only when he has produced several letters.

There are also disadvantages in creating two series of letters, one outgoing and the other incoming. A searcher has to keep both series going at the same time. This means that a historian, who is usually interested in a specific period, may have to run through very many items in the alphabetical series. While it is important to know the names of writers, they are often not of sufficient interest to warrant an alphabetical arrangement.

A fourth method of arrangement is the topical one. The above-mentioned Committee on Public Records also asked what factor is more important in arrangement: time or subject matter. Gaillard Hunt, of the Library of Congress, replied that time is the more important factor, and that records should therefore be arranged chronologically. "A subjective arrangement," he said, "is not feasible in the case of papers that cover more than one subject, and, moreover, depends upon the judgment of the archivist as to the subject to which a paper belongs, and that judgment cannot safely be depended upon. These remarks are specially true when applied to a series of correspondence." [10] Eckenrode endorsed these views:

Experience shows that time is of more importance in the arrangement of manuscript material than subject matter, because it is by far the easiest method for finding specific things. For instance, the investigator may not know under what subject heading to look for a document, but he usually has a pretty definite idea of its date and can find it by date. Letters should be arranged by years and the letters of each year grouped under certain subjects or classes.[11]

Aside from the fact that personal papers are difficult to group by subject, there are also difficulties in applying new filing systems. Subject and classified systems are more difficult to install than chronological and alphabetical systems. They are also less objective. To indulge in a poor pun, a subject arrangement is likely to be subjective, for it involves making a choice of subjects in relation to which records should be organized and a determination of the *main* subject dealt with in each letter where several subjects may be involved.

In the arrangement of correspondence items, enclosures are often removed from the particular letters with which they were enclosed. Since the relation of the letter and enclosure is usually meaningful, an archivist should show this relation by pencil, as is the practice at the Library of Congress.

Series of other record types

An archivist should arrange items in other distinct record types in whatever order best facilitates their use.

He may arrange them numerically, chronologically, alphabetically by name or subject, or in some other order.

He should arrange narrative accounts, such as minutes, proceedings, diaries, and memoirs, chronologically.

He should arrange sermons and speeches, if they had their origin in one person, either in reference to the times when they were given or to the places where they were given, depending on whether time or place is the more significant. If they had their origin in many persons, he should arrange them alphabetically by name of person.

He should arrange clippings chronologically, if they relate to a particular person or family. If they relate to a corporate body, he should group them into series by place or subject, and within the series arrange them chronologically.

He should group legal, financial, and business papers into series by type, and arrange them chronologically within series.

Series of bound volumes

An archivist should arrange volumes in whatever order best facilitates their use.

He should normally arrange letterpress books of outgoing letters, account books, order books, daybooks, diaries, journals, and the like in chronological order or, if numbered, in numerical order. The volumes, of course, may be grouped into series. Thus, Herbert A. Kellar grouped the bound volumes in the Mc-Cormick collection—daybooks, journals, ledgers, order books, sales books, and the like—into series "according to purpose and content, and within series in order of chronology." [12]

SERIES ESTABLISHED ON THE BASIS OF RELATION TO ACTIVITY

An archivist should arrange record items, in a series established on the basis of its relation to activity, in a straight chronological order. Such a series will generally be composed of a number of subseries established on the basis of record type. A series of records relating to the production of a book, for example, may contain notes, manuscripts, letters, and reviews pertaining to the book. The logic for creating a series on an activity or transaction requires that the items within the series, or within its parts, should be arranged in an order that will reflect the sequence of action, i.e., a chronological order.

Arrangement of Items in Collections

ARTIFICIAL COLLECTIONS

If items within artificial collections are arranged well, they should be kept in their original order, but if they are in disorder, they should be arranged either chronologically or alphabetically, depending on their nature.

COLLECTIONS OF MISCELLANY

The collections of miscellany under consideration may consist of either bound or unbound items.

Loose items

In the last century, the Massachusetts Historical Society established two collections of miscellaneous items: the first, in 1838, comprised of seven volumes of manuscripts ranging in date from 1632 to 1824; [13] and the second, in 1856, of six volumes, ranging from 1628 to 1805.[14] The society arranged items within the volumes chronologically.

More recently, manuscript repositories have arranged miscellaneous loose items alphabetically by name of author, as well as chronologically. In the Huntington Library, the Duke University Library, and the Clements Library, such items are arranged chronologically; in the manuscript divisions of the Library of Congress and the New York Public Library, alphabetically by author. Such items are usually placed in folders, which are filed in standard filing cases.

In my opinion, the advice given American librarians in London by the librarian of the British Museum in October, 1877, on the arrangement of miscellaneous manuscripts, is valid. Such an arrangement, the librarian said, "cannot be too simple." He therefore recommended the adoption of "a simple plan for finding each manuscript. This may be done by assigning to each manuscript a consecutive number as it is acquired, and then referring from an index of these numbers to the place occupied by the manuscript in the library." [15]

Each small accession of documents, in a word, should be registered, the documents placed in a folder, the folders numbered consecutively and placed in standard archival boxes. A numerical arrangement is the simplest and most practical method of arranging miscellaneous small accessions, just as it is the simplest and most practical method of arranging manuscript collections as such. It is an arrangement that permits the addition of material, without disturbing the relation of that already acquired. The register provides a systematic control of such accessions, which ordinarily are very difficult to manage. The register, or an index or catalog prepared at a later stage of work, will effectively show the relation of accessions to subjects, chronological periods, and geographical areas, if it is properly prepared. Such relations, in every instance, can be shown more effectively in descriptive documents than by physical placement.

Bound items

A collection of miscellaneous volumes should be arranged in the same manner as a collection of miscellaneous loose items.

The volumes should be registered, numbered, and placed on shelves in the sequence of the numbers assigned to them.

A collection of volumes of a given record type can readily be arranged in a simple alphabetical or chronological order, if items in such a collection are identifiable by author or date. The order given items in such a collection should readily make apparent the position of particular volumes in it. In the Manuscript Division of the Library of Congress, journals, diaries, and orderly books are arranged chronologically, while letter books are arranged alphabetically. In the Harvard School of Business Administration, certain account books are arranged chronologically. While at the University of North Carolina Library, Robert B. Downs considered three logical groupings of book records: one, by type; another, by author (corporate or personal); and a third, by place of origin. He questioned "whether a subject approach would be successful," and added that temporarily he was arranging volumes alphabetically by author, but that this scheme was only moderately satisfactory.[16]

In my opinion, if several collections of volumes are maintained, each consisting of a specific record type, volumes in each collection should be arranged in a numerical order, i.e., they should be registered, numbered consecutively as they are accessioned, and shelved. The numbers assigned to them will facilitate reference to them in indexes and catalogs, in which the multiple relations of particular volumes to subject, place, and time can be made known.

XIII

PHYSICAL ARRANGEMENTS

Records are not as easy to deal with as publications and must be dealt with differently. They consist, as we have seen in Chapter IV, of many record types that are brought together in many different ways and filed under many different systems; they are in all sizes; they are maintained during their current life in all kinds of containers; and they reach an archival repository in all kinds of conditions.

If an archivist is to accomplish his dual purpose of preserving and making available for use the records entrusted to his care, he should place them in the stacks in a neat and orderly manner. He should pack them in containers; identify the contents of containers on labels; number the stack rows and the compartments within them; identify the contents of stack rows on labels; and prepare control devices, such as accessions and location registers, to show their precise location.

To achieve the order and neatness found in library stacks, an archivist should pay attention to certain physical activities, namely, packing, shelving, and labeling. Since they involve mainly physical rather than intellectual exertion, such activities are often regarded as being not truly professional. Their importance, however, can easily be underestimated.

Packing activities serve to protect records physically. They keep them from the agents that shorten the life of records. They serve to reduce the hazards of fire. They also reduce the normal wear and tear on records.

Packing and labeling activities are the final steps in arrangement work. They reflect, outwardly, the order that has been given records as a result of a careful analysis of their inner relations.

Labeling activities are also a first step in descriptive work. They are, in a sense, intermediate between arrangement and description work and relate the two to each other. The way records are arranged and described should be made known through labels. Labels are a key to both their arrangement and their description. They make apparent the location of records by indicating (on end row labels) the place where a group or collection is deposited in the stacks, and by indicating (on container labels) the space in which the components of a group or collection are deposited. They thus serve to make records physically accessible for use.

Packing

REGISTERING AND ASSIGNING SYMBOLS

In order to control records in a repository, an archivist should assign symbols to identify archival groups and manuscript collections and to identify particular accessions to them. He should use symbols in registering accessions and later in identifying accessions while they are being arranged.

He should maintain an accessions register, which is an administrative record designed to provide information on the receipt of all documentary material. Its primary purpose is to provide an immediate, brief, and permanent record of how material came into a repository. This is vital to the effective administration of a documentary repository.

In regard to each accession, an archivist should record the following information, immediately after records have been officially received, in an accessions register: the symbol (number) assigned to the accession; its date; the source from which it was obtained; the terms under which it may be used; the name of the government agency, corporate body, or person that produced it; the place and date at which it was produced; and its quantity.

Manuscript collections

An archivist should assign the same symbol to a manuscript collection that he does to an accession of which it is comprised, for usually accessions are the equivalent of collections. If a collection is made up of several accessions, he should indicate their relation to the collection by the device discussed below.

If collections within a repository are organized in the numerical order of their receipt, he should identify them by simple numbers, i.e., 1, 2, 3, 4, etc.

If they are organized into classes and within classes are arranged in numerical sequence, he should identify them by a letter symbol (to denote class) as well as by numbers, i.e., A-1, A-2, A-3, etc.; B-1, B-2, B-3, etc.

He should identify accretions, or additions to a collection, by using two numbers, the first to denote the collection, and the second, after the decimal point, to denote the accretion, i.e., 1.1, 1.2, 1.3, etc.; A-1.1, A-1.2, A-1.3, etc.

He should identify an accession to a collection of miscellaneous bound volumes by a double letter "MV," as well as by number, i.e., MV-1, MV-2, etc.

He should identify an accession to a collection of volumes of a particular record type by double letters, the first denoting that it belongs to a collection of miscellany, and the second denoting its record type, e.g., A for account books, D for diaries, L for letter books, etc. The complete symbol should thus be: MA-1, MD-1, ML-1, etc.

Archival groups

An archivist should assign numbers to accessions either in the sequence in which they are added to the holdings as a whole or in the sequence in which they are added to archival groups. In the first case, the symbols consist of a sequence of simple numbers, i.e., 1, 2, 3, 4, etc.; in the second, they are comprised of two parts, the first denoting the archival group and the second the accession. The symbols used to designate archival groups may be either numbers or letters. In the National Archives, numbers are used to identify archival groups; [1] in the British Public Record Office, letters.[2]

PACKING

Manuscript curators, in the past, preferred binding to boxing. They concluded, after the New York State Library fire in 1911, that binding afforded "by far the best protection" from damage to records [3] and that it ensured them from loss or theft while in use. But their chief reason for binding was that it created record units that they knew how to handle, for they could catalog, index, and shelve manuscript volumes just as they could books.

The advantages of binding, however, are largely illusory, for archival containers can be handled as effectively as bound volumes. Containers have been regarded as the units of treatment in the French National Archives for many years, and are so regarded today in many American archival and manuscript repositories. Containers, in fact, should be considered the archival equivalent of library books. If properly designed, they can be manipulated as easily as bound volumes. If properly constructed and packed, they afford as much protection to records as bindings; perhaps even more from adverse effects of heat, humidity, or atmospheric pollution. And, while records may be loose in them, numbering individual items will safeguard them from theft or, at least, make possible a quick detection of theft.

An archivist should insert records in boxes carefully.[4] He should perfect their arrangement before packing them, for once records are boxed it is very difficult to rearrange them; their arrangement, for all practical purposes, is frozen. He should pack them neither too loosely nor too tightly. If he places them in a box too loosely, they will crumple; if too tightly, they will be difficult to remove for use and difficult to reinsert after use, and may be torn in the process.

Large record units

Before packing large record units, such as archival series and manuscript collections, an archivist should have clearly in mind how to arrange them in the boxes. He should understand the structure of the group or collection as a whole and know which series exist in it, how they are related, and what order should be given them.

In packing a manuscript collection or archival series, an archivist should place each collection or series in its own box or run of boxes. Certain collections and series will obviously extend over many boxes; others will not fill even one box. Ordinarily, only one manuscript collection should be placed in a box. In order to accommodate small collections, half-sized boxes should be available. Series within boxes should be clearly demarcated from one another.

Small record units

Many accessions consist of single documents or very small groups of documents, as is evident from the analysis in Chapter XI of certain American guides.

Whether a small accession should be embodied in a collection of miscellany or treated as a separate collection depends largely on the size of boxes used in a repository. In the Minnesota Historical Society [5] and the Wisconsin Historical Society [6] both full-sized and half-sized boxes are used, the full-sized containing about 5 inches and the half-sized about 2 ½ inches of records. In most respositories containers are used that hold about as much as the small-sized container of Minnesota and Wisconsin. Any accession large enough to fill the smallest container used in a repository should be treated as a separate collection; any accession that fails to do this should be embodied in a collection of miscellany. If the decision on the method of treatment is made without regard to the size of containers, any accession should be regarded as a separate collection if it contains 1 inch of records, or about 100 items; if it contains a smaller quantity or fewer items it should be added to a collection of miscellany.

If small accessions are embodied in a collection of miscellany, each accession should be placed in a separate folder. The accession should be registered, the folder in which it is placed should be numbered to correspond to the accession number given it, and the folder label should concisely identify the accession. The folders containing small accessions should be made of paper that does not contain injurious acids and should be packed in regular-sized archival boxes.

Bound material

An archivist should ordinarily shelve series of bound volumes directly, not pack them.

But if a manuscript collection contains both bound and unbound material, he may insert both in boxes, if the bound material is not too large. If he finds that bindings are so dilapidated that they do not serve to identify or protect their contents, he may place the contents of volumes in folders and box them.

CHARACTERISTICS OF CONTAINERS

Several characteristics of containers, relating to design, size, and substance of manufacture, will be noted briefly, though it is not my purpose to discuss their engineering features. Containers should serve to make records accessible for use and to protect them physically.

Design

Archival containers should be designed differently from those used in government offices for current records and in record centers for inactive records.

During the second half of the last century, when records became very voluminous in the United States, many new types of containers were produced for both governmental and commercial uses. The characteristic of these types that is particularly noteworthy here is their expansibility. The containers—filing cases, transfer drawers, document file holders, etc.—were designed to accommodate expanding files. They were designed to permit insertions of records at various points within filing systems that were developed concomitantly with the new equipment.

Here we are concerned with archival containers rather than containers designed for the handling of current files. There are fundamental distinctions between the two. Archival containers are designed to hold record units that will not ordinarily be enlarged by insertions; current record containers are designed for expanding files. Archival containers are designed to be handled as individual units, as are books. They are the units to be manipulated, to be packed and shelved, and made available for use. They are thus not stationary, as are filing cases into which current records are placed as they are created and accumulated.

Archival containers hold smaller lots of records than do standard file drawers designed for the maintenance of records in current use. A standard file drawer holds about 2 linear feet of records; an archival container about 5 inches, or one-fifth as much as the file drawer. If the contents of a file drawer are placed in archival containers, five containers of the type used in the National Archives are required. Offhand it would seem that the archivist's job of searching is complicated by this action, for presumably he will have to look in five places instead of one for a given item. But this is actually not the case, if the archivist does the work required of him. If the items within the containers are properly arranged, if the containers are properly labeled, and if the record group or series is properly described in finding aids, the archivist can go directly to a particular container to find what is wanted in a specific instance. By doing this, he can reduce his searching work and also reduce the physical wear and tear on his records while they are in use.

Record center containers are designed neither for current office use nor for archival use. They are designed to hold relatively inactive records that must be retained for long but not indefinite periods. They need be neither expansible, as are containers that hold current records, nor manipulable, as are containers that hold permanent records. The record center container used by the federal government of the United States is illustrated in Fig. 1.

Archival containers are designed either for the vertical or the horizontal storage of records. Slightly more than half of the documentary repositories in the United States store records vertically, and about one fourth store them both vertically and horizontally.[7] Old material and large material, in particular, is stored horizontally.

VERTICAL CONTAINERS. Containers in which records are stored vertically are placed side by side on shelves. Such containers must be packed fairly full, if the documents that stand in them in an upright position are not to crumple. The use of folders reduces crumpling. Crumpling is also avoided in a box in

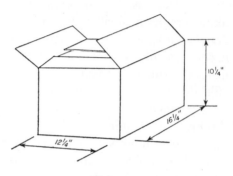

Figure 1

use at the Clements Library; this box contains a steel spring attached to the hinge cover, which when pressed against a loose stiff board flattens records on the inside against the opposite cover. In such a box, according to Colton Storm, "there is no danger of loose papers collapsing in a mess when the box is vertical." [8] Greater care must be exercised in packing vertical containers than is the case with containers designed for flat filing.

Ordinarily, records must exist in considerable quantity to enable an archivist fully to pack a vertical container so that documents within it will not crumple. Records, in a word, must exist in large series. For this reason, vertical containers are especially suitable for packing public records, which are usually in large series, and for packing large manuscript collections.

In general, vertical containers are well suited to the handling of records in quantity, and, if properly packed, they serve to protect records well. They also look neater and can be removed more easily from, and replaced on, the shelves than horizontal containers.

The first container designed for archival use was that of the

Iowa State Archives (Fig. 2). It was modeled after the Library Bureau pamphlet box and was "originally intended and designed

Figure 2

to lie flat and to be filed alongside bound records." [9] Waldo G. Leland described it as follows:

This box opens part way down the front and on the top; and by means of folders which are labeled, as in a vertical filing system, the contents of the box are classified so that on opening the top of the box you readily see what it contains. This system seems to me to be the most flexible and the most economical. Papers are filed flat— which is essential; and there is little, if any, waste of space. The boxes are placed on the shelves as if they were books.[10]

After several years of use, the Iowa State Archives box was changed to permit vertical instead of horizontal filing through a

Figure 3

change in its construction whereby only one hinge was used in the opening instead of two (Fig. 3). "By this change," according to Cassius C. Stiles, superintendent of the Iowa Public Archives, "we have a more compact, stronger, and practically dustproof box and a gain in economy of space in filing, and the advantages of the vertical file." [11]

Vertical containers now used in the National Archives are made of 50- and 60-gauge kraft cardboard (Fig. 4). For a num-

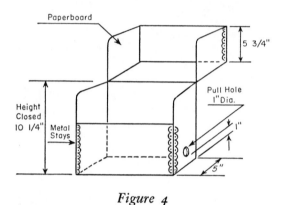

Figure 4

ber of years they were obtained with a patented metal edge, but recently stapled boxes are being used. They are cheaper and, being delivered flat, require less storage space while not in use. Stapled boxes are not as handsome as metal edge boxes but are just as serviceable.

HORIZONTAL CONTAINERS. Containers in which records are filed horizontally are placed one on top of the other on shelves, usually three or four to a pile. They are especially well suited to the needs of manuscript repositories, for even small collections can be deposited in them without danger of crumpling. They are more cumbersome to handle and less efficient in the use of space, but they protect records somewhat better than containers designed for vertical filing.

There are two types of archival containers designed for horizontal filing: a clam-type box and a slide box.

A clam-type box (Fig. 5) is used extensively in historical societies and state archives of the United States. The Historical

Society of Pennsylvania is among the important societies that use it.[12] Such a box opens as do covers of a book. Essentially, it consists of over-all covers that open from a bottom hinge.

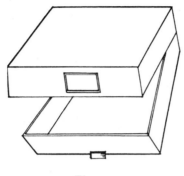

Figure 5

Another type of horizontal box, often used for the storage of private papers, is a slide box (Fig. 6). Records in such a box can

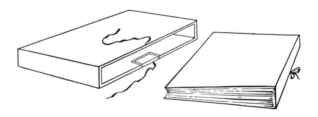

Figure 6

be deposited and removed with a minimum of friction. It consists of two parts: a portfolio or cover of cardboard, or stiff paper, with a stiff back, hinged with binder's cloth to the sides, and a box into which the portfolio can be slipped. This type of box was formerly used at the Library of Congress [13] and is now used at the Huntington Library,[14] as well as at other places.

Size

The record center containers used by the federal government of the United States are of one size only: 15¼ inches long, 12¼ inches wide, and 10¼ inches high. They accommodate legal-sized papers if inserted lengthwise, and letter-sized papers if inserted sidewise. They hold 12 inches of legal-sized records or 15 inches of letter-sized records. Since they weigh 30 to 40 pounds when filled, they are too heavy for any but male employees, and are suitable only for the storage of relatively inactive records.

Vertical containers designed for archival uses should hold 4 to 5 inches of records and therefore should be 4 to 5 inches wide. This quantity can be manipulated quite easily during packing, and when packed a container holding this quantity can easily be placed on a shelf. After it has been shelved it can be removed when needed without any trouble. This quantity is also about right for effective reference service work. If it is greater, too many documents must be manipulated to find the particular one wanted; if it is smaller, too many containers must be manipulated. Most unbound textual records in the National Archives are now packed in cardboard boxes of two sizes, with the following outside measurements: 15¼ inches long, 10¼ inches high, and 5¼ inches wide for legal-sized records, and 12¼ inches long, 10¼ inches high, and 5¼ inches wide for letter-sized records. Ordinarily, a container suitable for archival use should weigh about 8, but not more than 12, pounds when filled. Pressboard containers, of the type now used in the National Archives, weigh about 10 pounds when filled.

Horizontal containers designed for the storage of small manuscript collections should hold about 2 or 3 inches of records and should be in two sizes, one to accommodate legal-sized and the other letter-sized material. A large-sized container should also be available for large collections and should normally hold 4 to 5 inches of records, as do the regular-sized containers in the Minnesota and Wisconsin historical societies. In the Baker Library at Harvard University, a box that holds about 9 linear inches of records is used for large collections.[15]

Substance of manufacture

Archival containers should be made of a durable substance, either a paper product of a long life expectancy or a metal. Also, the substance of which the containers are made should not be harmful to records. It should not, for example, be a paper with a high acid content. Sixty-five percent of the documentary repositories in the United States now use containers made of paper.[16]

Metal containers have the advantage of being durable and nonflammable, but they are too heavy for archival use, unless aluminum, which is prohibitively high in cost, is used in their manufacture. If the steel used in the manufacture of a container is light enough to make it easy to handle, the container is likely to be too weak to stand up under the use to which it will be subjected.

When using metal containers an archivist, to a large degree, will be lifting metal instead of records. In order to have metal containers light enough for easy handling they have to be smaller than pressboard containers. A metal container ordinarily cannot hold more than 3 inches of records without becoming excessively heavy, while a pressboard container can hold as much as 5 inches of records without having this disadvantage.

LABELING CONTAINERS

As he packs records, an archivist should temporarily label boxes with a grease pencil or chalk. Normally, he should identify them with nothing more than the symbol assigned to the archival group or manuscript collection with which he is working, plus the box number.

As soon as he has records shelved, he should devise appropriate labels for boxes. He should affix to each box a label that identifies the archival group or manuscript collection and the specific series or part of the group or collection that is packed in it. Typically a label should contain the following information: the symbol of the collection or group; the title of the collection or group; the title of the subgroup, if such exists; the title of the series; data identifying the specific part of the series; and the box number.

When a series extends over a number of containers, the label on each container should identify the part of the series it holds. Thus, if a series is arranged numerically, the label should show the numbers assigned to the file units within containers; or if arranged alphabetically, the letters of the alphabet assigned to the file units within; or if arranged under a classified system, the classification symbols assigned to the file units within. The specific identification data, however, should not contain all of the information that is available in regard to the contents of a particular container. The data should not be too detailed, for the detailed information in regard to the contents of the container should be provided in finding aids.

Symbols or numbers that are used to identify an archival group or a manuscript collection should be placed in the upper left-hand corner of a label, while box numbers should be placed in the upper right-hand corner.

When dealing with very voluminous collections or groups, an archivist may find it desirable to have labels preprinted. On such labels, the number and title of a collection or group and the title of a subgroup (and, occasionally, of a series) are preprinted, so that each label need not be typed individually. All that remains to complete a label is to type on it the title of a series (or of its specific parts) and the box number.

Groove holders for labels are provided on some types of boxes, but are not available on the types used in the National Archives. While pasting labels to boxes may seem tedious and is often messy, pasted labels are generally the most practical and economical so far devised.

Shelving

SHELVING MATERIAL

Records should be shelved efficiently, and efficiency in shelving should be judged by the extent to which records are made accessible and to which stack space is fully utilized. Considerations of accessibility should always be weighed against considerations of space utilization.

Archival groups should be shelved so that records of a specific provenance are brought together. Their arrangement should be carefully planned, although even with the most careful planning it is often not possible to allocate the exact amount of space required for various components of an archival group, with the result that empty space pockets are developed in stacks.

Manuscript collections should be shelved so that space is utilized progressively as material is received. They should be shelved so that empty space pockets do not develop.

When dealing with small manuscript collections, it is more important to shelve them so they can be found than to shelve them so that every last inch of space is utilized.

Bound material presents special problems in shelving. Should it be filed side by side with unbound material to which it relates, or placed in a separate series? In 1914 this question was put to a number of archivists by the Committee on Public Archives of the National Association of State Libraries.[17]

Archivists gave various answers to the question. Thomas M. Owen (1866–1920), director of the Department of Archives and History of Alabama, thought bound material should be kept in a separate series.[18] He was supported by H. J. Eckenrode, who said that "bound records should not be filed side by side with loose manuscript documents of like content. Bound volumes are actually books and cannot be handled in the same way as loose papers." [19] Peter Nelson, assistant archivist of the New York State Library, stated that "documents of similar character, source and date, would be classified in the same series," but that it may "be necessary because of a physical form of these various records to shelve them in different parts of our archives . . . provided we do not lose sight of the connection of the documents." [20] Gaillard Hunt, chief of the Manuscript Division of the Library of Congress, stated simply that "bound records should be filed side by side with unbound records, but all records should eventually be bound." [21]

Bound volumes, in my opinion, should be shelved as follows:

Each bound volume from a specific source should be treated as a separate collection and should be shelved either in a collection of miscellaneous bound volumes, if such is maintained, or in its proper position among other collections.

If a bound volume is accompanied by unbound records, the entire lot should be treated as a collection and shelved as a unit.

Material that is larger than average in size should be shelved separately, if it cannot be shelved conveniently with the average-sized material to which it relates. It should be filed flat, either on open shelves, in packages, or in pull-out or map drawers.

TYPES OF SHELVING

It is not my purpose to discuss here the engineering features of stack equipment, its design, dimensions, and the like; information on such matters may be obtained from specialists in the field of equipment. But there are a few professional considerations that must be taken into account in shelving; these relate to certain features of stack equipment and to the identification of stack equipment.

Efficiency in space utilization is an important factor to be considered in the choice of stack equipment, and all engineering features of such equipment should be carefully considered to avoid loss of space or excessive use of space. Efficiency in space utilization is not as important in an archival institution as in a record center. In the latter, the success of operations is measured, to a large degree, by the efficiency with which space is utilized—for the savings effected by the centers are computed largely by the difference between the cost of storing records in the center and the cost of storing records in the offices in which they were held.

Because modern records are of various physical types, i.e., correspondence, reports, forms of all kinds, occurring in various sizes and shapes, the equipment should be sufficiently flexible to enable the archivist to place all types and sizes of records in proper relation to one another. Archival shelf supports should therefore provide for shelves that are adjustable by one-inch or two-inch gradation.

The term "stack" may be used both in a narrow and in a broad sense. In a broad sense it refers to a room within an archival building in which records are stored. In a narrow sense, and in the sense in which I shall use the term here, it refers to the supports (or frames) to which shelves are attached. A stack row, or, to use the more technical term, a range, consists of a series of adjoined compartments, each of which contains a tier of shelves.

Stacks may be made of either wood or metal. Wood, ordinarily, is not suitable for the construction of archival stacks because it is impermanent and inflammable. Under certain circumstances it may be used for the construction of stacks in storage areas for temporary records, such as record centers. Eighty percent of the manuscript repositories in the United States now use steel shelving.[22] Metal stacks may be either mobile or stationary. Both kinds are commercially available.

Mobile stacks

Mobile stacks are of two types.

A type well known in Europe is one in which entire rows are moved on tracks. The tracks, which are placed in the floor, run at right angles to the stack rows. The rows are placed compactly side by side, and for this reason the trade name "Compactus" has been given to this equipment. The stack rows may be moved along the tracks in an accordion-like fashion to provide access to any particular row that is desired. In a given block of stack rows, only one aisle space is thus needed.

A type of mobile stack well known in the United States is one in which stack compartments (instead of rows) are moved on tracks. The tracks may be attached either to the ceiling or to the floor, and run parallel to the stack rows (instead of at right angles to them). In each row, space as large as one compartment is left empty. The stack rows, just as in Compactus equipment, are placed compactly side by side. The compartments may be moved from side to side along tracks to provide access to any particular compartment desired.

Mobile stack equipment has found favor in certain European and American archival institutions, especially since it facilitates "tight packing." In the federal government of the United States, which very probably has produced more records than all other national governments of the world combined, movable equipment until now has been considered to be impracticable for archival purposes. The space savings realized by the use of movable equipment do not offset the increased costs of the equipment itself, of the construction necessary to accommodate it, and of the additional labor required in its use. Storage in record centers, microfilming, and double shelving are considered more economical alternatives.

Stationary stacks

Stationary stacks are of three main types: those with shelf supports in the form of vertical uprights that contain grooves

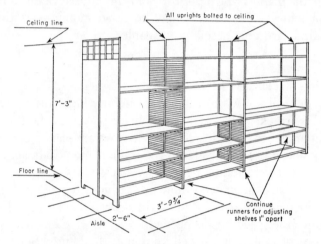

Figure 7

into which shelves can be inserted, those with shelf supports in the form of single stack columns to which cantilever shelves can be hooked or otherwise attached, and those in which the shelves are bolted to the shelf supports. These three types are known respectively as upright, bracket, and utility stacks. Upright stacks, with adjustable shelving, are used in the National Archives (Fig. 7). Bracket, or cantilever, stacks are illustrated in Fig. 8; utility stacks, in Fig. 9.

Considerable economy of space can be achieved if stacks are designed to make double shelving possible. This means placing one container behind another on a shelf. If two containers can be placed back to back on a shelf, instead of just one on a shelf, aisle space is obviously saved.

Double shelving is recommended only for large sequences of records that extend over a number of archival containers; not for small manuscript collections, each of which must be placed in a separate container, for such small collections may easily be

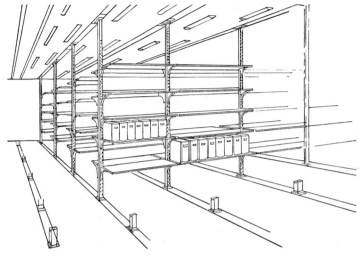

Figure 8

lost if shelved double. If records are shelved double, an accurate record of their location should be maintained.

Stationary stack equipment meets the needs of most documentary repositories. Bracket stacks are cheaper and easier to use than upright stacks. Most state repositories in the United States

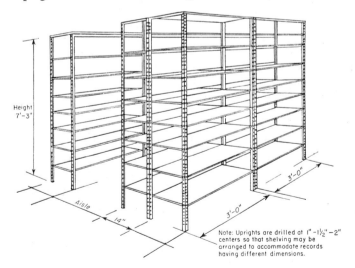

Figure 9

use the former; the National Archives uses the latter. Utility stacks are used mostly in record centers.

As a final step in arrangement, an archivist should develop devices by which he can control information on the location of records in his stacks. These are of two kinds: (*a*) symbols assigned to equipment and (*b*) location registers.

Assigning locational symbols

Symbols should be assigned to stacks in such a manner that a particular symbol will relate to one location, and one location only. The symbols should refer to the following elements: the stack area, the row within the stack area, and the compartment within the row. A complete symbol should thus read: 1-15-6. In this symbol, number 1 refers to the area, number 15 to the row within the area, and number 6 to the compartment within the row.

Maintaining location register

A stack numbering system enables an archivist to provide precise and accurate information on the location of various groups and series in his stacks in a location register. An entry in a register should show the following:

the symbol that identifies a record unit and its components
the title of the record unit and titles of its components
the symbol that identifies the stack area, row, and compartment
    in which the record unit is deposited
the symbols that identify the containers in which the record
    unit is packed

A location register is important to the effective administration of a large documentary repository. It is a means of keeping information up to date on the physical location of records, which is necessary when records are often shifted to accommodate new accessions. It is helpful in reference service work. By showing where every group or collection and its components are located, it can pinpoint the place in which searches should be made in response to specific requests.

XIV

PREPARATION OF ARCHIVAL
INVENTORIES AND GUIDES

A record inventory is, as its name implies, a stocktaking of records. It has a twofold purpose: to provide a preliminary analysis of an archival group and to provide an initial or provisional finding aid. It should also provide an archivist with information that is useful in the preparation of a guide, which represents a later and more refined stage in finding aid work.

A guide is a comprehensive finding aid to records in a repository or to records relating to some subject field. Its purpose is to provide a brief conspectus of such records, which a searcher can use to determine if particular record units are relevant to his subject of inquiry.

Inventories

In taking stock of a group of public records, an archivist must make a list of various record units found within the group. A question then naturally arises: What are the units of records that should be listed?

The record units that are listed in an inventory of public records vary in different countries.

In Europe, in which registry systems are usually employed in organizing current records, registered files are the units that are inventoried in an archival institution.[1] The German repertories thus consist of unpublished lists of individual binders or files, while the German inventories are simply repertories in published form, generally augmented by explanatory or bibliographical information. Similarly, registered files and registers are listed in

French inventories. The units or lots by which they are enumerated or described are usually containers, bundles, or volumes.

In the United States, in which modern filing systems are employed in organizing current records, the units that should be inventoried are series. Such record units, it will be recalled from Chapter X, are comprised of documents that are coherent because they are organized according to an integrated filing system, or because they are of the same type, or because they relate to the same matter of business.

PURPOSE AND SCOPE

An inventory of public records normally should cover all records that are assigned to a particular archival group. If a group is very large and can be conveniently divided into separable parts, each of which has well-defined limits by reason of its administrative or functional coherence, these parts may be covered by separate inventories. Thus, separate inventories may be prepared for records that were produced by subdivisions of the agency that created a group, or that relate to one or more of the major functions of the agency. If this is done, however, the parts should be carefully planned to permit complete coverage of all records in the group without overlapping.

While preparing an inventory, an archivist gains a knowledge of the origins, structure, and content of an archival group that is very useful to him in reference service and later descriptive work. Its preparation is a kind of discipline for him, for while preparing it he is required to do those things that are always necessary to acquire a knowledge of records. These relate to a study of the organization and function of an agency, which he must know if he is to understand the records it produced; a dissection of the archival group into its constituent parts, such as subgroups and series; and an identification of the record type and a description of the content of each of the series.

Two types of inventories should be prepared of public records in the United States: inventories in which record series are merely identified by title and inventories in which record series are described as well as identified. The former should be prepared for archival groups that have a limited or highly special-ized research interest; the latter, for archival groups that have a general research interest.

The former type, which may be called summary inventories, should contain an introduction in which the origins and prove-nance of the group as a whole are analyzed and a listing of series in the group by title, arranged under proper captions or heads. Instructions in this chapter on preparing entries for series are in two parts: those relating to title lines and those relating to de-scriptive paragraphs. Only the first part of these instructions apply when preparing summary inventories.

Inventories of the second type, which may be called descrip-tive inventories, should contain, in addition to an introduction and a listing of series titles, a descriptive paragraph on each series.

Both types of inventories should be provisional in character. They should serve merely as a means toward the end of prepar-ing comprehensive finding aids, such as guides, or specialized finding aids, such as lists. The information they provide about the administrative history of an agency should serve merely to show how an archival group was produced and to what func-tions it relates; it should not be a vehicle for a pedantic display of historical scholarship. Their entries on series should contain only essential information on type and content. While such entries should be compiled according to a standard style and format, the provisional character of the compilation should be recognized; it need not be editorially perfect.

Since inventories are provisional in character and are designed primarily for use within an archival institution, they should be published selectively. The first instructions on inventory work issued by the National Archives on February 28, 1941, stated that "after careful editorial revision," inventories "shall be processed in such form as to be available not only for internal distribution but also for use by searchers within the building or outside, as circumstances may make desirable." [2] In the course of time, however, inventories came to be regarded as finished finding aids intended primarily for external use. Because of this change, excessive attention came to be given to their composition and editing. For this reason, as well as because of increased reference service, the inventory program of the National Archives gradually bogged down. Normally, summary inventories should be reproduced in multiple copies for limited distribution; descriptive inventories should be published for general distribution.

While European archival institutions often produce a succession of inventories in which records are described in progressively greater detail, this is not a desirable practice for American archivists to follow. The latter should proceed from an inventory to some other type of finding aid. A succession of preliminary finding aids—as recommended by the National Archives committee on finding aids in 1941, i.e., first, preliminary checklists, then preliminary inventories—should not be prepared.[3] Such a succession simply results in a regurgitation of ill-digested information.

Information provided in various parts of an inventory should not be repetitive. Information provided in an introductory statement, captions or heads, series titles and descriptive paragraphs, and appendixes should, as a rule, be progressively more detailed, proceeding from the general to the specific.

INTRODUCTION

In an introduction to an inventory, an archivist should provide a general view of the character and content of an archival group. He should show how a group came into being by providing information about the agency that produced it and the functions and activities that resulted in its production. But his main purpose should be to throw light on records, not on their organizational or functional origins.

In a history of a government agency that created or assembled an archival group, an archivist should provide information that shows its administrative antecedents and its origins as reflected in the authorization for its establishment by law, executive order, or otherwise; its major organizational subdivisions; and its major functions.

He should group information on the agency's organizational structure and functions under the major heads selected for the grouping and description of series. Normally, he should provide information only in reference to its major organizational subdivisions and major functions; he should omit minutiae of its organizational and functional development that are not essential to an understanding of records.

If an archival group has very complex administrative origins, however, an archivist may find it advisable to provide historical information on the antecedents and development of each organizational subdivision that produced important bodies of records. He should place such information below the administrative heads under which he will group series for descriptive purposes. But he should not repeat, under such heads, information found in the over-all introduction.

He should place information on specific activities or transactions that resulted in the production of specific record series under entries for series. He should not include it in an introduction.

In an introduction, an archivist may provide information on an archival group that he believes will be helpful in understanding its character and content. The information would include the group's subgroups, subject matter, organization, arrangement, and relation to other archival groups.

An introductory statement should be objective and factual in content; it should be organized in a coherent system. The following outline is intended to be suggestive only:

(a) Administrative history of a government agency
   (1) Origins: administrative antecedents, authorization for establishment (law, executive order, administrative order, or other authority), dates
   (2) Major subdivisions of last (or current) organization
   (3) Major functions
       of agency as a whole
       of major subdivisions
(b) Records
   (1) Analysis by types, by major administrative subdivisions, or by functions

(2) Organization and arrangement
(3) Relation to other records

INVENTORY ENTRIES

An archivist should group inventory entries under heads or captions that show organizational or functional origins or follow some other logical pattern.

In the preparation of an inventory entry, two actions are involved: an identification of the record unit that is being inventoried and an enumeration of its attributes. An inventory entry consists, therefore, of two parts: (a) a title line in which a record unit is identified and (b) a descriptive paragraph in which its attributes are enumerated.

Title line

A title line should pertain to the following matters about a series: its record type, described in general or specific terms, as well as by its distinctive characteristics and by the method of its reproduction, if pertinent; its inclusive dates; and its quantity.

An archivist should observe the following rules in preparing title lines:

First, if a series consists of many record types, use *general terms* to describe its types, such as "records," "papers," or "manuscripts." The use of the word "files" should be avoided whenever possible, though the term "case files" may be used since it has a special meaning. For example, if a series consists of "legal records," it should not be identified as "legal files."

Second, if a series consists of a specific record type, such as correspondence, letters, reports, and the like, identify the *specific type* in a title line. Specific terms are always preferable to general terms in describing record types. Special attention has been given to the identification of record types in the chapter on "Record Attributes."

Third, whenever possible, further identify the record type in a series by its *distinctive characteristics*. These characteristics may be derived from the administrative origins of the series and the functions that resulted in its production, or may relate to its subject matter.

In devising a title for a series, an archivist should proceed on an *ad hoc* basis. The extent to which identifying information in a series title will be needed depends on the nature of the group heads and on the nature of the descriptive data that follow the title. Thus, if a number of archival series are analyzed under administrative or functional heads, the titles should not repeat information on origins and functions provided in such heads.

Information on the administrative origins of an archival series may be included if this information more specifically identifies the office or official that performed the action reflected in the series. A title, therefore, may indicate the origins of an archival series by naming the small administrative unit or the particular official responsible for creating it. If, for example, the type of the series is determined to be CORRESPONDENCE, other attributes that will serve to identify its administrative origins may be indicated as follows:

> PAYMASTERS' CORRESPONDENCE
> COMMANDANTS' CORRESPONDENCE

If the series consists of no specific types and is identified simply as RECORDS, the records may be attributed to an official by title or by name. For example:

> RECORDS OF JOHN DOE (a given individual)
> RECORDS OF MEDICAL OFFICERS (individuals of a given title)

A title may also include information on the function to which a series relates. This information will serve to identify more specifically the kind of action reflected in the series. If, for example, the type of the series is determined to be CORRESPONDENCE, further identifying attributes or specific activities may be indicated as follows:

> ADMINISTRATIVE (or FISCAL or POLICY) CORRESPONDENCE
> CORRESPONDENCE RELATING TO INVESTIGATIONS (or REQUISITIONS)

Or if the type is determined to be REPORTS, it may be indicated that they relate to specific activities:

PROGRESS (or INSPECTION or SURVEY) REPORTS

Or if the type of the series is determined to be APPLICATIONS, it may be indicated that they are of a specific kind or that certain actions were taken on them:

APPLICATIONS FOR COMMISSIONS
APPROVED (or CANCELLED) APPLICATIONS

A title may also include information on the character of the series as indicated by its subject-matter content, its frequency, or other attributes. For example:

MISCELLANEOUS (or GENERAL) CORRESPONDENCE
CORRESPONDENCE RELATING TO FARMLAND BOUNTY (or TRANSPOR-
TATION)

Or, by combining information on functions, a title would read:

MISCELLANEOUS FISCAL (or ADMINISTRATIVE or POLICY) CORRE-
SPONDENCE
GENERAL ADMINISTRATIVE (or FISCAL or POLICY) CORRESPOND-
ENCE

Correspondence may be further distinguished by the use of such terms as "incoming," "outgoing," or "reading" (or "chronological"), or designated as letters sent or letters received. Reports may be identified by indicating that they are narrative or statistical in character or that they were produced at annual, monthly, or daily intervals. A title, accordingly, would read:

ANNUAL (or MONTHLY or DAILY) NARRATIVE (or STATISTICAL)
REPORTS

Or, by combining information on functions, a title would read:

ANNUAL (or MONTHLY or DAILY) NARRATIVE (or STATISTICAL)
PROGRESS (or INSPECTION or SURVEY) REPORTS, or, in short,
ANNUAL NARRATIVE PROGRESS REPORTS

Information on the arrangement given an archival series should be included in the title only if it helps to indicate the substantive character of the records. Thus, "chronological correspondence" usually refers to letters accumulated on a day-by-day basis for reference in an office. The word "chronological" is therefore meaningful in a title. Ordinarily, such titles as "decimal file" or "alphabetical file," though used in the file rooms of the agency that accumulated the records, would not be considered as apt or meaningful for a devised series title.

Fourth, if a record type consists of reproductions, indicate the *method of reproduction*, thus:

> TRANSCRIPTS: MANUSCRIPTS
> MICROFILM: MEMOIRS
> PHOTOPRINTS: LETTERS

Fifth, give the *inclusive dates* during which the records were produced, e.g., 1850–90. If most of the records or unusually significant records were produced between particular dates, give such dates in parentheses between the first and last dates, thus: 1850(1876–84)1890. If significant gaps exist in the records, indicate this fact thus: 1891–1910, 1915–20. If the exact dates cannot be established, use the word "circa" in its abbreviated form, i.e., "ca.," to denote this fact. If dates in the title line need further explanation, supply it in the descriptive paragraph.

Sixth, indicate the *quantity* of records in the series. Show this in terms of the number of linear feet and inches records occupy on shelves, including in the measurement folders, envelopes, or containers in which they are inserted. Use the figure that represents the nearest full linear foot, unless the quantity is less than one linear foot, in which case give the figure in terms of inches, as follows: 40 ft.; 6 in.; or 40 ft., 6 in.; or 40½ ft.

Descriptive paragraph

Each entry should have, following its title line, one or more paragraphs that contain descriptive and analytical information not provided in the heads under which archival series are grouped or in the titles of series. If a series consists of a number of parts, it may be desirable to describe each of the parts in separate paragraphs. Information about each series should pertain to the following matters: its record types; its significant items, if any; its provenance; its content; and its composition.

In preparing a descriptive paragraph, an archivist should observe the following rules:

First, show the various *types of records* included in the series, if a general term such as "records" or "papers" was used in the title. If, for example, the word "records" is used in the title, the descriptive paragraph might begin with either of the two following expressions:

Correspondence, memoranda, reports, and other papers relating to . . .
Mainly correspondence and reports, but including . . .

Enumerate the *main* types of records included in the series, but do not necessarily identify every type. If occasional types are significant, however, refer to them, as in the following example:

Included are newspaper clippings relating to the dispute, in 1908, between President Theodore Roosevelt and Congress over limiting the scope of Secret Service activities.

Typical record types may also be enumerated to show the nature of a series, as in the following example:

POSTAUDIT CASE FILES

These case files, relating to applications for price adjustment that were submitted by service companies pursuant to Maximum Price Regulation 165, were transmitted to the national office for postaudit. A typical case file includes the following: (1) the application for adjustment of a maximum price for a service; (2) regional office memoranda relating to the processing of the application; (3) findings and recommendation of the price specialist; (4) correspondence with the service company relating to the granting or denying of the price adjustment; (5) the order and opinion of the regional administrator; (6) the transmittal memorandum for transferring the file to the national office for postaudit; and (7) a postaudit memorandum summarizing the review of the case. The case files are arranged alphabetically by name of company.

Second, identify *significant items* in the series. Unusually important items within a series should be singled out for attention, and the typical entry for such an item should show its producer, its type, the activity or transaction which resulted in its production, and, if necessary, the main subject to which it relates in terms of persons, places, things, or phenomena.

Third, provide information on the *provenance* of a series, using the term in the archival sense of its meaning. Such information should be supplemental to that provided in the title line. It may relate to the place of an office or official in the administrative hierarchy of an agency; to the relations of an office or official to other offices or officials, if these relations reveal the source or significance of the records; and to the status or the location of a class of offices or officials, if pertinent. The importance of determining the hierarchical position of an office in identifying GENERAL CORRESPONDENCE is readily apparent. Ordinarily, the head under which a series is described and the title of the series should show if such correspondence was maintained at a bureau, divisional, or sectional level. General correspondence, in a given archival group, for example, might cover the agency as a whole, in which case its administrative origins would probably be indicated by a head such as "general records"; or it might cover a bureau or division, in which case its administrative origins would probably be indicated in the head by the name of the bureau or division. If the administrative status of the office or official that created the general correspondence is not indicated in heads or titles, however, this information should be provided in descriptive paragraphs. Such a paragraph might read:

GENERAL CORRESPONDENCE.

Letters received, copies of letters sent, and related material pertaining to the affairs of the Bureau at the policy level, not including correspondence of subordinate divisions or specialized correspondence pertaining to contracts, requisitions, and specifications.

Or, if the administrative status of the office that created the general correspondence is indicated in a head, the position or the name of the particular official that created it may be indicated in the descriptive paragraphs, as follows:

GENERAL CORRESPONDENCE OF JOHN SMITH

Letters received and copies of letters sent by Mr. Smith, with related material pertaining to . . . . Mr. Smith served as Chairman of the Board, Aug. 22, 1941–Oct. 25, 1943.

Fourth, show the *content* of the series. The methods of showing content vary according to the kind of record series that is
being described.

To describe a series organized according to a subject system,
an archivist should enumerate the *main* subject heads under
which records are classified. In modern filing systems, administrative records are generally organized under subject heads. The
main classes of records are shown in heads on guide cards, while
the units of records that relate to specific transactions or topics
are shown in heads on folder labels. These heads, both general
and specific, often show the subject content of a record series,
and should therefore be taken into account in describing the
content of a record series in a preliminary inventory. The following example illustrates how to enumerate subject heads:

GENERAL CORRESPONDENCE.

Letters received and sent and such related records as memoranda,
reports, and circulars, documenting all activities of the Service, including new work on flood control, water facilities, drainage and
irrigation surveys, land utilization, and farm forestry. Project subjects (class 200) include research, watershed studies, sedimentation
studies, soil studies, water conservation studies, island research, conservation operations, agronomy, flood control, engineering, erosion-
control practices, conservation nurseries, wildlife, woodland management, and technical cooperation with the Bureau of Indian
Affairs. Records other than those relating to projects (class 200) are
divided into classes for administration and organization (100), accounts and disbursements (300), information and education (400),
personnel (500), equipment and contracts (600), legislation (700),
labor (800), and miscellaneous (900).

Formal filing or classification schemes should not be reproduced
in descriptive entries of inventories. If important, they should be
included in appendixes of inventories, or issued separately for
what they are, i.e., filing or classification schemes.

To describe a series of case files, organized numerically or
alphabetically, an archivist should describe the content of a *typical* file. Case files are the American equivalent of European registered files and are produced in large quantities in various regula-

tory, investigative, and adjudicatory programs of the federal government. They may be defined as aggregations of papers (not necessarily fastened together) constituting the complete record of a particular matter of business, representing all of the proceedings in relation to a single case or issue, or containing all the essential papers in relation to a particular problem, person, or organization. They may contain all kinds of documents—letters, memoranda, briefs, reports, and the like—but they have a similarity because the matters to which they relate are similar. Because they have common attributes, case files can be described effectively by showing the content of a typical file, as in the following example:

APPLICATIONS FOR ISSUANCE OF COMPLAINT

Applications that were docketed and assigned to examining attorneys for thorough investigation before issuance of formal complaint. A typical file includes correspondence stating the nature of the complaint; correspondence with the applicant and the proposed respondent; docketing directions; case assignments; reports on interviews; exhibits; reports and recommendations of the attorney examiner; report of the chief examiner with a statement of the facts, review of the law applicable, conclusions, and recommendations to the Commission; and the order of the Commission.

If a given series of case files is very voluminous, and is important from a research point of view, it may be desirable to identify individual case files by the subjects, persons, or corporate bodies to which they pertain. This should be done either in an appendix to an inventory or a special list.

To describe a series established on the basis of record type, an archivist should describe the content of a *typical* item. Record types are largely the result of repetitive action in governmental and corporate bodies. Because a given type contains the same kind of information about some matter or person, record types can be described effectively by showing what is in a typical item, as follows:

QUESTIONNAIRES AND RELATED RECORDS

Records received from each respondent government agency, consisting generally of: (1) correspondence, (2) lists of chiefs and supervisors, and (3) questionnaires, which contain seven sections or schedules as follows: A. Payroll classification by unit; B. Functions, activities, projects, processes, or services of the unit; C. Utilization of space: Office, file, storage, or other space per thousand square feet; D. Publicity and public relations; E. Employees for whom exemption from the draft has been requested; F. General testimony; and G. Mileage, transportation, telephone, and subsistence.

If records of a given type are voluminous and significant, it may be desirable to make known the existence of individual items in a series either in an appendix to the inventory or in a special list.

To describe a series established on the basis of its relation to a particular activity, an archivist should show its contents in terms of the *activities* that resulted in its production or to which it pertains, and/or the *objects of* such *activities,* such as the persons, corporate bodies, places, things, and phenomena that are involved in them.

Series of records in which subject content is not reflected by their arrangement, such as correspondence, should be described by enumerating the *main* activities to which they relate. For example:

GENERAL CORRESPONDENCE

Letters received from agents, private individuals and firms, other Treasury Department offices, other government departments (including the House and Senate), and others, relating mainly to counterfeit detection, protection of the President, special investigations, visits of foreign dignitaries, the assignment of agents, and expenses incurred by agents.

Or such series may be described by enumerating the *main* subjects to which they relate, as in the following example:

RECORDS RELATING TO THE BALLINGER-PINCHOT CONTROVERSY

Correspondence, reports, memoranda, maps, and other papers of the Office of the Forester and of the Office of Region 6 at Portland, Ore., relating to three major issues in the controversy: (1) Withdrawal of power-site lands from entry by private persons, (2) withdrawal of sites in national forests for administrative use by the Forest Service, and (3) administration of the Alaskan coal fields.

If series of files exist that were produced by offices that engaged in essentially similar activities, the contents of a *typical* office file should be described, followed by a listing of the offices. For example, during World War II, local boards of the Office of Price Administration concerned themselves with controlling prices and rationing commodities. During the selection of records of the agency for preservation in the National Archives, a limited number of the boards were designated as "record boards," whose records were preserved to illustrate various problems handled at the local board level. The records of these record boards were essentially similar in character, because they related to essentially similar matters, and they were therefore described by showing the content of the records of a typical board and by listing the boards for which records were available. If office files that are similar in character are very numerous and are significant for research use, the offices that produced them should be listed in an appendix to an inventory or in a special list.

Fifth, show the *composition* of the series. Information on composition may relate to the kind of file units in a series, i.e., whether folders, binders, volumes, and the like; or to the system under which such file units are arranged. Since most series of public records are arranged in some way, the system of arrangement should be specified, i.e., whether alphabetical, numerical, geographical, or subject. Information on composition may also relate to the size or other physical characteristics, or to the physical condition of records, i.e., whether disarranged or in a fragile condition.

APPENDIXES

An archivist should include in an appendix any readily available and useful information about an archival group that does not fit into the body of an inventory. This may relate to the history of the body that produced the records, the history of the records, or the character and content of the records.

Since it is provisional in character, an inventory is the first step in organizing information about an archival group. And part of the work of organizing this information consists of making known all extant knowledge that exists about it in an appendix. This information may consist of tentative finding aids prepared by the repository, such as checklists, shelflists, or lists of case files, record items, or subject heads. Or it may consist of agency classification schemes, lists, and other finding aids. Such information on the content of particular series should be included in an appendix whenever it is significant and whenever it is too extensive to include in series entries.

Guides

ORGANIZATION

If a guide to documentary material is to do what its name implies, i.e., to guide a searcher to records relevant to his inquiry, it should be schematized in some way. Its contents should be revealed in a table of contents, and its entries should be arranged in a logical order.

Table of contents

An archivist should provide a table of contents to a guide in which archival groups are listed by title and symbol (usually number). In view of its importance as a key to the contents of the guide, the table should appear as a preface; it should not be relegated to an appendix.

Archival groups should be listed in a table of contents under administrative heads or numerically, depending on the order given entries in the body of a guide. If entries in a guide are arranged in the order of the numbers assigned to archival groups, the table of contents should list such groups under administrative heads. If, on the other hand, they are arranged in an order that reflects administrative relations, the table of contents should list the groups in numerical order.

An example of a listing under administrative heads is found in Appendix D of the National Archives *Guide* (1948). This appendix contains a "Classified List of Record Groups" that is designed to provide the user "with a convenient and logical pattern of arrangement of the record groups, showing insofar as is practicable the hierarchical organization of the Government." [4]

Order of entries

In the body of a guide to public records, an archivist should describe archival groups either in an order that reflects their administrative relations or in a numerical order. If the table of contents lists archival groups under administrative heads, guide entries should be listed in the order of the numbers assigned to archival groups; if, on the other hand, it lists them numerically, the entries should be organized under administrative heads.

The National Archives *Guide* serves to illustrate the problems that arise in describing public records. The various archival groups of the federal government could have been arranged, for descriptive purposes, either in the numerical order in which they were established or in an order that reflected the governmental organizational structure. In the *Guide* they were arranged numerically—an arrangement that a reviewer said "cannot be described as anything but a national misfortune," and which served to emphasize the "disorganization and incoherence" of the federal bureaucracy.[5] While this disorganization and incoherence was made obvious by a numerical arrangement of guide entries, the strictures of the reviewer would not have been sound if such entries had been listed in a table of contents that revealed the organizational structure of the government.

ENTRIES

An archivist should describe each archival group in a separate entry. The entry should contain (*a*) historical information about the governmental body that produced the archival group and (*b*) a description of the series within the archival group. The historical part should be clearly separated from the descriptive part.

Historical information

In preparing historical information for a guide entry, an archivist should condense the administrative history of the inventory that pertains to the archival group under consideration. He should give only the essential facts about the organizational and functional developments of the government agency that produced the group, and he should regard as essential only those facts that help explain the character and significance of records. He should present these facts in either narrative or tabular form. If they are presented in narrative form, he should reduce them to one paragraph; if in tabular form, to a chronological table. A listing of the facts in chronological order is, on the whole, the clearest and most succinct method of presentation.

In the description of a large and complex archival group, it may be necessary to divide the guide entry into a number of parts pertaining to subgroups, produced by major organizational subdivisions of the agency that produced the archival group. If this is necessary, historical information should precede descriptive information on each subgroup.

If administrative history work will delay, for an indefinite period, the completion of a guide, an archivist should exclude historical information from the guide entries. Such information is not absolutely indispensable to the description of archival groups; it is, in fact, often not consulted when a guide is used. It is better to provide immediate information about records than to produce, after a long delay, a guide that includes administrative histories.

Descriptive information

In preparing a guide entry, an archivist should include only information that has a direct bearing on records. While important, explanatory information about the provenance or functional origins of series should not be substituted for specific information on their type, date, and quantity. And historical information should not be interlarded with descriptive information.

In preparing a guide entry, an archivist should summarize the descriptive information contained in an inventory and in other finding aids. The process of preparing such an entry is a process of distillation—of extracting the essence of descriptive data available in a repository. While this process cannot be reduced to an exact technique, there are several things that should be noted about it.

While an archivist should provide a separate inventory entry for each series, he should, in a guide entry, combine or condense inventory entries for all series that have common attributes or that are otherwise related. Series may have common attributes because they are the same type, the same kind of file unit, the same kind of file, or because they relate to the same kind of action or matter of business.

In many inventories an archivist will find a number of series that consist of letters, reports, journals, clippings, or other specific documentary types. Or he may find a number of series that consist of the same kind of file units, e.g., case files; or a number of series that consist of the same kind of files, e.g., office files; or a number of series, comprising various record types, that relate to essentially the same kind of transactions or activities. Or he may find series of indexes and registers that are related to series of letters and other documentary types.

The fact that record series are similar in character is of central importance in their description. It indicates the technique to be employed in preparing a guide entry for them, i.e., that series that have common attributes should be described collectively in regard to their common attributes, and singly only in regard to their variable attributes.

Thus, series of letters—a specific record type—should be described under a single guide entry as "letters of (listing offices or officials or other variable attributes)."

Case files—a specific kind of file unit—should be described under a single guide entry as "case files pertaining to (listing variable attributes)."

Office files—a specific kind of file—should be described under a single guide entry as "office files of (listing names of officials or offices)." In the National Archives preliminary inventory of the records of the National Recovery Administration, a number of inventory entries pertain to office files.[6] In a guide, these should be listed under a single entry, e.g., "Office files of Alexander

Sachs, Robert H. Montgomery, Leon Henderson, etc." The titles of the individuals should, of course, be included.

And series pertaining to the same kind of transaction or the same kind of activity should be described under a single guide entry. In the National Archives preliminary inventory of the records of the Special Committee of the Senate to Investigate the National Defense Program, a number of series are identified as "records relating to————." [7] In a guide, these should be listed under a single entry, e.g., "Records relating to aluminum, magnesium, lumber, paper, textiles, etc."

Series of indexes and registers should be described with the letters or other documentary types to which they relate.

Arrangement

In listing series (or important items within series) in a guide entry, an archivist should arrange them either in a narrative form or in a tabular form.

In the National Archives *Guide* (1948), series are listed in a narrative form. Narrative statements tend to become padded with verbiage. A good guide is characterized by an abundance of information about records and a paucity of words.

In the *Summary Guide to the Pennsylvania State Archives*, produced by the Pennsylvania Historical and Museum Commission in 1962, series are listed in tabular form, as in the following example:

RECORDS OF THE RECEIVER GENERAL OF THE LAND OFFICE, 1781–1809.
General Correspondence, 1781—(in process).
Summary Statements of Accounts, 1781–99. 1 vol.
Account Books; Land, Lots and Fees, 1802–9. 26 vols.
Certificates for Monies Received on Patents, 1786–1807. 3 cartons.
Funded Certificates Received, 1790–93. 1 vol.
List of Monies Received for Patents and Warrants. 1790–1794. 6 vols.
Tax Book, 1788–94. 1 vol.

A tabular listing of series is preferable to a narrative listing. It makes information about records more readily apparent, for it is easier to scan a list of series, line by line, than to read a narrative account of them. It also has a disciplinary advantage. It forces an archivist to identify record units by type, date, and quantity. It discourages him from substituting words for facts about records. It results in a presentation of more precise descriptive information about records. And it reduces this information to bare essentials.

INDEX

In a guide to public records, an index is the primary means of making known the relation of archival groups to subjects. Normally, it should include references to the following:

(*a*) All subjects, that is, persons, places, things, and phenomena, that are identified in guide entries. The extent to which subjects can be identified in an index depends upon the extent to which they are identified in guide entries. Usually, only subjects that are identified in guide entries are indexed, not subjects to which the records themselves relate. This limitation is important, for it points up the limitation of an index in showing subject relations. To protect the unwary user, an archivist should insert a prefatory note in his index to explain this limitation.

(*b*) All names of governmental bodies and of their organizational subdivisions.

(*c*) All activities and transactions that resulted in the production of series.

XV

PRELIMINARY DESCRIPTION
OF PRIVATE PAPERS

Many manuscript curators find it necessary to make some sort of preliminary analysis of newly acquired material. This analysis is embodied in documents that have been given various names. In the Duke University Library, the document is called a "sketch," which, according to Ruth K. Nuermberger, "has proved to be the most valuable part of our records." Dr. Nuermberger says that the sketch "arose from the realization that the knowledge gained from working through a collection was soon forgotten." [1] Katharine E. Brand, while at the Manuscript Division of the Library of Congress, developed an initial descriptive document that she called a "register." She devised two types: a short register, for single manuscripts, and a full-length register, for a group of manuscripts. [2]

When a new accession of private papers is received, it is obviously desirable to get an idea of its nature immediately. Two types of analyses should therefore be made of the papers: the first relating to their provenance, and the second to their character and content. The provenance of an accession should be recorded in a biographical sketch or corporate history. The character and content of an accession should be described on a work sheet or data sheet. The two types of documents, when combined, are similar to a National Archives inventory, and they may therefore be called an inventory.

In an inventory an archivist should record all facts readily available about an accession (which is usually the equivalent of a collection), including information about the person or corporate body that produced it, often extracted orally from the donor or seller or obtained from biographical reference works; the activities that resulted in its production; its record types, ascertained while arranging it; and the persons, places, things, and phenomena that are mentioned in it. The inventory should be like the Duke University "sketch," which, Dr. Nuermberger says, contains, first, biographical information on the person (except for outstanding persons written up in printed biographies or biographical dictionaries) or family represented in the collection and, secondly, information on any subjects of particular interest to which the collection relates. The sketch concludes with some evaluation of the material as a source for historical, literary, economic, or social study. In the writing of a sketch, all available reference works are used, and a reasonable amount of time is expended in seeking biographical information.

The information thus compiled should be used to label the containers or folders in which the new accession is packed. After the accession has been packed and fitted into its proper place in the stacks, the information should be used to prepare catalogs and guides. Two copies of an inventory should be made, one inserted in the container or folder with the papers to which it pertains, and the other in a loose-leaf binder to serve as a provisional finding aid.

An inventory of private papers should be prepared mainly for internal use. The inventory technique, as applied to private records, was borrowed, as a reviewer has observed, from the procedures of the National Archives in analyzing its record groups. The practice of publishing inventories, or registers, was presumably also borrowed from the National Archives practice of issuing preliminary inventories in near-print form. The problem of publication, however, is different in respect to public and private records. Publication of inventories of public records is feasible, because the record groups to which they pertain are few in number; very voluminous, often encompassing as many records as hundreds of manuscript collections combined; and much more comprehensive and disparate in their subject matter than manuscript collections. While the National Archives may

thus be justified in publishing inventories of its record groups—
and it is justified in doing this only on a selective basis—there is
little justification for publishing inventories, or registers, of
manuscript collections, unless such collections are unusually significant or voluminous. The publication of inventories for the
innumerable manuscript collections that exist in American repositories will not facilitate a bibliographical control of the
manuscript resources of the nation, for innumerable separate inventories are difficult to handle bibliographically.

An inventory of private papers should, however, serve as a
means toward the end of establishing bibliographical control
over the holdings of a particular repository, but this control
should be in the form of catalogs and guides.

Analysis of Provenance

If an accession was produced by a person, information in regard to him should be in the form of a biographical sketch; if by
a corporate body, in the form of an administrative history.

BIOGRAPHICAL SKETCH

Information provided in a biographical sketch is suggestive of
the content of a manuscript accession in the same way as an
administrative history of a government agency is suggestive of
the content of an archival group. The sketch of the person
should indicate the main activities in which he engaged, in relation to which papers probably exist. It should show the persons
with whom he dealt, the places at which he was active, and the
years of his life. It will thus refer to most of the elements pertinent to an analysis of the substance of an accession—its dates,
places, the subjects or activities to which it pertains, and the
persons mentioned in it.

A biographical sketch should be similar in its content to that
provided in biographical dictionaries. It should show the following:

(a) The dates (day of month and year) of the subject's birth
and death
(b) The names of the subject's father, mother (maiden name),

wife (or husband), and children; names of brothers and
sisters and grandparents, if significant; changes in family
name or in name of subject

(c) The highlights of the subject's career, including, if significant, information on the following:
the occupation and economic status of parents
schools, colleges, universities attended and degrees received
(in course and honorary)
occupation or profession
activities, with dates of the various activities
positions held, with dates of incumbency
organizations or institutions with which associated
productions (writings, inventions, etc.)
notable events or episodes with which associated

(d) The places with which the subject was associated

The following is an example of a biographical sketch prepared
by members of the Institute on Archival Management held at
the University of Texas, July 18–August 12, 1960:

Bedichek (June 27, 1878–May 21, 1959) was born in Cass Co., Ill.;
son of James Madison and Lucretia Ellen (Craven) Bedichek; mar-
ried Lillian Greer, Dec. 25, 1910; children, Mary Virginia, Sarah
Craven, and Bachman Greer. Educated at the Bedichek Academy
and University of Texas (B.S. 1903, M.A. 1927). Reporter, Ft.
Worth Record, 1903–4; teacher of English in high schools, Hous-
ton, 1904, San Angelo, 1905–8; secretary, Chamber of Commerce,
Deming, N.M., 1908–13; editor, Deming *Highlight*, 1910–12; secretary, Y.M.B.L., Austin, 1913–14; city editor, San Antonio *Express*,
1916. Known chiefly for his work with the University Interscholastic League, 1917–56, of which he was athletic director, director, and
director emeritus. Known also as a naturalist and author, producing
the following books, most of which appeared after his retirement in
1928: *Adventures with a Texas Naturalist* (New York, 1947),
Karankaway Country (New York, 1950), *Educational Competition: The Story of the University Interscholastic League of Texas*
(Austin, 1956), *The Sense of Smell* (New York, 1960).

ADMINISTRATIVE HISTORY

If an accession was produced by a corporate body, an administrative history of the body should contain the following:

(a) The dates of its establishment and dissolution
(b) The names of persons associated with it, including names of
     founders and officers
(c) The highlights of its development, including, if significant,
     information on the following:
         the kind of business, institution, or organization
         the kind of products it made, services it rendered, or func-
             tions it performed
         the significance of its products, services, or activities
         its organizational development
         notable events or episodes with which it was associated
(d) The places at which it functioned

Analysis of Records

A work sheet, or data sheet, should be prepared for each sizable new accession. A single item, or small lot of items, that is
received separately should be added to a collection of miscellany
and should ordinarily be described in an accessions register;
however, if a small accession is so complicated that a more complete description of it is desirable, it should be described on a
work sheet.

The work sheet on an accession should be in two parts: the
first pertaining mainly to its title, and the second to a description
of its contents (see the suggested format on the accompanying
work sheet). On Part I of the work sheet, information should be
entered that is needed (a) to compile a title line or title paragraph for an accession or separate body of material (entries 3–
10) and (b) to show the relation of an accession to geographical, subject, and chronological heads (entries 11–13). Information in entries 11–13 should be used to compile a table of contents to a guide and to organize catalog cards under appropriate
heads, as will be explained in the next chapter.

Instructions on the preparation of Part I of the work sheet are
presented in reference to the numbers assigned to entries on the
form.

1. Give the number assigned to the accession or collection.

2. Give the name of the accession, in accordance with instructions that apply to entry 3. Information on the name, in entry 2,
is designed to facilitate the use of the work sheet.

WORK SHEET

Part I: Title Line

1. Number assigned	2. Name of collection	11. Name of state
3. Name of producer___ Last First Middle		12. Subjects
		Agriculture
		Business
4. Place of production ___		Education
		Fine Arts
		Foreign Affairs
		Government & Politics
5. Kind of producer___		Labor
		Military Affairs
		Religion
		Science
		Social Affairs
6. Record type___		Travel & Exploration
		13. Chronological periods
7. Distinctive characteristics of record type___		Pre-1492
		1492–1550
		1550–1600
		1600–1650
		1650–1700
		1700–1750
8. Form of reproduction___		1750–1800
		1800–1830
		1830–1850
9. Dates of the records___		1850–1870
		1870–1890
10. Quantity ___		1890–1910
		1910–1920
		1920–1940
		after 1940

Part II: Descriptive Paragraph

Acc. No.   Name of collection

14. Content   15. Receipt and use   16. Bibliographical information

3. Devise a name for an accession or collection as follows: The producer of a manuscript collection may be a person, family, or corporate body, such as a school, business, or organization of one kind or another. Examples:

ADAMS, JOHN QUINCY (a person)
FARNSWORTH FAMILY (a group of persons)
AMERICAN COLONIZATION SOCIETY (a corporate body)
CHASE NATIONAL BANK (a corporate body)

An artificial collection (one brought together from various sources by a collector) should be named after a collector, that is to say, a person who brought it together rather than the one who produced it, only if it cannot be named after a producer. An example follows:

ROSENBLUM, SAMUEL (a collector)

4. Give the name of the place in which the accession was produced. Indicate place by giving the name of a specific state or states; or if produced within a locality within a state, give the name of a city, town, village, or county.

5. If an accession was produced by a person, indicate the person's occupation or profession; if by a corporate body, the kind of body, that is, whether an institution, organization, or business —unless this information is apparent from its name. Entries in biographical dictionaries show how this may be done. Examples, taken mainly from the National Historical Publications Commission guide, follow:

ANDERSON, SHERWOOD (Ill., Va.; novelist, poet)
ANTHONY, HENRY BOWEN (R.I.; journalist, Gov. U.S. Sen.)
ILLINOIS CENTRAL RAILROAD
BIRMINGHAM MANUFACTURING COMPANY (Ala.; electrical equipment)

If an accession is acquired from a collector, the word "collector" should appear in the title line instead of words showing occupation or profession, thus:

ROSENBLUM, SAMUEL (N.Y.; collector)

6. Indicate the kind or type of records that are found in the accession.

If an accession consists of many record types, use general terms, such as "records," "papers," or "manuscripts." The term "records" should be used to refer to material produced by corporate bodies or government agencies; the term "papers," to refer to material produced by persons; and the term "manuscripts," to refer to compositions that are normally published, whether produced by a person, corporate body, or government agency. Thus, a manuscript, using the term in a restricted sense, is the unprinted version of a book or an extended writing, such as a memoir, autobiography, essay, sermon, or the like. Examples of a specialized use of general terms follow:

ABBE, CLEVELAND (D.C., meterologist) PAPERS

BIRMINGHAM MANUFACTURING CO. (Ala.; electrical equipment) RECORDS

HAWTHORNE, NATHANIEL (Mass.; author) MANUSCRIPTS

If an accession consists of a specific record type, identify the type as accurately and precisely as possible. Avoid the use of terms that have several meanings or that are obsolete.

7. Identify a record type by its distinctive characteristics, if it has such.

If an accession is identified by general terms, such as "papers" or "records," provide information about the activity or action to which it relates. Thus, records may be identified in relation to general activities, as follows:

PERSONAL RECORDS

BUSINESS RECORDS

Or they may be identified somewhat more specifically in relation to a specific kind of activity, as follows:

BANKING RECORDS

WAGE RECORDS

Or they may be identified even more specifically in relation to a specific action, thus:

PHILIPPINE INSURRECTION RECORDS

If an accession consists of a specific record type, identify the type in relation to its provenance, the activities or transactions that resulted in its production, or its subject matter, as in the following examples:

LETTERS OF INQUIRY
PRICE LISTS
ARLINGTON COUNTY TAX LISTS
PURCHASE JOURNALS
ESTATE ACCOUNT BOOKS

8. If records are in the form of typewritten or handwritten transcriptions, identify them as transcripts; if in the form of photographic reproductions, as microfilms or photoprints. Place the information on the form of reproduction before the information on record type, and separate it by a colon, thus:

TRANSCRIPTS: MANUSCRIPTS
PHOTOPRINTS: LETTERS
MICROFILM: MEMOIRS

9. Give the first and last dates during which an accession was produced.

If most of the papers or unusually significant papers were produced between particular dates, give such dates in parentheses between the first and the last dates, thus: 1850(1876–84) 1890.

If significant gaps exist in the papers, indicate this fact thus: 1891–1910, 1915–20.

If exact dates cannot be established with certainty, use the word "circa" in its abbreviated form, i.e., "ca." to denote this fact.

10. Show the quantity of material in an accession in terms of (a) linear feet and inches, (b) items, and (c) volumes.

If an accession is sizable, indicate the space it occupies on a shelf in terms of the number of linear feet and inches, including in the measurement folders, envelopes, or containers in which it is contained. Since private papers are usually smaller in quantity than public records, linear measurements are often inadequate in showing volume. The following practices should therefore be observed.

If an accession occupies less than 3 inches of space, indicate the number of items in it, as well as the number of inches it occupies, as follows: 3 in. (112 items), or 3 in. (ca. 100 items). If the space occupied by a body of records is negligible, report only the number of items and enclose the number in parentheses, as follows: (3 items).

If an accession consists partly of bound volumes, indicate this fact by stating that it includes a specified number of volumes, as follows: 4 ft. (incl. 3 vols.).

If an accession consists wholly of bound volumes, indicate this fact as follows: 4 ft. (14 vols.).

Indicate the quantity of microfilm by specifying the number of feet of film, or the number of reels if more than one, thus: 40 ft. (positive); 2 reels (negative).

11. Give the name of the state or states to which the accession relates.

12. Check the pertinent box (or boxes) to show the subject (or subjects) to which the accession relates. Subjects should be identified by thinking in terms of the fields of activity that resulted in the production of an accession. Was it, for example, produced as a result of military activity, or educational activity, or activity in the field of fine arts?

13. Check the pertinent box (or boxes) to show the chronological period (or periods) to which the accession relates.

Part II of the work sheet should contain a heading to identify the accession and collection. Its entries—pertaining to the content of the record unit, its receipt and use, and bibliographical information in regard to it—should be entered as sideheads, and placed as they are needed.

Part II should be used to record information that is needed to prepare a descriptive paragraph (or paragraphs) for a catalog or guide entry.

Instructions on the preparation of Part II are presented in reference to the numbers assigned to the entries on the form.

14. Indicate the content of an accession by providing information on its (a) functional origins and (b) subject matter.

(a) In analyzing functional origins, list the activities and transactions that resulted in the production of the accession. Ascertain first if manuscripts exist in relation to the activities and transactions recorded in the biography or the administrative history prepared for the inventory. For example, if a biography shows that a person produced a book, ascertain if there are manuscripts relating to its production. Or if an administrative history shows that a business firm engaged in a number of specific activities, try to identify records that relate to them.

Sometimes information in a biography or history is inadequate. Sometimes papers that should exist in relation to various activities and transactions recorded in it are missing. In such cases, try to identify papers in relation to activities of an occupational or professional nature, such as farming, teaching, or mining activities, or medical or journalistic activities; activities conducted in carrying out specific enterprises, such as the development of an invention or the production of a book; or specific transactions, such as the settlement of an estate or the litigation of a dispute. In the case of business records, try to identify papers that relate to specific activities, such as the manufacture of a specific kind of product or the keeping of accounts.

(*b*) In analyzing subject matter, provide information on the objects to which activities or transactions relate. The objects are of four kinds: persons, places, things, and phenomena.

List the names of *persons*, which may be either corporate or personal bodies, selectively, including the following:

(1) Names of all important persons who are mentioned in an accession or who contributed to its production. Obviously, it is important to know that a record unit relates to Washington, Jefferson, or Lincoln, and most archivists will call attention to such a relation. They will invariably indicate that an accession relates to personages such as Presidents of the United States, federal cabinet members, and, more generally, persons important to the history of the nation. If their knowledge of history is extensive, they are also likely to identify persons whose influence on the course of events, though less widely known, is nonetheless considerable. They should always identify the persons significant to the development of the agencies with which they

were associated—if a state government, the persons important to the history of the state; if a church, the persons important to the history of the church; and so forth.

(2) All names in highly important accessions. This is the practice in some repositories, such as the Clements Library. While, in old personal manuscript collections, all names are important for genealogical and perhaps also for historical research purposes, an archivist should not list names in an inventory that have only a genealogical interest, for this is too time-consuming. He should list such names in an index, to be prepared at a later stage in his finding aid program.

(3) All names of corporate bodies, except in large accessions of business or professional records.

List the names of all *places* mentioned in an accession, including names of countries, cities, towns, and villages.

List the important *things* mentioned in an accession, such as buildings, bridges, classes of manufactured goods, topographical features of the land, minerals, animals, and other man-made and natural objects that are the main subject of the records.

List only the main *phenomena* to which an accession relates, not all the incidental matters that are mentioned in it. Identify the phenomena, which may involve either persons or things, in specific terms, as particular acts, events, or conditions.

The content of an accession may be shown in one of two ways.

If it consists of several record types that are identified in the title line by a general term, such as "papers" or "records," an archivist may enumerate the activities and transactions, and the objects of such activities and transactions, as follows:

Correspondence, manuscripts, clippings, and other papers relating to . . . (followed by an enumeration of activities and their objects).

Or he may separately describe each series, as in the following example prepared by members of the Institute on Archival Management held at the University of Texas in 1960:

REFERENCE MATERIAL ("Contest File"), 1913(1953–56)56. 1 ft.

Mainly handwritten notes compiled anterior to the first draft of *Educational Competition*, but included also are clippings, reprints, correspondence, notes, and other record types. While few documents are reproduced verbatim in Bedichek's book, the notes contain the first expression of his ideas on competition, and the material, as a whole, reflects how he collected and organized his information. Among the letters is one from E. D. Shurter, 1913 (File no. 37) on the founding of the University Interscholastic League, and one from Bedichek's daughter Sarah, 1941 (File no. 82). The material was numbered after it had been accumulated and is roughly arranged according to subject. Unindexed.

15. Provide information on how the accession was acquired and under what terms it may be used. If it consists of original material, show whether it was bought or given to a repository, who the seller or donor was, and when and where it was acquired. If admission to the accession is restricted, indicate the nature of the restrictions. State if literary rights to the accession have been either reserved for a specified period or dedicated to the public.

16. Provide references to finding aids, both published and unpublished, and to articles and books in which the accession is described. If an accession is relatively obscure in its origins, refer also to articles and books relating to its producer.

XVI

DESCRIPTION OF
MANUSCRIPT COLLECTIONS

The first finding aids for manuscript collections that an archivist should prepare are guides and catalogs, which should provide a brief conspectus of the holdings of his repository.

Both catalogs and guides should ordinarily be comprehensive. They should cover all holdings of a repository—pictorial and cartographic, as well as textual. They should include all forms of records—reproductions as well as originals. They should describe photographic, typewritten, and handwritten copies of documents, for such copies, if properly and accurately made, are quite as valuable for research purposes as are originals, and their existence ought to be made known. They should include general descriptions of artificial and miscellaneous collections, though items within such collections may be cataloged separately.

Catalogs should be kept current, while guides should be issued at periodic intervals. Catalogs are growing finding aids—aids that expand as the holdings of a repository increase. Since they are on cards, they lend themselves to expansion. Card entries on new collections can be intercalated at appropriate places in a catalog when such collections are received.

Catalogs differ from guides because they are finding aids designed primarily for internal use. They cannot be duplicated and distributed easily for external use.

The subject heads, in relation to which entries (descriptions of collections) are organized, should be the same in guides and catalogs. Information in entries 11–13 of the work sheet, discussed in the previous chapter, should be used to prepare a table of contents to a guide and guide cards for a catalog.

The entry slips, on which collections are described, should also be the same for guides and catalogs. Information in the inventory, discussed in the previous chapter, should be digested, edited, and transcribed onto 5 x 8 slips, which should be used as copy for both guides and catalogs.

Selection of Subject Heads

The method of selecting subject heads, under which entries of guides and catalogs should be organized, was suggested by Hubert H. Bancroft. In the latter half of the nineteenth century, Bancroft collected a large quantity of books and manuscripts for his history of Western America. His manuscripts, which now repose in the library named after him at the University of California, consist of letters, diaries and journals, autobiographies, interviews, narratives of participants in historical events, and other kinds of personal papers, as well as copies of statutes and other archival material. In his reminiscences entitled *Literary Industries*, he referred to "tons of unwinnowed material" [1] on his shelves such as "had never before been collected, collocated, eviscerated, and re-created by one man, unassisted by any society or government." [2] His great trouble, he wrote, was to get at what he had, for in its present shape it was of little use to him or to the world. He set his staff to work in indexing it in the conventional library manner, but he discovered that this method of indexing was impracticable. He wrote that "besides absorbing an enormous amount of time and money in its making, when completed it would be so voluminous and extended as to be cumbersome, and too unwieldy for the purpose designed." [3]

Bancroft therefore chose a limited number of broad subjects that formed the basis of his new index. These subjects, which he said embraced "the whole range of practical knowledge," [4] related to such matters as agriculture, antiquities, art, bibliography, biography, botany, commerce, drama, education, and so forth. There were between forty and fifty of them, for each of which he devised an abbreviation.

After having selected his major subjects, Bancroft devised a system to show the subtopics (or specific subjects) that fell within each of them. In the subject "Agriculture," for example, he included "stock raising, soils, fruits, and all other products of farm cultivation." [5]

With both major subjects and subtopics selected, Bancroft described the indexing operations as follows: [6]

A list of subjects, with their subdivisions and abbreviations, was placed before an assistant, who proceeded to read the book also given him, indexing its contents . . . . When he came to a fact bearing on any of the subjects in the list he wrote it on a card, each assistant following the same form, so as to produce uniform results. For example, the top line of all the cards was written in this manner:

Agric. Cal., Silk Culture, 1867

Antiq. Chiapas, Palenque. . . .

The second line of each card gave the title of the book, with the volume and page where the information was to be found; and, finally, a few words were given denoting the character of the information. Herewith I give a specimen card complete:

Ind.   Tehuan.   Zapoteca.   1847

Macgregor, J. Progress of America. London, 1847. Vol. I, pp. 848–9.

Location, Character, Dress, Manufactures.

The point of Bancroft's indexing operations is that he first indexed in relation to major subjects, similar to those listed in the work sheet discussed in the previous chapter, and within each of the major subjects he enumerated a number of topics in relation to which he desired to obtain information. The device he hit upon, he wrote, "is at once ingenious, simple, and effectual." [7] The index, he said, directed him "at once to all the sources of information concerning his subject, and the orderly treating of innumerable topics, otherwise impossible, is thus made practicable." [8] He concluded that "hundreds of years of profitless uninteresting labor may be served by this simple device." [9]

Bancroft's method of organizing his source material suggests, I believe, the method of organizing information on manuscript collections in card catalogs and guides. It involves the choice of two kinds of subjects: first, broad subjects (to be shown on guide cards and in a table of contents), in relation to which entries on collections should be organized, and secondly, subtopics, or specific subjects, that are subdivisions of the broad subjects (to be shown in descriptions of collections in catalog and guide entries).

The broad subject heads should relate to classes of human activity and should encompass most activities that result in the production of records. While it is difficult to compile a list of subject heads that is completely satisfactory, the following heads will cover the holdings of most repositories:

Agriculture	Foreign Affairs	Religion
Business	Government and Politics	Science
Education	Labor	Social Affairs
Fine Arts	Military Affairs	Travel and Exploration

If a repository collects material that relates to a special field of activity, a special list of subject heads should be developed for describing its holdings. Such heads should be chosen on an *ad hoc* basis. Thus, if the holdings of a repository pertain to business, this field of activity should be divided into a number of smaller areas. This is done in describing the business records of the Baker Library of Harvard University. In its guides, the Baker Library described records in relation to classes of industries, beginning with genetic industries, followed by extractive industries, manufacturing industries, engineering and construction, the various types of services, such as marketing and financial services, and ending with governmental services.[10] Or if the holdings of a repository relate to a specific phenomenon, such as the Civil War, a special list of subject heads should be developed relating to various aspects or events of the war.

Subject heads should be mutually exclusive, should be coordinate in importance, and should remain fixed, once they have been chosen. If they are not mutually exclusive, collections will have to be described under all heads that are approximately alike. And if subject heads are changed or added after a guide or catalog has been partially completed, they will be misleading and inaccurate.

While it may be argued that an analysis of manuscript collections in relation to broad subject heads is meaningless, this is actually not true. For information on subject, under the procedure here proposed, is combined with information on time and place. And this threefold analysis of collections by time, place, and subject is merely intended to guide the user to descriptions of particular collections that may interest him. The detailed analysis of the collections will be found in descriptive entries of guides and catalogs and in other finding aids.

A scholar can ordinarily use records effectively if they are identified in broad terms, that is to say, in relation to large classes of phenomena, to chronological periods, and to geographical areas. He can ascertain for himself if records relating to a given phenomenon, time, or place contain information that is pertinent to his subject of inquiry if he is properly trained in research method. He will seldom rely altogether on an archivist, or on the finding aids an archivist produces, to provide him with this information.

Preparation of Entry Slips

A form, 5 x 8 inches in size, should be devised for the production of copy for entries in guides and catalogs. The form should be preprinted, in multiple copies, with interleaved carbons, and with the following heading:

Acc. No.	Places	Subjects	Dates

A separate entry slip should be used for the description of each collection. One set of the slips should be used for the production of a guide; another for the production of a catalog; and a third should be held in reserve.

DESCRIPTION OF ACCESSIONED COLLECTIONS

Organic and artificial collections received as accessions should be described in the inventories discussed in the preceding chapter. The information in such inventories should be used to prepare entry slips in two parts: (*a*) a title line and (*b*) a descriptive paragraph (or paragraphs).

Title lines

A title line should contain information that will properly identify a collection. Normally, the information should be adequate enough to enable a user to determine if a particular collection is pertinent to his subject of inquiry. It should therefore provide the most important facts about the collection.

Detailed information, or information not relevant to an understanding of the content and character of a collection, should be omitted from a title line. Thus, the dates of the producer, showing the life span of an individual or a corporate body, while significant, can more appropriately be placed in a descriptive paragraph, since one set of dates, i.e., those during which the records were produced, should always be included in the title line. Information on the receipt of a collection, i.e., on the person from whom acquired, and on the terms under which it may be used, is also not relevant to an understanding of its content and character, and should be reserved for a descriptive paragraph.

A title line, digesting the information contained in entries 3–10 of the work sheet, should contain information on the following: the name of the collection; the place at which it was produced; the kind of producer; the form of reproduction, if other than original copy; the type of records, identified by their distinctive characteristics; the date of the records; and the quantity of records. A title line for a collection of personal papers should thus read:

BEDICHEK, ROY (Texas; educator, writer, naturalist), Papers and Manuscripts, 1890–1959, 5 ft., 5 in.

Descriptive paragraphs

While most collections are too small or insignificant to require more than one paragraph for their description, an archivist may find it advisable to describe a very large or important collection in several paragraphs instead of just one. He may then wish to use sideheads to highlight information in various paragraphs.

A descriptive paragraph should contain information about the character, content, and significance of a collection, supplemental to that provided in the title line. This information should pertain to the following:

(1) The *provenance* of the collection. An archivist should condense the information contained in a biographical sketch or administrative history of an inventory. This information, reduced to one paragraph, should contain the following essential information about the producer of a personal collection: the dates of his birth and death, enclosed in parentheses immediately after his name, and the salient facts about his career. An example follows:

Bedichek (1878–1959) is known chiefly for his work with the University Interscholastic League, 1917–56, which he describes in *Educational Competition* (Austin, 1956), and for his interest in nature, which is reflected in his books on *Adventures with a Texas Naturalist* (New York, 1947), *Karankaway Country* (New York, 1950), and *The Sense of Smell* (New York, 1960).

An archivist should similarly condense the information contained in an administrative history, including only salient facts about a corporate body. These should pertain to the dates of its establishment and dissolution; its organizational and functional developments; the persons associated with it, particularly the names of its founders and officers; and the places at which it functioned. An example follows:

The Birmingham Manufacturing Co. (1921–37) was founded by John Doe, who became its first president. It was the first firm to produce dynamos, motors, and transformers in the South. It established branch offices in Knoxville and Nashville, when the Tennessee Valley Authority became operative.

If a collection is small, an archivist will find that it is adequate merely to identify, by kind, the personal or corporate body that created it and to show the dates of its existence. Descriptive paragraphs in the Duke University guide by Tilley and Goodwin contain a sentence that indicates the name of the creator of a collection, the dates of his life (if available), and his occupation or profession.[11] For example:

Legal, business, and personal correspondence of Edward Lucas (1780–1858), lawyer, merchant, and politician, a member of the Virginia House of Delegates, 1818–22, 1830, 1831, and of the U.S. Congress, 1833–37.

(2) The *content* of the collection, described in terms of the activities and transactions that resulted in the production of the records, and the objects (persons, places, things, and phenomena) to which such activities and transactions relate. Information, contained in entry 14 of the work sheet, should be reduced to one paragraph, if the collection being described is large; or to one sentence, if small. An example follows:

Bedichek's papers consist of personal correspondence, 1907–59; literary manuscripts, 1947–59, including notes, references, drafts, and copyright correspondence; reference materials, 1913–56, used in compiling *Educational Competition;* clippings, 1911–16, 1918–19, 1929, and annotated publications pertaining to the University Interscholastic League, the latter consisting chiefly of its Constitution and Rules, 1911–54 (with gaps).

(3) The *receipt and use* of the collection, condensing information contained in entry 15 of the work sheet.

(4) *Bibliographical information* regarding the collection, condensing data contained in entry 16 of the work sheet.

DESCRIPTION OF COLLECTIONS OF MISCELLANY

The collections of miscellany organized within a repository ordinarily will not be described on work sheets, so that information in regard to them should be obtained from accessions registers or catalogs, if such have been prepared.

A collection of miscellany that is organized by record type

should be named after its type, e.g., ACCOUNT BOOKS. A collection of miscellany that is organized by subject should be named after the subject to which it pertains, as in the following examples taken from the New-York Historical Society guide: LOYALISTS; and AMSTERDAM, Montgomery Co., N.Y.

In describing a collection of specific record types on an entry slip, an archivist, in the descriptive paragraph, should list items alphabetically by name and in tabular form. In listing such items, he should enumerate only their variable attributes, i.e., the attributes that distinguish one item from another. Thus he should show for each item, while listing account and receipt books, the name and kind of firm that produced each book, the place at which the firm operated, and the book's date; while listing diaries, memoirs, and other personal accounts, the name and occupation or profession of the writer, the place at which the writer lived, and the item's date; and while listing logbooks, the name of the vessel that produced each logbook, the departure and arrival ports of the voyages recorded in it, and the dates of the voyages.

In describing a collection of miscellaneous letters, an archivist should list each accession chronologically and in tabular form. For each item, or small lot of items, he should give its dates, the name of its producer, the occupation or profession of the producer, and the main subject to which it relates.

In the lists, an archivist should cite the accession numbers assigned to items in order to facilitate reference to them, as in the following examples:

ACCOUNT BOOKS:
Potomac Farm Market, produce merchants, 1821–41 (MA-17)
Smith & Darrow, merchants, 1789–1824 (MA-15)

Organization of Guides

While most recent guides produced in the United States cover all holdings of the repositories to which they pertain, certain of them do not include descriptions of particular kinds of material. Some exclude material of a corporate or archival character, as does the Minnesota Historical Society guide by Nute and Ackermann.[12] Others exclude material on the basis of its record type. The Wisconsin Historical Society guide by Harper and Smith contains no descriptions of single biographies, local history sketches, and manuscript genealogies;[13] the Massachusetts Historical Society guide, none of account books, small diaries, short journals, and logbooks;[14] and the Ohio State Archaeological and Historical Society guide, none of single letters, broadsides, circulars, and posters.[15] Other guides exclude material on the basis of its quantity. The Huntington Library guide by Cuthbert contains references neither to miscellaneous material, regardless of its importance, nor to collections containing less than forty pieces.[16] The Wisconsin Historical Society guide by Smith excludes collections of less than ten pieces.[17] And still others do not describe material because it consists of reproductions rather than originals. The Huntington Library guide by Cuthbert contains no references to facsimiles;[18] the Minnesota Historical Society guide by Nute and Ackermann, none to photostats and typewritten or handwritten transcripts.[19] The Ohio State Archaeological and Historical Society guide by Biggert includes references to photostats of manuscripts in private hands, but not to photostats of manuscripts the originals of which are in other libraries.[20]

Special guides may, of course, be prepared for records relating to specific subject fields, such as the economic, genealogical, or scientific.

Guides may be differentiated from each other on the basis of the amount of descriptive information they contain. They may be either summary guides, in which record units are identified merely by title, or descriptive guides, in which record units are described as well as identified. The kind of guide that should be prepared by a repository staff depends on the time available for its preparation. A sketchy guide is better than none at all. A summary guide may be prepared by using the information contained in Part I of the work sheet discussed in the previous chapter; a descriptive guide by using also the information contained in Part II.

Information in the heading of the entry slips (relating to place, subject, and time periods) should be used to prepare a table of contents to a guide. Such a table should help a searcher to narrow down the area of searching among the innumerable collections that may be described in a guide, and should be the point of departure in looking for more specific information on particular collections. If a searcher is interested, for example, in military affairs in Virginia for the period 1800–30, he should be able to find out which collections pertain to this subject by looking under the appropriate head in a table of contents.

In view of its importance, a table of contents should be given a prominent place in a guide. It should appear immediately before its descriptive entries, and should not be relegated to an appendix, as has often been done in recent guides produced in the United States.

Two actions are involved in preparing a table of contents: first, the use of lists of geographical, subject, and chronological heads, and secondly, the identification of collections that pertain to each of the heads.

A table of contents may be arranged first by place, then by major subject, and then by chronological period, as follows:

VIRGINIA
 Foreign Affairs
  1700–1750
   (Numbers of pertinent collections)
  1750–1800
   (Numbers of pertinent collections)
  Other chronological periods
 Military Affairs
  1800–1830
   (Numbers of pertinent collections)
 Other Subject Heads
WEST VIRGINIA, etc.

Geographical heads should be omitted if information on the areal relations of manuscript collections is unimportant. If they are omitted, the table of contents may be arranged by major subject and then by chronological period, as follows:

FOREIGN AFFAIRS

1700–1750
    (Numbers of pertinent collections)
1750–1800
    (Numbers of pertinent collections)
    Other chronological periods
MILITARY AFFAIRS, etc.

American manuscript curators have used lists of subject, chronological, and geographical heads in various ways in the guides they have produced.

In the Library of Congress *Handbook of Manuscripts* (1918), collections are identified by name under broad subject heads in a prefatory note. The heads are: [21]

Artists	Indians	Religious
Bibliography	Languages	Revolution
Civil War	Law	Scientific
Colonial	Library	Social
Constitution	Medical	Theatrical
Diplomatic	Mexico	Travel
Economic material	Military	Washington City
Education	Naval	
Finance	Political	

Under the head "Artists," to illustrate, collections are identified by name as follows:

Du Simitiere	Pulaski
Jefferson	Thornton
Latrobe	John Trumbull
Mills	

In the Library of Congress *Checklist of Personal Papers* (1918), information on manuscript collections is organized into two parts: an alphabetical list and a chronological list.[22] In the latter, collections are identified by chronological periods, thus:

1610–1620: Argenteau Family—Conner, Powell, and allied Families —Davenport, John—Delassus, Charles Dehault—Fenner—Mather,

Samuel—Stanwood, James Rindge—Usselinex, William—Van
Rensselaer–Bowier—Washington, George—
1620–1630: Argenteau Family—Conner, Powell, and allied Families
—Davenport, John—Delassus, Charles Dehault—Esten—Fenner—
Mather, Samuel—Miller, Samuel—Stanwood, James Rindge—Us-
selinex, William—Van Rensselaer–Bowier—Washington, George
—Wheatland, Henry—

In the Clements Library guide, by Peckham, an appendix contains a "Topical and Chronological List of the Collections,"
which is "designed to serve the student who wishes to know
what collections are available in a given field of interest." [23] The
list is divided into two heads, the first being British and North
American History and the second Hispanic American and
Philippine History. Each of these major heads is in turn subdivided into chronological periods, under each of which a number of topics are listed. For example, under the head British
and North American History, there is a period from 1744 to
1754 under which the following topics are enumerated: King
George's War, Treaty of Aix-la-Chapelle and the aftermath in
British Politics and Diplomacy, and others.

ORGANIZATION OF ENTRIES

An archivist should organize guide entries so as to facilitate
reference to them. There are two ways of handling entries that
will help accomplish this objective. They relate to (*a*) the sequence of entries and (*b*) grouping collections under a single
entry.

Sequence of entries

As a rule, an archivist should arrange entries in a guide in an
alphabetical-numerical order. Most guides to private papers that
have been published in the United States follow the pattern outlined in the Historical Records Survey manual, *Preparation of
Inventories of Manuscripts.*[24] In this pattern, guide entries are
arranged alphabetically by name of collection and are numbered. The arrangement given entries in Historical Records Survey guides is one that is, all things considered, the most satisfactory.

An alphabetical-chronological arrangement is the easiest method of organizing guide entries. As entry slips for particular collections are prepared, they should be placed in an alphabetical file. When all have been completed, the slips should be numbered. If properly prepared, the slips may be used as copy for photo-offset reproduction (in a manner similar to that employed in producing the bound volumes of the Library of Congress union catalog of manuscript collections). If they are so used, the headings of the slips should not be reproduced, but should be trimmed off after they have served the purpose of providing information for a table of contents to the guide.

An alphabetical-numerical arrangement of entries is essential if a table of contents, of the kind discussed above, is to be prepared, for it permits an easy reference to entries on various collections.

An alphabetical-numerical arrangement, moreover, permits a progressive production of guides as new accessions are received. In the guides produced in Minnesota and Wisconsin, entries are numbered in sequence from one guide to the next. Thus, the Kane and Johnson guide [25] to the holdings of the Minnesota Historical Society takes up where the Nute and Ackermann guide [26] leaves off; and the Harper and Smith guide [27] to the holdings of the Wisconsin Historical Society, where the Smith guide [28] leaves off.

An archivist should not group entries under subject heads to show the relation of collections to subjects. The use of subject heads introduces difficulties in the production of a guide that should be avoided.

It is difficult, in the first place, to describe collections in relation to any particular list of subject heads, for collections often do not fit exclusively into any one subject class. This difficulty is pointed out by Elizabeth Ring, who observed in the preface to her *List of Manuscripts Relating to the History of Maine* that "many of the large miscellaneous collections contained a variety of subjects and covered a wide chronological range, making impossible what might undoubtedly have been a more useful subject classification." [29] If such heads are used, the fact that a particular collection relates to several subjects must be made known either by repeating entries for the collection under each head to which it relates or by inserting cross-references under various heads.

It is difficult, moreover, to prepare a guide in which entries are organized under subject heads. If such heads are used, entry slips must be placed in several alphabetical sequences rather than in a single one.

As a guide is always difficult to produce, anything that makes its production more difficult or complicated should be carefully evaluated from the point of view of its utility. Since its production is complicated by inserting subject heads in it, other methods of showing subject relations should be followed.

Grouping collections under single entries

If a guide is to give a user a proper perspective of the holdings of a repository, the descriptive information it provides about various record units should be properly balanced. More information should be provided about large collections than about small ones. While single documents, or small lots of documents, may be quite important from a research point of view, they should not receive as much attention as sizable collections. By having separate entries for such documents, too much attention is given to too little.

An archivist may therefore find it advisable to group under single entries a number of collections that are comprised of the same record type or that arise from the same kind of institution. The following record types, among others, may be appropriate for grouping under single entries: account books, diaries, genealogies, logbooks, memoirs, order books (or orderly books), and sermons. In the New-York Historical Society guide, single entries are found for the following record types: [30]

ACCOUNT BOOKS:
Ames, Ezra, artist, Albany, N.Y., 1790–1826.
Arthur & Deall, merchants, N.Y.C., 1783–85.
Baltimore, Md., unidentified, 1785–86; 1788–92.
Bancker Family, N.Y.C., 1718–1812. 14 vols.

. . . .

ORDERLY BOOKS:

    1748–57, Quebec Campaign. Wolfe.

    Aug. 12–Oct. 12, 1758, Oneida Station (Fort Stanwix).

    April 24–Aug. 25, 1759, Niagara Campaign.

    . . . .

RECEIPT BOOKS:

    Arthur & Deall, N.Y.C., 1783–85.

    Bayard family, 1762–74. 3 vols.

    Bishop, Ezekiel, N.Y.C., 1811–32.

    . . . .

Collections from a particular kind of business, from churches, from fraternal organizations, and from other similar kinds of institutions may also be appropriate for grouping under single guide entries. In the Pennsylvania Historical Society guide, the account books of forges and furnaces, and the record books of fire companies, are thus grouped.

The extent to which the number of guide entries can be reduced by grouping collections for descriptive purposes is shown in an analysis of the Kane and Johnson guide to the Minnesota Historical Society collections. This analysis reveals that of the total of 1,190 guide entries, 31 relate to account books, 59 to diaries, 81 to genealogies, and 58 to reminiscences. These four record types account for 229 entries, or about one fifth of the total.

Grouping collections for descriptive purposes brings like things together in guide entries; by reducing the number of entries, it makes a guide easier to use. But such a grouping complicates the production of a guide, for it involves organizing entry slips, while copy is being prepared, into type classes or institutional classes. The relationship of collections to such classes may, perhaps, be shown more easily in indexes.

PREPARATION OF INDEXES

The relationship of manuscript collections to broad subjects can be made known quite effectively in a table of contents; but their relationship to specific matters should be made known, if desired, in an index.

An index to a guide to manuscript collections should include references to the following: the activities that resulted in the production of collections, or to which collections pertain; and the objects of these activities, such as the persons, corporate bodies, places, things, and phenomena that are involved in them.

The extent to which references on specific matters can be included in an index depends on the extent to which they are identified in guide entries. Usually, only a few of the matters to which collections pertain are identified in such entries. In regard to personal names, for example, the compiler of a guide may have identified only names that he ran across; this is the usual practice. Or he may have included all names of persons, regardless of their importance; or only names of important persons. If names are not identified consistently and completely in guide entries, the name index will be misleading. This is even truer of topical indexes, which refer to matters, such as things and phenomena, that are much more difficult to identify than are names of persons and places.

Because of the limitation of indexes—because they refer only to matters identified in guide entries, not to matters dealt with in records—manuscript curators often have not prepared indexes to their guides. In his excellent *List of Business Manuscripts in Baker Library*, Robert W. Lovett does not attempt subject indexing, though his index refers to the various kinds of industries in relation to which descriptive entries are arranged.[31] Ordinarily, the broad subjects to which collections relate should be shown in a table of contents; the specific matters to which they relate, in guide entries. Card indexes on specific matters should be prepared in response to a definite need for them.

If an index to guide entries is prepared, an archivist should insert a prefatory note to explain its limitation, i.e., to show the extent to which topics, and names of persons and places, are identified in guide entries.

Organization of Catalogs

Manuscript collections are well suited to cataloging. They are quite numerous, for a large repository may have thousands of them in its custody, and a small one may have hundreds. They are, moreover, discrete entities that can be separately identified and described on catalog cards.

Archival groups, in contrast, are relatively few in number, and for this reason can be described more easily in finding aids in page form. The very largest archival institutions have only a few hundred of them in custody—the National Archives of the United States about 300, the Public Record Office of England about 80, and the French National Archives about 50—while small institutions have less than a score.

Every manuscript repository should prepare a catalog of its manuscript collections for its own use and for use in cooperative cataloging projects. A catalog is the only type of finding aid that facilitates a pooling of information about the documentary resources of a nation. Indeed, it may be questioned if the archival profession will follow the lead of the library profession in replacing printed catalogs by card catalogs.

To prepare a catalog, a sufficient number of cards should be reproduced from each entry slip, described above, to permit cards on a particular collection to be filed under the various geographical, subject, and chronological heads to which they pertain.

In arranging his cards, an archivist should follow library methods of duplicating and intercalating. In a library catalog, the "main entry" for a book ordinarily occurs under the name of its author. If it has more than one author or if it relates to more than one subject, "added entry" cards are made that are inserted at the proper alphabetical points in the catalog. The additional names or subjects are simply typed on the "added entry" cards above the first line of type. The typewritten lines then determine where in the alphabet the cards shall be placed. Under this procedure, information is provided at every point in the catalog at which a book would presumably be sought.

Instead, however, of organizing his cards into one alphabetical file only, an archivist should arrange his cards into three major files: one arranged by geographical areas, another by subject, and a third by chronological periods. If a particular collection relates to more than one place, subject, or period, he should insert cards under several guide cards (pertaining to place, subject, and period) to show its multiple relations.

XVII

PREPARATION OF INDEXES
AND ITEM CATALOGS

Records pertinent to studies of social, economic, or political phenomena should be described collectively, not singly; for the user of such records will be able to pursue his investigations by consulting collective descriptions of them in guides and inventories. Records pertaining to the suppression of piracy on the high seas or to blockade running during the Civil War, for example, need not be described singly, for the searcher using them is interested in the phenomena reflected in them collectively, not in specific manifestations of the phenomena that are shown in a single document.

But some records should be described in reference to particular matters. Records pertaining to persons can be used by the genealogist, and those pertaining to things can be used by the antiquarian and local historian, only if the particular information they contain is disclosed in finding aids. Such records should be described so as to reveal where information may be found on specific persons, places, or things.

The question remains, of course, as to how items that are used singly should be made known to users. Should they be cataloged, indexed, listed, or calendared?

Indexes and item catalogs, which are discussed in this chapter, are designed mainly for use within a record repository, since they cannot be duplicated readily for general distribution. They should be prepared on cards instead of pages.

The terms "indexes" and "catalogs" are often used interchangeably, because the finding aids to which they refer are in some respects similar. They have the same physical form, and they contain the same information in respect to the subject content of records.

But there is a difference between them as to the way records are identified that is quite important. In catalogs, records are identified by providing information on their producer, their type, the place and date of their production, and their quantity. In indexes, records are merely identified by symbol or by the name of the producer, and only the relation of records to some subject is indicated. No biographical or bibliographical information is ordinarily provided in them.

The difference between indexes and catalogs arises from the purposes they are intended to serve. Indexes are designed merely to point the way to subject content, to indicate where information on subjects may be found in records. They are not designed to describe records, as are catalogs, but only to identify them in relation to subjects. Indexes are thus locating media; catalogs are descriptive media, though they too, obviously, may be used to locate information.

Indexes

Record indexes should be distinguished from indexes to publications. The techniques that are followed as well as the subjects that are identified in preparing indexes to records are different from the techniques and subjects taken into account in indexing publications.

In order to show where information may be found in records, an index card should contain two things: a subject (person, place, thing, or phenomenon) on which information exists and a reference to records in which information on a subject exists. The reference may be in the form of a symbol or an abbreviation of the title of a record unit.

The identification of record units, in which information on particular subjects can be found, is easy to the degree that an archivist has properly arranged and identified his holdings. If he has arranged the collections, small lots of material, and single items in his custody in proper sequence, and has properly identified them by symbol, he can identify records on index cards merely by citing the symbol assigned to them. Proper arrangement and proper notation are thus essential preliminaries to effective indexing work.

Since it is necessary merely to identify records to accomplish the purpose of indexes, no descriptive information about records should be provided in them other than that required for their identification. If unnecessary descriptive information is provided on index cards, the advantages of the indexing technique are largely dissipated.

Indexes are very useful tools in the hands of an archivist. Since records are merely identified, not described in them, they can be prepared more easily than can other types of finding aids. For this reason they can become particularized in regard to both the matters and the record units to which they refer.

They are the best means of providing information on the subject content of individual record items, especially of single documents. They can be prepared to advantage in regard to items with titles that are not essential to an understanding of their nature and significance. This is often the case with respect to the titles of single documents, for the names of their producers, their types, and the places and dates of their production need not be given to facilitate their use. But the title of account books or diaries may be essential; and catalogs rather than indexes should be prepared for such items.

Indexes are also the best means of providing information on specific matters in all kinds of record units. They are the medium by which information on persons, places, and specific topics can be most easily made known.

PERSONAL INDEXES

An index to personal names is primarily useful to genealogists and biographers, though it may also be useful to historians. It should be compiled for every record unit (group or collection) in which names are the key to its effective use. The name indexes to various record units in a repository should be combined into a single index.

If an archivist wishes to avail himself of the advantages of the indexing technique, he should provide, on an index card, the bare minimum of information essential to identify a person and the record unit in which information is found about a person. A card ordinarily should contain only the name of the person and the symbol (or abbreviated title) of the record unit.

In a large index, containing very many names, supplemental information may be necessary in order to identify persons properly. The extent of such information depends on the size of the index. When one is dealing with very many persons, certain surnames, such as Jones and Smith, lose their quality of uniqueness. A list of names that are represented by at least one hundred persons in the 1790 census is found in a book, entitled *A Century of Population Growth*, published by the Bureau of the Census.[1] Certain surnames, moreover, have many variants, such as Snyder, Snider, Schneider. A list of them is found in a book entitled *Standard Cross References of Proper Names*, published by the Polk Directory Company.[2] In order to identify persons with surnames that occur very often or that have many variants, the place and date of the items in which they are mentioned should be noted, in addition to their surnames and given names.

While compiling an index, an archivist should initially spell personal names exactly in the way in which they are spelled in records, even when the spelling is obviously incorrect. In collating entries on a particular person, he should try to ascertain and use the spelling recognized as the correct one. If he cannot positively associate a particular name with a particular person, he should give the name exactly as it appears in records.

While a name index should normally point the way to records in which personal information is found, it may be made to serve other purposes. It may actually provide personal information that is so extensive that reference to the original records is unnecessary. When it does this, it becomes more than an index; it becomes a new record of personal information. It is then similar to the "index-record cards" produced in the War Department under Fred C. Ainsworth (1852–1934), late in the last century. These "index-record cards" contain information on the military service of individual soldiers, abstracted from muster rolls, pay-rolls, returns, and other types of military records.[3] They were compiled to handle pension applications.

The name index cards prepared at the Illinois State Library are similar to the "index-record cards" of the War Department. They are described by Margaret C. Norton, former archivist of Illinois, as follows:

One card is made for each name appearing in a document. This card gives on the top line the name, inverted, and written in capitals. On the second line are given the county and town of residence. Beginning on the third line there is a digest of any biographical information given in the document—brief, yet sufficiently full to avoid the necessity for direct reference to the original document. On the last line a full bibliographical citation is given.[4]

Indexes that supplant original records, or that make reference to them unnecessary, should be compiled for genealogical purposes only when they are needed to protect the original records from excessive use or to reduce the reference service work load, and then only if financial resources are available to ensure their completion. If an archivist must choose between preparing an index that provides full information about a few names and preparing one that provides little information about many, he should choose the latter, for genealogical searches involve reference to many names.

PLACE INDEXES

In preparing title lines for entries in finding aids, an archivist will usually provide geographic information, for he will show the places with which the producers of records are associated. If he follows correct procedures, he will show the geographic relation of manuscript collections in guide entries and, occasionally, in the table of contents of a guide. He will, similarly, show geographic relations in a catalog. The geographic information thus provided will ordinarily be adequate to direct searchers to records relating to places in which they may be interested.

Some collections, however, are significant primarily because of their information on places, and an archivist may therefore find it desirable to prepare place indexes to them.

An index card to a place name should contain two entries: the name of the place and the symbol (or abbreviated title) of the record unit in which information in respect to the place is found.

While compiling an index, an archivist should initially spell place names exactly in the way they are spelled in records, even when the spelling is obviously incorrect. In collating entries on places, he should try to ascertain and use the correct spelling. If the spelling of an out-of-the-way place is not ascertainable, he should give the place name exactly as it appears in records.

TOPICAL INDEXES

An unconscionable amount of time can be spent in topical indexing if topics are not properly chosen. Perhaps the best illustration of an indexing project on which endless time was spent is that involving the papers of George Clinton, first governor of the state of New York. Clinton's papers were purchased by the state in 1853, and money was appropriated for "arranging, indexing, and binding and lettering the same."[5] A calendar, which listed Clinton's papers in chronological order and gave a brief statement of their nature or principal subjects, was prepared by 1855.[6] In 1881 the state again appropriated money for the "arranging and indexing of the Clinton and other historical papers."[7] Judge George W. Clinton, a grandnephew of the first governor, was employed for this work, which he began "with patriotic as well as filial zeal."[8] In his first annual report he discussed his conception of an index as follows: "An index ought, like a great river, the carrier of commerce and creator of fertility, to be 'without overflowing full.' It ought to be so framed as to yield readily the answer, if there be one in the body of papers, to every question of every reasonable questioner."[9] In a subsequent report he indicated that his index should provide information about "the minor matters" found in the Clinton papers, about "the argument and spirit of the writers," about "their remarks and opinions about individuals," and the like,[10]

He confessed, however, that his undertaking "has proven far more severe" than he had anticipated when he began it. He died in 1885, leaving his work—two bundles of about two thousand sheets—"in a condition which made it of very little use to historical investigators," [11] according to George Roger Howell (1833–99), the first archivist of the New York State Library. Howell's successor, Arnold J. Van Laer, had a somewhat more favorable impression of it.[12]

In view of the fact that research interests are indefinable and expansive, and vary from one generation to the next, an archivist may properly question what he should do in indexing records in relation to detailed or specific topics. Should he identify records in relation to every specific topic in which there may be a conceivable interest? Or is there a point of diminishing returns in indexing records in relation to specific topics—a point at which an analysis of records in further detail becomes profitless?

In my opinion, an archivist should have a limited objective in indexing records. His objective should be neither to indicate every conceivable topic referred to in his records nor to elaborate on highly specific research topics. No matter how detailed his indexes are, he is not likely to reveal all topics in relation to which inquiries may be made. And if his indexes are detailed, he is likely to provide information on topics in relation to which no inquiries will be made. The exclusion of topics in which there is an interest, as well as the inclusion of topics in which there is no interest, makes the work of indexing records comprehensively in relation to topics a questionable undertaking. An archivist should not make a general practice of indexing particular matters on a comprehensive basis.

Before preparing a topical index, an archivist should know in what specific things or specific phenomena an interest exists, for a topical index may relate either to material things, such as structures, manufactured articles, topographical features of the land, or the flora and fauna of a region; or phenomena, such as conditions, activities, events, and other actions that affect persons and material things. Once he has determined which things and phenomena should be indexed, an archivist should prepare index cards in relation to them in the same way as he does in relation to names of persons and places. The cards, in short, should identify the thing or phenomenon; the date and place at which the record was produced; and the record unit, by symbol, in which information is found on the thing or phenomenon.

If there is need to index particular things on a large scale, modern information retrieval methods should be employed. The Henry Francis du Pont Winterthur Museum, near Wilmington, Delaware, used such methods in preparing an index to manuscripts that referred to its museum objects. The museum has a very large collection of American decorative arts, especially of furniture, in relation to which manuscripts were accumulated in the Joseph Downs Manuscript Library. Since the manuscripts in the Downs Library were expressly acquired for the information they contained on the museum objects, a detailed index to the manuscript references to such objects was necessary. The method employed in compiling it is described in an excellent article by Elizabeth A. Ingerman.[13]

An archivist will encounter difficulty in indexing phenomena, for they are ordinarily not easily identifiable. To avoid excessive difficulty, he should not attempt to index phenomena that are indefinite and intangible, such as ideas, opinions, feelings, and concepts of all kinds. If he attempts to index "the argument and spirit of the writers," and "their remarks and opinions about individuals," as did George W. Clinton, he is not likely to complete his index.

Item Catalogs

In one of his short stories, Anatole France wrote about a friend whose "mania . . . was compiling catalogues. Week in, week out, he catalogued and catalogued and catalogued." [14] This mania has possessed many persons working with documentary material, for often catalogs of manuscript items have taken years of time and have never been completed.

Item cataloging generally requires more time than is available to manuscript curators. "Much remains to be done to keep the general catalogue of manuscripts abreast of accessions," the librarian of the Massachusetts Historical Society wrote in 1927.[15] "Our uncatalogued manuscripts are . . . almost as numerous as the sands of the sea," he wrote in 1935.[16] In order to obtain a general knowledge of the holdings of the society, he began, a few years later, to prepare a comprehensive guide to his collections. The experiences of other large repositories in the United States are similar to those of the Massachusetts Historical Society.

The guides produced by the WPA Historical Records Survey in the 1940s show that item catalogs in a number of well-known repositories were but partially completed during that period. Statistics show that less than 10 percent of the items were reported as cataloged in the California Historical Society, the Connecticut Historical Society, the Duke University Library, the Hoover Library, the Huntington Library, the Illinois State Library, the Maryland Hall of Records, the Nebraska State Historical Society, the University of Virginia Library, the West Virginia University Library, and the Wisconsin Historical Society; about 25 per cent of the items in the Florida Historical Society, the Indiana State Library, the Minnesota Historical Society, and the North Dakota Historical Society; about 35 percent in the Arkansas Historical Commission Library, the Detroit Public Library, the Missouri Historical Society, the Historical Society of Pennsylvania, and the Princeton University Library; and about 50 percent in the Chicago Historical Society, the Clements Library, and the Newberry Library.

This situation still prevails. A recent report by the American Association for State and Local History states that, as a result of the steady growth of manuscript collections, the situation "has almost gotten out of hand, for two-thirds of the agencies said that they had large back-logs of uncataloged manuscripts." [17]

Individual record items do not ordinarily deserve the attention required in the cataloging process, which is rather slow and difficult. They are generally too insignificant for cataloging, unless they comprise a highly important collection. To give each of them the full cataloging treatment, which has acquired complexities through years of refinement, results in a waste of energy and effort, and is likely to divert the staff of a repository from more constructive work.

Catalogs should be prepared first of manuscript items that lack organic characteristics. During the last century, many collections were acquired that were comprised of discrete items, each of which could be treated as a separate physical entity. Artificial collections, brought together by collectors from many sources, and collections of miscellany, brought together by archivists from many sources, have this character. Items in such collections should be cataloged, provided, of course, that they are of sufficient importance to justify giving them such attention.

Catalogs should be prepared of manuscript items that have an organic relation to one another only after the items have been described collectively, and then only if they are of sufficient importance to justify giving them such attention. Such items lack the attribute of discreteness that makes it possible to treat them individually on catalog cards. If they are the product of activity, they cannot stand alone, for they have a relation to all other items that are the product of the same activity. They do not, moreover, require individual treatment in order to describe them effectively. Their content and significance can be made known in a collective description.

Catalogs of record items are not an effective means of generally making known the holdings of a repository. They hide the woods for the trees by focusing attention on single items, without revealing the nature of the collections of which such items are a part. They are like catalogs of pages of a number of books, which describe the contents of individual pages but fail to identify the books of which such pages are a part. They are not a substitute for comprehensive finding aids, such as guides and catalogs of collections. They cannot, in fact, be used effectively if a general conspectus of the holdings of a repository is unavailable. For example, the voluminous catalogs of the Massachusetts Historical Society, produced at various periods since 1791, can be interpreted only by means of the guide to its collections, issued in 1949.

Catalogs are also not an efficient means of revealing the existence of records on important or highly significant topics. If information on such records is compiled, it should be made known generally; not only to visitors to a repository. It should be made known in published lists, not in catalogs.

ORGANIZATION

Various types of catalogs have been created by manuscript curators. The commonest are catalogs in which record units are identified by their authors or writers. Among the important repositories that have produced author catalogs are the Massachusetts Historical Society, the Huntington Library, the Clements Library, and the New-York Historical Society. Certain of these—the Clements and the New-York Historical—also have catalogs for recipients of documents. The Huntington Library has, in addition to an author catalog, catalogs for persons other than authors, for subjects, and for record types.[18] The New-York Historical Society also has a catalog of record types, such as diaries, account books, and letter books.[19] The Duke University Library, the practices of which are modeled somewhat after those of the Huntington Library,[20] has prepared an author catalog of its collections, which it calls the "main file" of its catalog; an author catalog of letters within each collection, which it calls the "autograph file"; and a geographic catalog, in which collections are listed "by the state around which each centers."[21] Dictionary catalogs, similar to those found in a library, have not been prepared extensively, though their use is regarded as "the best practice" by one manuscript curator.[22]

Catalogs of items in collections of miscellany that consist of specific record types, such as account books, diaries, and genealogies, should be organized alphabetically by author. Catalogs of miscellaneous letters should be organized into two files: one arranged alphabetically by author, and the other chronologically.

ENTRIES

When record items are cataloged, the information most commonly provided on a card relates to author, place, date, subject, physical characteristics, and location. While entries in the WPA Historical Records Survey guides are not completely revealing of the content of catalog cards prepared by various repositories, the accompanying tabulation will show, in general, the kind of information that was provided. A number of the repositories

	Author	Place	Date	Subject	Physical description	Location
Buffalo Historical Society	x	x	x	x		x
Chicago Historical Society	x	x	x	x	x	x
Clements Library	x	x	x		x	x
Detroit Public Library	x	x	x	x		x
Duke University Library	x	x	x			x
Florida Historical Society	x	x	x	x		x
Huntington Library	x		x		x	
Kansas State Historical Society	x	x	x	x	x	
Long Island Historical Society	x	x	x	x	x	x
Missouri Historical Society	x			x		
Newberry Library	x	x	x	x	x	x
New York State Library	x	x		x		
North Dakota Historical Society Library	x			x	x	x
Oregon Historical Society	x	x	x	x		
Oklahoma University	x	x	x	x		x
Oklahoma Historical Society	x		x	x	x	x
Pennsylvania Historical Society	x		x	x		x
Princeton University Library	x			x		x

listed provide more information than is indicated in the tabulation. For example, the life-span of the author is indicated on cards produced at the Missouri Historical Society and the Newberry Library. The recipient of items or pieces is indicated by the Clements Library, the Florida Historical Society, the Huntington Library, the Kansas State Historical Society, and the Historical Society of Pennsylvania. Information to show location may relate to a collection or accession number or to a place in the stacks.

While cataloging techniques have not been standardized, a number of repositories have developed rules of their own that, with a little collaborative effort, could be formed into standard rules, for they vary only in unessential details.[23]

A catalog entry for a record item should normally consist only of a title line that identifies the item that is being cataloged. If an archivist wishes to provide descriptive information also, he should add a brief statement on the content of an item.

Title line

An archivist should provide information in the title line in the following manner.

First, give the *name of the producer or author* of the item. If the item was produced by a particular person, give his name; if it was produced anonymously in an office, give the name of the office, thus:

> Doe, John (an individual)
> National Resources Planning Board (a corporate body)

Spell the author's name in the manner that is recognized as the correct one. If an author signs his name in several ways, follow the commonest signature. Do not reproduce misspellings of names, which may appear in signatures. Always reproduce an author's name fully, though his signature may appear in the form of an abbreviation, or initials, or a nickname, or some other designation. For example, list a letter written by Czar Nicholas II, signed "Nicky," and addressed to "Willy" (Kaiser Wilhelm II) as: Nicholas II to Wilhelm II. Similarly, list a letter signed "T. R." as that of Theodore Roosevelt; and list a letter signed "brother" or "sister" by the name of the person signing himself or herself thus.

Second, indicate the *place* at which an item was written or with which its author is identified. Place may be indicated by referring to a state, region, city, county, town, or village. Spell the names of out-of-the-way places in the manner that is recognized as correct, if the correct spelling is readily ascertainable. If it is not, spell the place name exactly as it appears in the item itself. Show the place thus:

Jones, John (Tuscaloosa, Ala.)

Third, indicate the *kind of producer*. Do this by showing the occupation or profession of the item's author, i.e., whether he is a farmer, teacher, or what not. Show the kind of producer thus:

Jones, John (Tuscaloosa, Ala.; Confederate cavalry officer)

Fourth, identify the item by its *record type*. The following record types are most likely to require individual cataloging:

Account books	Manuals	Proceedings
Diaries	Memorials	Reminiscences
Histories	Messages	Reports
Journals	Minutes	Scrapbooks
Letters	Minute books	Sermons
Letter books	Notes	Speeches
Logbooks	Order Books	Studies

Fifth, show the *distinctive characteristics* of the record type, whenever possible. Almost every record type has characteristics that distinguish it from other types, and these should be noted in identifying it. The characteristics may relate to the activities that resulted in the production of a record item or to its subject matter.

Sixth, show the *form of reproduction*, if pertinent. Show if the record item was reproduced as a photoprint or microfilm, thus:

Photoprinted letter
Microfilmed reminiscences

Seventh, give the *dates* of the item. If the item is a single document, show its actual date, thus:

Business letter, Jan. 1, 1861

If the item consists of a file unit or a volume, such as a diary, letter book, or minute book, which has covered a period of time longer than a single day, give its first and last dates, thus:

Personal letter book, Jan. 1–March 30, 1861
Monthly narrative progress report, March, 1861

If the item is significant for a specific period, or if most of the material contained therein was written within a specific period, emphasize the dates of the period by including them in parentheses between the first and last dates, thus:

Diary, 1861(1863–67)78

Eighth, indicate the item's *recipient,* if readily identifiable. Reproduce his name in the same manner as the author's name, i.e., correctly spelled and not abbreviated. Indicate the fact that the item was addressed to a person or corporate body by using the word "to," thus:

to Richard Roe
to War Production Board

Ninth, indicate the *number of pages* in the item, if it has more than one page.

Tenth, indicate by *symbol* the manuscript collection (or series and archival group) in which the record item is found. Place this information in the first line above the title, thus:

> 56-4
> Doe, John (Harrisburg, Pa.; farmer), Account book

Descriptive paragraph

Normally, a record item should simply be identified, not described on a catalog card. If a cataloging system is excessively complicated by reason of its descriptive information, it may become so difficult to complete the catalog that it will lag behind the growth of collections that need cataloging or it may become so expensive to prepare that it may infringe upon funds that can be spent more judiciously on other finding aids.

For this reason, information in a descriptive paragraph should be limited to the main activity to which an item relates, or to the main object of such an activity, indicated in terms of the person, corporate body, place, thing, or phenomenon involved in it.

An archivist should therefore follow the rule that *information on the subject content of an item should always be limited to its most important or main matter,* not to incidental or relatively unimportant matters to which it may relate.

Supposing, for purposes of illustration, that the following item is being cataloged:

Ursuline Convent,
Columbia, S.C.
11 December, 1865

Mr. Minister,

I am a French woman, and I apply to you, as the Representative of my Nation, to obtain any indemnity from the Government at Washington, for my losses, and not only for mine, but also for those of my father who resides near Nimes. I estimate these losses at fifteen thousand dollars.

Our Convent, an institution where a large number of young ladies of the best families in the country have been educated, was burned by General Sherman's army. On the General's approach, our Mother Superior wrote to him, informing him of our situation. Our sisters for the most part strangers, having no relative on this side of the Atlantic, having left their country to come with all apostolic zeal, to serve God and their neighbor, in this strange land, what could they do, where would they go, if their Convent was burned? Our Superior represented all this to him; she had addressed him with confidence; as she had had his own daughter and her sister-in-law as pupils. He answered that the Convent would be protected, and advised the mother of one of our young ladies to leave her with us. The city was burnt, and the next day, we and our eighty boarders had to take refuge in the cemetery, the only safe asylum in a city given up to flames and pillage. There they came to offer their services; but alas it was too late—they forgot us in the hour of danger. And since that terrible night on the 17th of February, we have suffered—no language can give an idea of it! Our friends of the North are doing all they can with the Government to obtain an indemnity. We read in the annals of Our Order, that European Governments have acted thus, in similar cases, and if our petition is advocated by you, Mr. Minister, it will only have more importance. Mr. Seward and Mr. Stanton already seem to favor it.

Accept,
(Signed) Sister St. Etienne Vassas

This item should be identified under the above rules as follows:

Its *producer* or *author*, about whom information is required under rule 1, is obvious, i.e., Sister St. Etienne Vassas.

Its *place of production*—Columbia, S.C.—is significant and should be indicated in accordance with rule 2.

The *kind of producer* should be indicated in accordance with rule 3.

Its *record type*, which should be specified in accordance with rule 4, is a Request for indemnity.

The record type is indicated in specific terms. The document could have been termed a "letter," but this term is not particularly descriptive of its content. A term that shows its *particular attributes* was therefore chosen.

Since the document is an original, not a *reproduction*, rule 6 does not apply.

Its *date*, about which information is required under rule 7, is obvious, i.e., December 11, 1865.

The title, rather than the name, of the *recipient* is significant, and therefore should be provided under rule 8.

Since the item is a one-page document, no information about *pagination* should be provided under rule 9.

The archival group in the National Archives in which the item is found is number 56. Since the series within groups have not been numbered, the numeral 4 is hypothetical.

A completed title entry should thus read:

56-4
Vassas, Sister St. Etienne (Columbia, S.C., French nun), Request for indemnity, Dec. 11, 1865, to French minister

The subject content of the item is a phenomenon, i.e., the burning of Columbia by General William Tecumseh Sherman's army. This is the main subject of the item, a subject of interest to every historian. It should be revealed in connection with the matter that impelled the author to write the document. Incidental information in the item about Sherman's religion and family, about conditions in Columbia and the like, should not be included in the descriptive paragraph.

An additional sentence should therefore be added to the title entry, as follows:

56-4
Vassas, Sister St. Etienne (Columbia, S.C., French nun), Request for indemnity, Dec. 11, 1865, to French minister, for losses incurred during burning of Columbia by Sherman's army, Feb. 17, 1865.

Notation

Any symbols used should be simple. They should serve only to identify the collection of which the item is a part.

PREPARATION OF LISTS
AND CALENDARS

Lists and calendars are finding aids that are designed for external as well as internal use. Since ordinarily they are published, they should be more finished and more formal than indexes and catalogs. They are, moreover, finding aids that are difficult to prepare, for the record items described in them are very small units of description, and an enumeration of their attributes is a tedious task. They should therefore be prepared selectively, in response to immediate or well-defined anticipated needs. And they should be prepared only after guides and catalogs of collections have been completed, only when it is necessary to provide supplementary information to that contained in such guides and catalogs, and then only when such information needs to be made known generally.

Lists

LISTS OF DISPARATE RECORD ITEMS

A list of disparate record items is an enumeration of documents that may be scattered among various collections or record groups, or that may be dissimilar in character. The purpose of such a list is twofold: to facilitate the immediate use of particular record items, and to reveal their existence and significance for potential use. Item descriptions will help accomplish this objective in either of two ways: by bringing together information about all items relating to some subject of importance without regard to the relative importance of the particular items, or by singling out for special mention items of importance in relation to a particular subject, thus bringing to the attention of the user the best sources of information on that subject.

The items to be described separately may be chosen because of their association with heroes, dramatic episodes, or places where significant events took place. The subjects to which they relate may thus be important phenomena, such as specific historic events or episodes, important things, such as historic sites or buildings, or important persons, such as Presidents of the United States. In the National Archives, lists of items relating to important subjects have often been prepared in response to service requests, such as lists of Lincoln and Jefferson items that were found dispersed among many groups and series.

Or the items to be described separately may be important because of their content or nature. Important items of this kind are often interfiled in the run-of-the-mill documentation of an office. Their importance can be judged partly by the amount of the information they contain, the authority or competence of the persons with whom they originated, and the influence or effect they had. The following classes of records have an importance that may make them appropriate for listing:

(1) Policy documents—such as staff studies and special reports relating to organization, program, and policy—that reflect top-level decisions with respect to organization, function, interagency relations, and relations outside the government; legal and economic briefs; memoranda delegating or defining powers and responsibilities or showing working relations with other federal agencies, state and local governments, industry, or private organizations; and speeches.

(2) Procedural documents that represent a codification of instructions, such as operational handbooks, manuals of procedure, style manuals, file classification manuals, and staff studies and special reports relating to techniques and procedures.

(3) Documents that summarize accomplishments, such as agency histories, annual reports, progress reports, minutes of meetings and conferences, transcripts of hearings, and reports on

substantive investigations (including compilations of statistical data and research reports).

Organization

Since a description of individual record items is a very time-consuming process, the question may be raised as to whether such items can be listed in a meaningful way without enumerating all the attributes of each of them.

In lists of discrete items, this can be done by grouping them under subject heads. If they are listed separately, without regard to possible relationships that may exist among them, each item must be fully described to make it meaningful. All its attributes, substantive as well as physical, must be enumerated.

If, on the other hand, such items are grouped under various subject heads, the heads will give meaning to the individual items appearing under them. They convey information that is common to all of them. *Subjects heads*, then, *reduce the amount of descriptive information that needs to be provided about individual record items*. The technique to be employed is that of *indicating subject content by means of subject heads and simply identifying record items*.

Record items may be grouped in relation to various kinds of subjects: the persons to whom they in any way pertain; the geographical localities to which they refer, or in which they were made or accumulated; the things to which they refer; the phenomena to which they refer; and the chronological period in which the items originated or to which they otherwise relate. The method of grouping should be devised, in each instance, by the archivist after carefully analyzing the items that he proposes to list.

The way in which the significance of items can be revealed will vary according to their nature. If the items have their source in many persons or corporate bodies, they should perhaps be grouped for listing according to their source. For example, in dealing with a collection of speeches, the speeches should first be grouped by the persons who gave them. If, however, the speeches all had their origin in one person, they should be grouped either in reference to the times at which they were given or in reference to the places at which they were given, depending on whether time or place is the more significant.

Introduction

An introduction to a subject list should usually contain information on the provenance of the record items that are being listed; the reasons for listing them; the way in which they are listed, explaining the groupings that are made of them and any symbols or unusual abbreviations that are used in listing them; their relation to other records; and restrictions on their use, if such exist.

Entries

In the body of a list, record items should be grouped under subject heads, and under each head each record item should be identified and described.

In the description of record items, the descriptive procedures employed in cataloging, discussed in the preceding chapter, should be followed. These procedures are recapitulated here for purposes of emphasis only.

First, identify the item by its *record type*, i.e., whether a letter, report, or account book, etc.

Second, show the *distinctive characteristics* of the record type, which may relate to the activities or transactions that resulted in its production or to its subject matter.

Third, indicate the *method of reproduction*, if the item consists of a reproduction. If it is a typewritten or handwritten transcription, identify it as a transcript; if it is photographically reproduced, identify it as a photoprint or microfilm.

Fourth, give the *name of the producer* of the item. If it was produced by a particular person, give his name; if anonymously in an office, give the name of the office.

Fifth, indicate the *place* at which the item was written or with which its author is identified.

Sixth, indicate the *kind of producer*. If the item was produced by a person, indicate his occupation or profession; if by a corporate body, indicate the kind of body.

Seventh, indicate the *date* of the item.

Eighth, give the *name of the recipient* of the item, if readily available.

Ninth, indicate the *number of pages* in the item, if it has more than one page.

Tenth, indicate by *symbol* the record unit in which the item is found.

Examples of complete list entries follow:

Request for indemnity, Sister St. Etienne Vassas
(Columbia, S.C.; French nun), Dec. 11, 1865, to French minister.
(56-4)

Personal diary, John Doe (Tuscaloosa, Ala.; Confederate cavalry officer), 1861(1863–67)1878, 24 pages.
(M-5)

LISTS OF ITEMS HAVING COMMON ATTRIBUTES

Items having common attributes are found among both public and private papers. In a manuscript repository, such items consist of specific record types, e.g., account books, diaries, journals, letter books, logbooks, minute books, and sermons. Such types are often brought together into collections of miscellany in large repositories.

Normally, an archivist should keep a register of items embodied in a collection of miscellany and, when preparing a guide, should group such items for the purpose of describing them in guide entries. But if there is an interest in a specific type of record, he may find it desirable to list all items of a given type, including those embodied in personal or corporate collections, as well as those embodied in a collection of miscellany. Thus, he may wish to list all account books, or diaries, or sermons in his repository.

In an archival institution, records that have common attributes may consist of files of offices that engaged in essentially similar activities, or case files of a specific type, or items of a specific record type. A list of such record units may be nothing more than a detailed analysis of the contents of a particular series, though occasionally it may cover more than one series if items in a number of series have some degree of similarity.

Introduction

An introduction to a list of record units having common attributes is quite important and should be prepared very carefully. It should relate mainly to the common attributes of the records that are being listed. In the interest of economy and convenience, it should describe the listed material collectively as far as possible, bringing together all common facts about the records, so that the list entries can be reduced to the briefest possible form.

The fact that records are similar in character is of central importance in their description. It indicates the technique to be employed in listing them, i.e., that records that have certain common attributes should be described collectively in regard to their common attributes and singly only in regard to their variable attributes. If records consist of a specific record type, the collective description should show the contents of a typical item; if they consist of case files, the description should show the contents of a specific case file, both in terms of the subjects to which it relates and in terms of the record types it contains; and if they consist of office files, the description should show the contents of a typical office file.

Often, while preparing a list, it will be necessary to group items with common attributes and to assign symbols or abbreviations to various groups, in order to facilitate reference to them in the body of a list. Such symbols or abbreviations should be explained in an introduction. In the "List of Climatological Records in the National Archives," for example, various types of reports are grouped, and symbols are assigned to each group, which are explained in the introduction to the list as follows:

SI: Monthly reports of voluntary observers for the Smithsonian Institution, 1840–73 (contained in series VO)

Reg Sta: Weekly (until 1881) and monthly reports of regular stations of the Signal Office, 1870–91, and of the Weather Bureau, 1891–98

VO: Monthly reports of voluntary observers for the Signal Office, 1874–91, and for the Weather Bureau, 1891–92, and monthly reports of Army surgeons stationed at military posts, 1860–93

An introduction should also briefly show the relation of the listed items to other records and should indicate restrictions on their use, if such exist.

Entries

Entries in the list proper should be made as succinct as possible in the light of the summary information given in the introduction. They should pertain solely to the variable attributes of the items that are listed. Information on variables will be different in each list.

Items of a given record type may be identified in lists by showing only the places and times to which they pertain. They may also be identified, on occasion, with respect to the persons, things (other than places), and phenomena to which they pertain, and with respect to their variant types. An example of list entries for items of a given record type, taken from the National Archives meteorological list, follows:

ALABAMA

ASHLAND—VO: April, 1889

AUBURN—SI: Jan. 1855–Jan. 1858; VO: Feb. 1881–Feb. 1884; Reg
Sta: Jan. 1889–June 1893 (3d order)

BERMUDA—VO:Jan. 1889–Dec. 1892

An example of a list of case files, produced in the National Archives, is that pertaining to wage stabilization cases referred to the National War Labor Board, 1942–45. In the body of the list, the individual case files are identified by the firm involved and by case number, thus:

Acme Fast Freight, Inc.	2-69332
Allegheny Ludlum Steel Corp.	3-40648
American Laundry & Cleaning Co.	4-13195

An example of a list of office files, produced in the National Archives, is that pertaining to the diplomatic and consular posts of the State Department. Since the records of foreign service posts relate to essentially similar activities, the records were described collectively, and the collective description was supplemented in an important way by a list of the posts, with dates for which records exist at each of them. The entries in the list are as follows:

Aachen, Germany. 1879–1917. 12 ft.

Aaran, Switzerland. 1800–1907. 2 ft. See also Lucerne.

Aarhus, Denmark. 1917–19. 7 ft.

Alberton, Prince Edward Island, Canada. 1883–1906. 2 vols.

Albert Town, Long Cay, Bahamas, British West Indies. 1884–1912. 1 ft.

Calendars

Calendars contain substantially more information about records than lists and always relate to individual documents, not to aggregations of documents, such as binders, folders, or volumes. In calendars, such documents are listed in chronological order, and each document is identified by the names of its writer and recipient and described by a digest of its contents.

Calendaring is a time-consuming and expensive procedure. It may be justified only with regard to highly significant documents. Such documents should have great research value to warrant the extensive treatment given them in calendars. This is the reason why the State Department, when the records were in the custody of its Bureau of Rolls and Library, prepared calendars to the papers of Jefferson, Madison, and Monroe.

If calendar entries are in the form of a reproduction of the exact phraseology of the original on essential matters, they can often be used instead of the original documents; but, if the purpose of calendaring is to obviate the use of the originals, a cheaper and more accurate modern way of doing this is to microfilm them. And it is better, from the point of view of research, for it provides a full text, not merely an abstract.

If calendaring is done in the form of paraphrasing the language of the main facts and ideas of the documents, perhaps a better and more efficient way of providing information in regard to the documents is to compile subject lists of them. In such lists, documents are described in relation to subject heads, not merely enumerated in chronological sequence. The information provided in them about the record type, the provenance, the dates, and the content of individual documents is usually quite adequate to meet all scholarly needs. Lists, obviously, do not provide the window dressing that is provided in calendars, but it matters little to the scholar whether a particular document is identified as a letter signed or an autographed letter signed, for the scholar wants to know simply if the document is pertinent to his subject of inquiry. And this, in lists, will be indicated in the subject heads.

A second reason for calendaring is to make records accessible that would otherwise be inaccessible because of their physical character. A perfect example of calendars that accomplish this purpose are those prepared to the medieval rolls by the British Public Record Office. These rolls, or registers, which contain the copies of documents either in abridged or complete form, consist of pieces of parchment fastened end on end and often quite long. As a result of the neglect accorded public records before the nineteenth century, many of the rolls are in poor physical condition and are difficult to use. The writing in them is often almost indecipherable and in languages difficult for many present-day scholars to interpret. Calendars of the rolls, therefore, are highly useful documents.

A third reason for calendaring is to protect records of great intrinsic value. Calendars provide a means of precisely identifying the documents not only by author and date but also by substance. This precise identification reduces handling, although the same purpose can be accomplished as well and perhaps more cheaply by microfilming the documents and, for that matter, by properly arranging and numbering them.

Calendars have a peculiar appeal to historians. They provide information about documents in chronological sequence—the sequence in which historians must read them to understand how things actually happened. They provide enough information about documents to enable an historian to know if any one of them is pertinent to his inquiry. They almost relieve historians of note-taking, and often relieve them of the necessity of consulting the originals of documents.

INTRODUCTION

The introductory section of a calendar should contain a collective description of the record items that are being calendared, including information on their source and significance.[1]

ENTRIES

Calendar entries should have three parts.

The first is a title line for each document, indicating its date, the names of the writer and the recipient, and the name of the place at which the document was written. In the case of calendars, the names of the writer and the recipient should be reproduced exactly as they appear in the original. If the names are misspelled, they should be reproduced in their misspelled version; if they are shortened, they should be reproduced in their shortened form; if nicknames, they should be reproduced as nicknames. If information on the identity of a person is supplied, it should appear in brackets, thus: "Nicky" [Czar Nicholas II], "Willy" [Wilhelm II], "T. R." [Theodore Roosevelt], "Brother" [John Doe], "Sis" [Mary Roe], etc.

The second part of a calendar entry is a paragraph in which the content of each document is indicated. This has been done in various ways. The first calendars are far skimpier in their content than those of recent vintage. In his discussion before the Bibliographical Society, Worthington C. Ford observed: "The two extreme limits are a mere list of papers, and the full and complete publication of every paper. The former is too general and misleading; the latter is unnecessarily expansive and expensive."[2] In recent years, content has usually been indicated in one of two ways.

The paragraph may contain a digest of the main facts and ideas of a document. Its contents, in such a case, are summarized in the words of the person compiling the calendar. This method was recommended by the British archivists in their instructions on compiling the *Calendars of State Papers*.[3]

The contents of the document on the burning of Columbia, S.C., reproduced in the preceding chapter to illustrate the cata-

loging process, may be summarized under this procedure somewhat as follows:

1865   Sister St. Etienne Vassas, Columbia, S.C. To Marquese of
Dec. 11   Montholon, French minister, Washington, D.C.
  Requests indemnity for losses incurred in destruction of Ursuline Convent during burning of Columbia by General
  Sherman's army, Feb 17. Indicates Superior petitioned Sherman with confidence to spare convent on the ground that
  his daughter and her sister-in-law had been students there,
  that during burning, its inmates sought asylum in a cemetery, and that Seward and Stanton seemingly favored the petition for indemnification.
   A. L. S. 1 p.

The paragraph of a calendar entry may also summarize the
contents of a document on essential matters in the language of
the original, and on nonessential matters in the language of the
compiler. Historians, who are the chief users of calendars, prefer
this form of calendaring. A digest of a document in the language
of the compiler "does not satisfy their requirements, since it does
not furnish them with the writer's words, upon which alone a
scholarly interpretation must rest," according to the conference
of Anglo-American historians.[4]

The contents of the document on the burning of Columbia,
S.C., may be summarized under this procedure somewhat as
follows:

1865   Sister St. Etienne Vassas, Columbia, S.C. To Marquese of
Dec. 11   Montholon, French minister, Washington, D.C.
  Requests indemnity for losses incurred in destruction of Ursuline Convent "burned by General Sherman's army," Feb.
  17. Indicates Superior petitioned Sherman "with confidence" to spare convent on the ground that his daughter
  and her sister-in-law had been students there, but that the
  "city was burnt" and that the inmates of the Convent took
  "refuge in the cemetery, the only safe asylum in a city given
  up to flames and pillage." Indicates further that Seward
  and Stanton seemingly favored the petition for indemnification.
   A. L. S. 1 p.

The third part of a calendar entry contains a reference to the physical character of the documents by means of letter symbols, the most common of which were listed on page 155. While many letter symbols have been added to indicate other record types, modern record types are so numerous that symbols can be used to a limited degree to designate them. They have a meaning only in reference to a few of the more common record types— types that were dealt with most often during the last century, when record items were generally described separately in calendars and catalogs.

INDEXES

Indexes should include the names of persons and places mentioned in documents that are calendared. They are a key to the contents of the documents, and actually give a calendar the character of a finding aid.

XIX

ARRANGEMENT AND
DESCRIPTION OF
CARTOGRAPHIC RECORDS

The methods of dealing with cartographic records vary according to their volume, the use that is made of them, and their variety. A select group of maps of North America, made before 1800 and used only for research, does not require all the techniques of arrangement and description followed in a repository of public maps covering all parts of the world, made by many different agencies, and used for extensive investigations of broad subject fields or for specific personal projects.

Persons who have charge of map libraries and cartographic archives ordinarily develop their methods on the more general foundations of the archival and library disciplines, geography, the history of cartography or of particular map-making organizations, and the various subject fields in which maps are commonly utilized.

An archivist who deals with maps as an adjunct to his manuscript holdings and who, for this reason, has no special knowledge of maps may find it profitable to read Erwin Raisz's textbook on *General Cartography*, or some other text.[1] A cartography text will help him acquire a general understanding of maps, though it may not help him understand maps as records.

It should be noted that particular classes of material often associated with map libraries and cartographic archives have been excluded from the following discussion. Archivists may find themselves in charge of construction drawings and architects' plans, which, because of their physical form, are often most easily stored in map drawers. Textual material, such as surveyors' field notebooks, mathematical computations, statistical tables, and map project files, is best kept near the cartographic material to which it relates. Aerial photographs, the basis of modern mapping, are most conveniently used by persons trained in geography and photogrammetry in close proximity to maps of the areas photographed. Maps that are illustrations in books or that are interfiled with textual records are ordinarily not the direct concern of those responsible for separate bodies of maps and cartographic records. In the interest of their better preservation and only when adequate cross-references can be made should such maps be brought into the cartographic section of a repository.

Attributes

Cartographic, as well as textual, records may be considered from substantive aspects, i.e., their organizational origins, their functional origins, and their subjects, and also from physical or structural aspects, i.e., their type, form, scale, size, and other technical attributes.

Because many maps are printed and have an author, a title, a date, and a publisher, it may seem reasonable to deal with them as if they were books. But this approach overlooks their areal character and ignores the methods of map compilation and the differences between the development of map printing and book printing. The visual character of a map can be grasped by considering the amount of text required to explain the spatial relations on even a simple map. Difficulties begin shortly after the title is read.

Map attributes are those general features that, taken together, make it possible to provide information about maps, or to identify and describe them, as a substitute for actually seeing them. The attributes are the elements that should be taken into account in their arrangement and description.

SUBSTANTIVE ATTRIBUTES

There are four substantive attributes to be considered.

Organizational origins

The factor of organizational origins or provenance is of major importance only in large repositories with organized cartographic archives. Cartographic records are, of course, produced by the same kinds of entities that produce textual records— government agencies, corporate bodies, and individual persons. In the federal government of the United States, several agencies have map making as an essential function. Among these are the Aeronautical Chart and Information Service, the Army Map Service, the Coast and Geodetic Survey, the Geological Survey, and the Naval Oceanographic Office, formerly the Navy Hydrographic Office. The Bureau of Indian Affairs and the former General Land Office, which is now part of the Bureau of Land Management, early in their history found maps necessary for the conduct of their business. In other agencies, such as the Bureau of the Census, the Forest Service, the Soil Conservation Service, and the Weather Bureau, maps play a significant functional and public role. Separate bodies of cartographic records for about 130 federal agencies, with their more than 500 smaller organizational units, are in the National Archives.

Throughout the United States, other organizations regularly produce maps. Many state and local governments have map-making units that provide maps for public distribution and for use in the conduct of official business. Among private corporate bodies that produce extensive quantities of specialized maps are the air, bus, and railway companies and oil and gas companies. Several major commercial map makers produce a variety of atlases, road maps, and maps for educational use. There are also a number of organizations engaged in the production of facsimile reprints of maps of particular historical interest.

The following elements of map description relate to organizational origins:

ORGANIZATIONAL AUTHOR. In archival systems and library cataloging, this is the agency or corporate body that produced the map.

INDIVIDUAL AUTHOR. There are few modern maps made by one person, although older maps are nearly always listed by author.

OTHER PERSONS CONNECTED WITH MAP MAKING. It is not always easy to determine who should be considered the author of a map, since many maps mention the work of a cartographer, compiler, draftsman, editor, engraver, leader of an expedition, person authorizing the work, publisher, surveyor, and topographer, to name the most common. There may be significant associations for one or all of these, and they should be considered in map description.

Functional origins

When taken as individual items for the information they contain, maps have a quality of discreteness not characteristic of textual records. When considered as a group in relation to the activities for which they are auxiliary tools, they display organic qualities similar to those of textual records. Most federal maps in the National Archives were produced in connection with specific activities, e.g., providing navigation aids for the benefit of foreign and domestic commerce, surveying the public domain for land disposal, making western explorations for geographical knowledge to assist settlement, surveying roads and railways for the extension of transportation facilities, and conducting geologic studies for the development of mineral resources.

Subjects

A map always has a primary subject, i.e., the area to which it pertains. But there is always an additional subject with the area subject, even in an outline map that shows only the configurations of the continents. This additional subject will be referred to as the secondary subject.

The area, or primary subject represented on a map, may be part of the earth's surface, the air and heavens above it, or the oceans and seas around it. It may be a natural geographical area, such as a continent, river basin, or region; it may be a more artificial political area, such as a country, state, or county.

The particular information about an area, or the secondary subject of a map, is ordinarily reflected by its type. Secondary subjects relate to such matters as the climate, communications, geology, land use, military operations, political divisions, and topography of an area; these subjects are, of course, indicated by map types: climatic, communications, geologic, and other types. The secondary subjects may be further subdivided. The variety of subjects to which maps may relate is reflected in the "Subject Classification Schedule," provided by Boggs and Lewis in their *Classification and Cataloging of Maps and Atlases,* published by the Special Libraries Association.[2] The variety of subjects dealt with by federal mapping agencies is reflected in the map holdings of the National Archives.

Title, date, edition, and place of publication

Many maps, especially printed ones, have a title given by the person or corporate body that produced them. The title usually indicates the subject of the map, i.e., the area shown and something about the particular features of it which are mapped. The date and place of publication often appear on a map with the imprint, which also includes the name of the publisher. But the date and indication of edition may also appear separately or as part of the title. For maps that are corrected frequently, the date may mean not only the year but also the month and day. Ordinarily, the date of a map refers to the time of its creation; this is usually also the date of the information shown on it. It is sometimes necessary to distinguish when a map was made from the date of the information shown on it. A map compiled and printed in 1962, for example, showing the routes of the vessels of Columbus in 1492, would properly be called an historical map, although not necessarily one of historic interest.

PHYSICAL AND STRUCTURAL ATTRIBUTES

The following elements of map description relate to their physical form and structure:

General types

The commonest general types of graphic presentation are maps and charts, on which information is shown by letters, lines, curves, colors, bars, shadings, dots, and other symbols. In common parlance, a map refers to land areas and a chart to water or air; thus, a topographic map, but aeronautical, hydrographic, and nautical charts; a weather map for conditions near the surface, but an upper air chart. Other general types, which should be distinguished from maps and charts, are cartograms and other more abstract presentations of statistical data, globes, and relief or terrain models. Plats, plans, and index maps are also usually separately noted.

Specific types

The principal graphic type, i.e., the map, which is our primary concern, may be divided into a number of specific types. A specific map type may ordinarily be identified by asking: What kind of map is it? Is it a cadastral, climatic, communications, geological, land use, military, political, or topographic map? Such specific types, as noted earlier, reflect the secondary subjects to which maps pertain. In this respect, cartographic records differ from textual records, in which types are identified in relation to activity, not subject content.

Technical attributes

The principal graphic type, i.e., the map, has technical attributes that relate to its form of production, composition, system of projection, scale, and size.

The *forms of production* to be distinguished among maps are: manuscript, printed, overprinted, processed, and annotated. Manuscript and annotated maps are unique and, for this reason, should be arranged and described differently from processed maps. Processed maps are in many forms, for modern map-making methods are very complex. The terms used to designate such forms have not been standardized, and, except in highly specialized repositories, an archivist need not identify them. But photostatic copies, which form part of the reference collections of many repositories, should always be identified as such in descriptions.

The *composition* of maps, here as in regard to textual and pictorial records, refers to how they were brought together. Atlases, bound volumes, sets, serial publications, and single items should be distinguished, and they usually receive appropriately different handling in arrangement and description.

The *system of projection* used in a map is ordinarily an element of its description only in detailed and comparatively technical studies. Texts on cartography treat projections in detail.

The *scale* of a map is an important element in the arrangement of topographic sets and should always be mentioned in item descriptions. Scale is the relation that exists between a distance on a map and a corresponding distance on the earth's surface. It is generally expressed as "inch to the mile" or some similar ratio, or as a natural or numerical scale, sometimes referred to as a representative fraction, such as 1:1,000,000.

Size should always be given in item descriptions. The vertical and horizontal dimensions of a map are taken from its neat line, border line, or edge, and expressed in inches or centimeters. If maps have been dissected into several sheets, that fact should also be noted.

Arrangement

From the point of view of the principles of archival arrangement involved, maps should be dealt with in the same way as textual records.

Public maps ordinarily fall into the same kind of series as public manuscripts, i.e., series that have a value primarily because they contain information of various kinds on geographical areas, and series that contain evidence of organic activities. Such series should be arranged in accordance with the archival principles of provenance and original order.

Maps held by private institutions may also be in series, but they ordinarily consist of single items or small groups of items brought together from various sources. Such items and groups are usually formed into heterogeneous map collections. Items in such collections should be arranged in the same way as items in artificial manuscript collections. Since such items have no organic or other relation to each other, they may be arranged according to library methods of classification.

Essentially, then, there are two basically different systems of arrangement that should be applied to maps: one is an archival system, the other a library system. The system to be applied depends on the nature of the maps and the use that is made of them. Series of maps should be arranged by provenance; disparate items derived from various sources, by area.

ARRANGEMENT BY AREA

Maps are arranged by area in most public, university, and historical society libraries and in private collections, and this is in accord with their use. A 1953 survey of 360 map libraries in the United States, made by the Geography and Map Division of the Special Libraries Association, showed that 74 percent of requests for maps were by area, 24 percent by subject, and 2 percent by title, publisher, scale, date, and the like.[3]

Area arrangement is recommended by Raisz in his *General Cartography*,[4] by Boggs and Lewis in their *Classification and Cataloging of Maps*,[5] and by most librarians who have written on the arrangement of maps.[6]

Area arrangement is suited to a collection of cartographic records that is brought together from many sources, generally as single items or in small groups. It is thus an arrangement that is suited to heterogeneous collections of maps in libraries and historical societies. It is also an arrangement that may be imposed on map items for their current use in a government agency.

Establishing classes

In arranging map items in a heterogeneous collection, an archivist should establish a number of geographical classes into which he will place individual items. The classes will vary, according to the quantity of cartographic records that is being accumulated in a repository. An archivist in a small state or local history society will need to choose geographical classes that are different from those in relation to which a librarian, dealing with a large map collection, will organize his maps.

Raisz suggests that maps of a geography department of a university should be arranged by broad geographical classes. Boggs and Lewis recommend a classification of maps according to the following scheme:

100	World	600	North America
200–300	Europe	700	Latin America
400	Asia	800	Australia, New Zealand, and East Indies
500	Africa	900	Oceans

Within these broad classes they have innumerable subdivisions, established chiefly on a political basis. They use a decimal system of notation to designate major areas and their subdivisions. Essentially, the Raisz method of arrangement involves a broad classification of maps; the Boggs and Lewis method, a close classification.

If the collection of maps is a small one, a broad area classification is adequate. The broad areas may be continents. If a collection pertains only to a particular continent, the areas may be countries; if only to a particular country, the areas may be regions. In larger repositories, a more refined area-subject arrangement is usually required, so that maps can be found even when a catalog of them is not available.

The areas for which classes are established should ordinarily be geographical areas, not political; for political boundaries often change, with the result that classes established in relation to them are not stable. A standard American geography book or atlas will suggest the areas that should be chosen in grouping map items in a small collection. For a large collection, the map classification schemes that have been developed for use in map libraries will be more useful than geography texts or atlases.

Once classes are established, they should remain fixed.

When dealing with maps in a repository that has custody of both state maps and maps from private sources, an archivist may decide that both systems of arrangement should be employed, i.e., that the public maps of the state should be arranged by provenance and private maps by geographical area. If the total number of maps is not large, all maps, whether public in origin or not, can be arranged by area. But even in a small repository, maps that have been grouped into a well-defined series, e.g., a series of maps relating to real estate values in a particular state, should be preserved within that series rather than be broken up and arranged under counties or cities with other maps that also cover those areas.

Filing

An archivist should normally file maps flat in map cases. The map storage equipment used in most repositories consists of stacked cases containing four or six horizontal drawers each. Maps are placed in manila paper folders, and the folders are labeled with the appropriate filing notation. The diversity of size encountered among any large number of maps requires a variety of folders, but usually full-sized, half-sized, and quarter-sized folders can accommodate all diversity. The number of maps per folder and folders per drawer will depend on the size, shape, and weight of the material being filed.

An archivist should earmark either map cases or map drawers, depending on the size of his collection, for maps falling into particular geographical classes. He should employ a filing system that will permit him to add maps progressively to the geographical classes he has established. If, for example, he receives an additional map that falls into a particular geographical class, he should be able to insert it in the appropriate folder and drawer without disturbing maps in other classes.

Notating

An archivist should devise a notational system that will identify maps and show their location within a repository. The elements of this system for maps arranged according to area are:

    symbols (abbreviations of areas, letters, or numbers)—to designate the geographical classes into which maps should be placed;
    numbers—to designate folders; and
    numbers—to designate maps within folders. Maps within folders should be numbered in the sequence in which they accumulate.

Each map should be identified by a symbol composed of three parts, thus: Eur.-11.2. In this symbol, an abbreviation is used for a geographical area, i.e., Europe; 11 refers to the eleventh folder of European maps; 2, to the second map in the eleventh folder. Under this system, maps will be filed progressively in each geographical class as they are received. Raisz recommends a slightly different system of numbering that accomplishes the same results.

ARRANGEMENT BY PROVENANCE

Large accumulations of maps can be handled more easily if kept by provenance than if classified by area. A regrouping of a large quantity of maps by area is almost, though not quite, as difficult as regrouping a large quantity of textual records by subject. It is not quite as difficult because maps ordinarily can be arranged in relation to a single subject, i.e., place, while textual records, when they are rearranged, must be grouped in relation to a number of subjects, i.e., persons, places, things, or phenomena. While it is theoretically possible, it is impractical to rearrange federal maps in the National Archives, which number about 1,800,000, in a unified area-subject system.

While maps, as a whole, do not reflect activity to the degree that textual records do, series of public maps often contain evidence of organic activity. Survey plats and field notes, for example, contain data on surface features and establish legal boundaries of land subdivisions, but also show the date and progress of the surveys, the names of surveyors, and the names of approving officials. They are thus as organic as textual material. The same is true of many of the early engineering maps in the National Archives, which record progress of explorations, military activities, and public works.

In regard to cartographic records, the principle of provenance should be applied in the following ways: Groups should be kept in separate units that correspond to their source in government agencies. Each group should be treated as an integral unit and should be kept intact. Records from one source should not be merged with those from another. Series that were created by the agencies should also be maintained intact. They may be placed in any conceivable relation to each other within groups.

The principle of original order may be applied with considerable latitude to cartographic records. Maps within series may be placed in an order that makes them most accessible to use. The order given the maps within series during their current life should be preserved, especially if it permits an archivist to find records when they are wanted and to describe records effectively. But there should be no compunction about rearranging map items, or other graphic record items, if by such a rearrangement they can be made more intelligible and more serviceable. The test here is a very practical one of usability.

Maps are arranged by provenance in the National Archives and in other repositories that handle a large quantity of maps. The units of arrangement, which are analogous to the continents with their geographic subdivisions in an area arrangement, are the record groups, which are bodies of maps received from particular agencies of the federal government. Certain parts of the stack are set aside for the records of agencies, rather than for areas, and within each record group the maps are further arranged by subgroups, which are organizational levels within particular agencies. The next levels of arrangement, the series, are often area-subject classifications. Series created in the agencies and individual maps within series are maintained in the arrangement given them by their creators. In the stacks, related record groups are in close proximity, e.g., the cartographic records of the various bureaus of the Department of the Interior are in one section, those of the Department of Defense in another.

General control devices are maintained that relate the records to their physical location. By means of one set of symbols it is possible to show the record group, subgroup, series, and file to which a specific map belongs. The method employed in doing this is described by Herman R. Friis in an article in the *American Archivist*.[7] By means of another set of symbols it is possible to show the precise drawer, compartment, row, and area in which the specific map is located. The two sets of symbols are keyed or related to each other by means of a location register.

Description

Since maps often lack organic qualities, and generally have the quality of discreteness, they can be described individually, to a greater degree than textual records, in catalogs and lists. But they should also be described collectively. Guides and inventories should be prepared for organic map series. The descriptions provided by guides and inventories are a more effective approach than the listing of individual items in organic map series. Descriptions of individual items obscure relationships and common characteristics that may be inherent in a map series, and to this extent detract from the ability of the person using the descriptions to comprehend the over-all nature of the series.

KEY CONTROLS

Since area and subject are the two things that must be known initially to handle 98 percent of the requests for maps, if the information yielded by the Special Libraries Association survey, to which I have already alluded, is correct, certain types of controls should be established that provide information on those two things only. Such controls are not, in the true sense of the word, descriptive documents. They simply show what maps exist for a given area and on a given subject. They are of two types: (*a*) index maps and (*b*) card indexes.

Index maps

The use of index maps to show what maps exist in a repository on a given area was explained by Francis H. Parsons, director of the U.S. Naval Observatory, as early as 1895 in the *Library Journal*.[8] Parsons stated that maps can be effectively controlled

by the use of key charts, which on a single map of large scale, show at once all a library possesses relative to any given locality. And the fact that it has nothing can be ascertained with a much smaller expenditure of time and patience than is required to read many cards about which a seeker cares nothing. By introducing schemes of color and similar devices in the limits of maps, as shown upon the "key," a great deal of information may be graphically imparted, as, for example, nationality of authorities, where maps of exploration are concerned; or the approximate date of maps around cities, where resurveys are frequent; or any other class of information especially needed by the librarian. In this one respect maps hold an advantage over and above all other treasures of the library.

Index maps may be used effectively in making known what maps are available in series of public maps with a similar content. Since such series often pertain to particular subjects, such as the soil, topography, or geology of an area, index maps to such series provide information on both area and subject—the two most important initial elements in their use. "Graphic mediums, such as the index maps so often used for published maps issued in series, are particularly helpful finding aids," observes Friis while commenting about National Archives practices in handling maps.[9] But maps of varying size, scale, and subject can be indexed only with great difficulty.

Card indexes

Since index maps cannot be employed effectively in respect to heterogeneous collections of private maps or series of public maps of a disparate character, card indexes should be prepared to items in such collections and series. The matters in reference to which such items should initially be indexed are limited in number, i.e., area and subject. If index cards are encumbered with information on other attributes that are not essential for searching, the advantage of indexing will be dissipated, and this advantage, it will be recalled, is derived from the fact that indexes merely show the way to information in records; they do not describe them.

If cartographic records are arranged by area, an index card should be developed that will show what types of maps are available for particular areas. Each card should be designed to contain entries (on separate lines) on a number of maps. A typical entry on a map should show the folder number in which it is found, the number assigned to it, the secondary subject to which it pertains, and its date. The geographical areas in reference to which maps are indexed should be the same in relation to which maps have been arranged. A card should look somewhat as illustrated:

Geographical area:			
Folder No.	Map No.	Subject (or Type)	Date

INDIVIDUAL DESCRIPTIONS

Maps may be described individually in catalogs and lists. Catalogs are designed for use within a repository; lists for external distribution.

Both catalog and list entries should be grouped by the geographical areas to which maps pertain. In catalogs, cards should normally be grouped under geographical guide cards; in lists, under geographical captions. Occasionally it may be necessary to have subject rather than geographical heads.

The information provided about individual maps should be the same in catalogs and lists. An archivist may question, however, whether full bibliographical and technical information should be given about all maps, or whether it should be provided only for certain classes of maps, such as rare maps, manuscript maps, or annotated printed or photoprocessed maps.

There are, I believe, two kinds of catalogs and lists that should be prepared: (*a*) descriptive lists and catalogs and (*b*) summary lists and catalogs.

Descriptive lists and catalogs

Library rules for cataloging maps should be followed in preparing descriptive lists and catalogs, in which full information is provided about each individual map.

Parsons, writing in 1895, stated that

the same general catalog rules that apply to books apply equally to maps, the following being the essentials to be noted: locality; title; date; scale; projection; author; if compiled, the authorities; if great accuracy is desired, the engraver; and if a reproduction, the particular character of the process. The size of the neat line and the geographical limits of the sheet, in latitude and longitude, should always be given.[10]

In recent years, librarians have questioned if maps should be cataloged as books, according to author-title, or according to the elements most important to their use, i.e., area-subject. Arch C. Gerlach, chief of the Map Division of the Library of Congress, states: [11]

The author-title entry for books is a useful approach for catalogers and acquisitions personnel but not for map reference use, so alternate rules of entry must be provided for control over map reference collections. A map lies in character between a book and a picture and combines some features of both. The main entry for cataloging maps should begin with geographical area, followed by subject, date, size or scale, publisher or authority, and notes on edition, series, number of sheets and classification number. The main entry heading should be one that can be applied to every kind of map and one that is useful in the information it provides.

In the National Archives, descriptive lists have been prepared of items in a number of important map series. The following entry from a list of Civil War maps illustrates the descriptive technique that was employed.[12] The entry is in two parts: a title of the map and a descriptive paragraph or annotation, which is indented.

MOUNTAIN REGION OF NORTH CAROLINA AND TENNESSEE.
Compiled by W. L. Nicholson & A. Lindenkohl, 1863. U.S. Coast Survey. . . . Drawn by A. Lindenkohl, H. Lindenkohl & Chas. G. Krebs, Lith.

1 inch to 10 miles. 25 x 42 inches. Published with color. Also includes parts of Alabama, Georgia, Kentucky, South Carolina, and Virginia. State boundaries and railroad lines are in red. Drain-

age features, roads, and place names are included. Relief is indicated by hachures. A list of authorities is included.

Summary lists and catalogs

Summary lists and catalogs should be prepared for most map collections of recent origin. In them, maps should be identified, first, by the area to which they pertain and, secondly, by the kind of information about the area, i.e., by secondary subject. Other attributes should be enumerated in the order of their importance, and such attributes should be enumerated only if information about them is essential to the use of the maps. Bibliographical and technical attributes are relatively unimportant as keys to their use. Information about them is useful only after a specific map has been identified by a user as pertinent to his inquiry and then only for the purpose of determining the accuracy or authenticity of the data in the map or for the purpose of preparing a citation to the map. Besides information on area and subject, an entry on a map should normally pertain to its date, author, size, and scale. Information on its title, imprint (place and date of production, publisher, engraver, and the like), and form of projection is not essential in determining if it should be consulted. Such information is often confusing, for catalogs and lists in which maps are identified by their full title are difficult to use. The important information on area and subject is often buried in a title and cannot easily be disinterred. A user has to read an entire title, often quite lengthy, to obtain the particular information he desires.

COLLECTIVE DESCRIPTIONS

The two major kinds of collective descriptions are guides and inventories. A guide may cover all cartographic records in a repository, or portions thereof based on maps in several record groups related by organization, function, or subject. Partial guides, for example, may cover the records of the bureaus of the Department of Agriculture, maps related to natural resource planning, or maps of western explorations. If guides are planned that cover only parts of a repository's holdings, provision should be made for eventual complete coverage without repetition. An inventory ordinarily covers all the maps in a record group, as, for example, the cartographic records of the American Expeditionary Forces, 1917–21.

Administrative histories

In an administrative history of an agency, an archivist should provide succinct information on its map-making activities. For major map-making agencies, the administrative history should provide enough detail on the functions of the agency to make clear the general circumstances in which its cartographic records were created. For agencies in which maps play a lesser role, less explanation is necessary. In either instance, the administrative history should be relevant to the records described and should mention only in general the agency's other activities. In some instances, portions of the administrative history should precede those descriptions in the guide or inventory to which it particularly applies.

Administrative history data may be presented in the form of a chronological table in which functional and organizational developments are listed after the date at which they occurred. In the National Archives finding aids, administrative history data are presented in narrative form.

Guide entries

The usual entry in a guide covers a subgroup, i.e., all the records of a major organizational unit below that represented by the record group. The textual description may consist of a succession of series title lines, which are explained below, with particular emphasis on those elements of description that appear useful. The period covered by the maps described and the number of items should also be given with the name of the organization.

Inventory entries

The usual entry in an inventory covers a series.

An archivist will find some series readily identifiable in the arrangement given records by their agency; intensive study and grouping, which does not necessarily entail changing the arrangement, may be required for records that have difficult or obscure arrangements. Series are usually established on the basis of the following factors: their type or secondary subject, such as road, city, soil, geological, topographical, or cadastral maps, or diagrams and charts; their production in connection with some particular activity, such as a survey, exploration, or engineering project; or their relation to a particular geographical area.

Each series entry should consist of a title line and a descriptive paragraph.

In a title line, an archivist should provide for the maps in the series the following information: the area, the type or subject, the date, and the number of items. As a general rule, specific terms should be used; for example, if all the maps show the distribution of precipitation, they should not be called weather maps but precipitation maps. Much rephrasing may have to be done before the most appropriate title is found.

In a descriptive paragraph, those elements of map description not covered by the entry title should be mentioned; for example, specific areas if the title area had to be a general one; information shown on the map to extend or modify the subject; method of production; details of especially useful items; reasons for the creation of the maps; their use by the agency; personnel associated with their creation; etc.

All series entries in a given record group or major portion thereof should, when taken as a whole, provide a balanced description and a concise characterization of the records. The same kinds of maps should be described the same way, although they may not necessarily all be found in the same series.

The following entry, taken from a preliminary inventory, illustrates the techniques employed at the National Archives in describing series: [13]

NAVAJO (NAVAHO) INDIAN RESERVATION. 25 items.   362

Map composed of parts of state maps of Arizona, New Mexico, and Utah, dated 1882–84, and annotated to show the Navajo Indian Reservation with various additions from 1878 to 1886. Maps of the Navajo Indian Reservation, one of which shows a proposed extension. Maps of part of Utah and adjoining States showing the Navajo Reservation, subdivisions, additions, routes of survey and travel, roads, railroads, railroad lands, and sites selected for schools. Map, dated 1925, of the Navajo country in Arizona, New Mexico, and Utah which shows Indian allotments and forest reserves. Maps of the San Juan Navajo Reservation showing topography, grazing lands, farming lands, and bad lands. Photostat of map of Boundary Butte Dome, San Juan County, Utah, showing land ownership.

In arranging series entries in an inventory, an archivist should group them, on the first level, either by the administrative sub-groups that produced them or by the areas to which they relate. On secondary levels, they should be ordered in some fashion that gives a general view of the record group and facilitates rapid identification of series that are wanted. Series of maps covering larger areas may precede those covering smaller, printed series may precede manuscript series, maps from surveys may precede office compilations, or subjects may be put in alphabetical order. In descriptive works containing many similar series, separated by organization or area, the order should be parallel.

The use of 5 x 8 cards enables an archivist to write provisional series entries, while trying various ways of ordering the series. Neither the series entry nor its place in relation to other series will be evident at once, although it is usually possible to determine what is an adequate and useful series description and its best position. The series order may, but does not have to, follow the physical arrangement of the records.

Indexes and appendixes

Inventories generally do not have indexes, although there may be much material, particularly single variable elements, that can be extracted from series entries for treatment in appendixes. A guide is indexed in the same way that any other work is indexed; the major classes of headings will be organizations, areas, and subjects. It should be noted that an index serves to supplement rather than repeat the table of contents and the internal arrangement of the guide.

XX

ARRANGEMENT AND
DESCRIPTION OF
PICTORIAL RECORDS

Pictorial records are maintained by various kinds of organizations—libraries, archival institutions, and museums, as well as business and industrial firms.[1] Since they are difficult to interpret without the aid of iconographic literature, a custodian of such records should have available books containing reproductions of pictures; directories of pictorial source material, particularly the "Picture Sources" of the Special Libraries Association, which is now in process of revision; bibliographies and reference books relating to pictures; and auction, trade, and exhibit catalogs.

The methods of arranging and describing pictorial records have not been fully defined, much less standardized. The Special Libraries Association is giving attention to them, as are other organizations concerned with iconographic records. The methods, obviously, should be developed in reference to the distinctive attributes of such records.

Attributes

PHYSICAL ATTRIBUTES

The physical attributes of pictorial records relate to their type, the media on which they are produced, their size, their composition (or the way in which they were brought together), and their quantity.

Types

Pictorial records may be divided into a number of types. The general types are photographs, original productions, and press productions. Each of these may be divided into a number of specific types.

The term "photographic," from which the nouns "photographs" and "photography" came, was first used by Sir John F. W. Herschel, noted English astronomer, in 1839. Several years later, in 1852, the term was criticized by the editor of the *Photographic Art Journal*, who said it was not good but "it is too firmly fixed in the public mind to attempt a substitute." [2] The term "photograph" should be applied to all pictures made by exposure to a camera equipped with a light-sensitive medium. Excluded are pictures made by the camera obscura, a process first described by Leonardo da Vinci but probably known from very early times, and the camera lucida, invented in 1806. If unique, pictures made by these processes should be classed as "original productions"; if represented in some form of graphic presentation, as "press productions." While ambrotypes and daguerreotypes, which represented photography for all practical purposes from 1830 to 1856, were not made by a negative-positive process, they should nonetheless be included among photographic record types. [3] The two main types of photographs are negatives and prints, but there are many special types of both. Slides, for example, may include film, glass, and stereopticon slides for magic lantern, all intended for projection.

The term "orginal productions" should be applied to all pictures that are created manually by drawing or painting. The Library of Congress uses the term "original works" for this class, and the term "hand productions" is also used. The specific types in this class are paintings, which include oils and water colors, and drawings of various kinds. Several additional specific types are listed in the Library of Congress *Rules for Descriptive Cataloging: Pictures, Designs, and Other Two-Dimensional Representations.* [4]

Since pictures made by other than photographic processes, or made manually, are usually produced on presses of one kind or another, the term "press productions" may be applied to them. Press productions should be distinguished from the original productions that, usually, must be created before copies of them can be made on presses. The pictures made by hand for reproduction by etching, engraving, or lithographic processes, for example, fall into the class of "original productions," but the copies of them into the class of "press productions." Similarly, pictures made exclusively by photographic processes, though produced in many copies, fall into the class of "photographs." The specific types of press productions with which an archivist is concerned are cartoons, engravings, etchings, lithographs, posters, figurative and pictorial maps, and woodcuts.

Pictorial record types, it should be noted, can be distinguished by taking into account the technical processes that were used in their production. A specific type can be identified by asking: How was the record produced? If it is a photograph, is it a slide, or an ordinary photographic print or negative? If it is an original production, is it a painting or drawing? If it is a press production, by what process was it made? This is in contrast to textual record types, which can be distinguished by asking what organic activities resulted in their production; and to cartographic record types, which can be distinguished by asking what is the major subject in relation to which they were produced.

Before he describes them, an archivist should understand the processes by which any and all pictures in his care were made. He should, in a word, recognize, if he should chance upon it, one of the lost engravings of Thomas Jefferson, produced in numbers by Quenedy in 1801; a likeness made from the physiognotrace of Joel Barlow, made in 1801; an aquatint of Washington, D.C.; or a copperplate of the Battle of Lexington.

Other physical characteristics

Among other physical characteristics of pictorial records, which are important in arrangement and description, are the following:

The *physical media* on which they are produced. In the photographic class, negatives and prints may be made of paper, film, glass, celluloid, metal, or other substances; in the class of original productions, various media are also used; while in the class of press productions, the chief medium is paper.

Their *size*, which may range from a small picture a few inches in dimensions to a panoramic photograph many feet in length.

Their *composition*, or the way in which they were brought together, which may be as loose pictures (mounted or unmounted); as aggregations of pictures in albums, scrapbooks, volumes, binders, envelopes, or folders; or as organized files.

Their *quantity*.

SUBSTANTIVE ATTRIBUTES

From a substantive point of view, pictorial records are different from both cartographic and textual records.

Provenance

Information on the provenance of pictorial records in some government agency, corporate body, or person is relatively unimportant, for such records do not derive much of their meaning from their organizational origins. Such information is useful mainly in helping to interpret pictures—to identify the time and place at which they were produced and the subjects to which they relate.

Information on the functional origins of pictorial records is also relatively unimportant. While they may relate to activity, such records are ordinarily not produced for purposes of action and are often not truly organic in character. They are usually produced to record information or to stimulate emotional response. Thus, a photographer or an artist may produce pictures for artistic pleasure and a caricaturist may create drawings to arouse a humorous or sarcastic response.

Subject matter

Pictorial records, as well as cartographic records, are mainly important from the point of view of their subject matter, not from the point of view of their provenance and functional origins.

But they differ from cartographic records in one important

respect. Pictorial records relate to multiple subjects; cartographic records, to one main subject. While cartographic records can be analyzed fairly effectively in relation to place or area, pictorial records must be analyzed in relation to a number of subjects, such as persons, things, and phenomena, as well as places. This difference has an important bearing on how pictorial records should be arranged and described.

Dates

The dates, in this context, refer to the time during which a picture was produced.

Arrangement

Because of their variety and complexity, pictorial records are arranged in many ways in American repositories. The three major classes of such records are quite different from each other, and each presents special problems of management. The photographic class, which is of primary interest to us here, has several characteristics that complicate work with it. Photographs exist in many sizes; they are found in two distinct forms, as negatives and prints; and prints are used for two distinct purposes, for reproduction and for reference service.

An archivist obviously should maintain the major classes of pictorial records separately because of their distinctive characteristics. He should arrange original productions in one class, press productions in another, and photographs in another.

An archivist should maintain photographic negatives separately from prints. Negatives are used for reproduction, not for search purposes, and for this reason are often housed in areas adjacent to laboratory facilities.

An archivist should group negatives and prints by size. In small repositories he should establish two groups: an oversized group, to be maintained in special containers, such as map cases; and a regular-sized group, to be maintained in archival containers. In large repositories he may find it advisable to establish a number of groups on the basis of size. Thus, he may file photographic negatives, when in quantity, in a number of groups according to their common sizes, such as 4 x 4, 5 x 7, 6 x 8, 9 x 11, etc.

An archivist, furthermore, should maintain unique prints, i.e., those for which negatives are unavailable, separately from reference prints. He should treat such prints as if they were negatives, using them for reproduction, not for reference purposes.

Whenever funds are available, an archivist should make a copy negative of each unique print and a reference print of each negative as a part of the accessioning procedure. He should treat copy negatives as if they were originals.

ARRANGEMENT OF NEGATIVES AND UNIQUE PRINTS

Negatives and unique prints should be regarded as the archives of a pictorial repository. They should be maintained in its stacks and should be used solely for reproductive purposes. There are three systems of arranging them that should be noted: (*a*) numerical arrangement, (*b*) arrangement according to provenance, and (*c*) classification by subject.

Numerical arrangement

While librarians, who are accustomed to classifying material by subject, may contend that "any numerical system is fatal," a numerical arrangement is actually the one best suited to a collection of pictorial records brought together from many sources, usually as single items or in small groups.

Whenever records—whether textual or pictorial—relate to multiple subjects, they should not be arranged, or classified, in relation to a particular subject. They should be dealt with in the way in which case files are handled. A particular case file on a railroad labor dispute, for example, may relate to many subjects —to the disputants, to wages or other matters under dispute, to the railroad, and the like. Such a file cannot easily be organized in relation to any particular subject. It is therefore given a number, and its multiple subject relationships are revealed in indexes that are keyed to the number assigned to it. Similarly, photographs, or pictorial records generally, should be filed by number, and their multiple subject relationships should be revealed in indexes (or other finding aids). Such records cannot be arranged in relation to a single class of subjects, i.e., place or area, as can cartographic records.

In view of the difficulties in classifying pictorial records, an archivist should, in all except very large repositories, arrange accessions of negatives and unique prints numerically. A numerical arrangement is a simple system of arrangement. No classification is involved in it, simply a progressive addition of negatives and prints to the groups established for them.

An archivist should register each accession, regardless of how small it may be, and number it in the order of its receipt. Since an accession record is "often the only record a library will have of the source of a photograph," says W. J. Burke, "the accession number will be the only accurate identification of the photograph."[5]

An archivist should handle accessions of negatives and prints as follows:

He should place a small accession of unique prints in a separate folder and maintain it in a collection of miscellaneous prints. He should label the folder to show the place or subject to which the accession primarily relates, the dates of the prints, and the accession symbol. He should place a large accession of unique prints in separate containers, label the containers, and shelve them with other accessions of prints.

He should file all negatives individually in envelopes, the substance of which will not react with the chemicals of the negatives. He should place a small accession of negatives in a separate folder, label the folder, and pack it in a collection of miscellaneous negatives. He should place a large accession of negatives in containers suited to their size and weight, and conducive to their preservation and to efficiency in use.[6] He should label the containers and shelve them, placing the accession in the numerical sequence in which it was registered, either with a single series of accessions or in one of several series established on the basis of the size of negatives.

He should develop a notational system for pictorial records similar to that devised for textual records, which is discussed in Chapter IX. If a repository collects original and press productions as well as photographs, he should use letter symbols to denote classes, as follows: P for photographs, OP for original productions, and PP for press productions. If a repository collects only photographs, he should use two sets of symbols: one for large accessions and the other for small. He should assign simple numbers, i.e., 1, 2, 3, to large accessions, and prefix the letter M to numbers assigned to small accessions. To avoid making his notational system too complex, he should not use symbols to differentiate between negatives and unique prints and between various sizes of negatives, though such records will be separated in the stacks.

In addition to using letter symbols to denote classes of pictorial records or to denote miscellaneous collections and to using number symbols to denote the sequence of accessions, an archivist should number all prints and negatives in each accession in serial order. In an accession with the symbol 3, he should assign the following symbols to individual items: 3-1, 3-2, 3-3, etc.; in an accession with the symbol M-3, the following symbols: M-3-1, M-3-2, M-3-3, etc.

If his holdings are sizable, an archivist should maintain a location register to show precisely where negatives and unique prints are deposited in the stacks.

Arrangement by provenance

Large groups of negatives and unique prints produced by a government can be handled more easily if kept by provenance. Such groups of records should be kept in separate units that correspond to their source in administrative agencies. Each group should be treated as an integral unit and should be kept intact. Records from one source should not be merged with those from another. Series that were created by agencies should also be kept intact and should be placed in a convenient relation to one another within groups.

Within groups and series, an archivist should maintain negatives and unique prints in the order given them during their current life, if it is a serviceable one. If it is not, he should arrange them numerically, as recommended above.

If records are arranged by provenance, an archivist should

employ two sets of symbols: one relating to the records and the other to physical location. By means of one set of symbols, he should show the record group, subgroup (if any), and series to which a particular picture belongs. By means of the other set of symbols, he should show the precise area, row, compartment, and container in which the particular picture is located. The two sets of symbols should be related to each other in a location register.

Classification by subject

In commercial firms large files of negatives and prints are often classified by subject while in current use. The classification practices of such firms are ably discussed by Ben Melnitsky in an article on "Classifying Negatives and Prints." [7] The subjects used to classify photographs are usually chosen to fit the special needs of a particular firm. W. J. Burke says that picture classification "is no exact science," and that "each picture collection presents its own peculiar problems." [8]

In classifying negatives and prints, commercial firms usually devise a notational system that identifies the subject class, the subclass within the subject class, and the serial number of a print or negative. The Standard Oil Company of New Jersey, for example, uses an adaptation of the notational scheme of the Cutter Expansive Classification system. In this system, the initial letter denotes a main subject, and numbers denote divisions within the main subject. It is illustrated by the following excerpt from the system:

L10   Laboratories
L101   Laboratory, Baton Rouge
L11   Laboratory, Bayway
L112   Laboratory, Bayway, Aviation fuel testing
L1142 Laboratory, Bayway, Esso Research Center opening

Other systems of notation may be employed to accomplish the same purpose. A commercial airline employs two digits to denote main subjects:

01   to denote airplanes in flight
03   to denote company officials

These digits are followed by the serial number of a particular print or negative, e.g., 01-0045 or 03-0091. Dewey's decimal notations may be used similarly.

ARRANGEMENT OF REFERENCE PRINTS

Reference prints should be regarded as tools for searching the archives of a pictorial repository. They should be placed in its search room, so that they are immediately accessible to a user. They may be maintained in loose-leaf binders or in vertical files, either in folders or envelopes. They should be keyed by symbol to the negative or unique prints from which they were made.

Reference prints of pictorial records are vitally important for effective reference service work. Pictures are difficult to describe verbally, and only by seeing copies of them can a user tell which specific picture meets his needs. If reference prints of pictures in a series or collection are available, a user can view individual items and thus identify the specific items of which he wishes reproductions made for his own use. By having reference prints available, an archivist can reduce the amount of time required for searching or for personal consultation, for normally he should give extensive time only to inquiries that are unusually difficult, broad in scope, or significant.

Types of prints

An archivist should determine which type of reference print is best suited to meet the needs of his repository and, once this is done, should systematically produce the type of his choice for use in his search room. The three types that should be considered are full-sized, miniature, and multiple prints.

Full-sized prints are rather expensive to produce, and should be produced in a large repository only for series that are unusually significant or active. In a small repository, full-sized prints are easier to produce than miniature or multiple prints.

Miniature prints are simply small-sized photographic copies of pictures that are placed on cards containing caption data. Certain commercial firms, notably Time, Incorporated, maintain reference files of miniature prints. Their size is 3 x 5, and the cost of their production is fairly reasonable. Certain military libraries of the federal government have developed files of 8 x 11 cards for reference use containing copies of pictures and information about them.

Multiple prints are miniature prints of pictures placed on a single sheet. The cost of their production is very high, and normally it is difficult to place on them the caption data that are necessary to make a print file meaningful.

Methods of arrangement

If reference prints are arranged in a rational order during their current life, an archivist should maintain the original order, especially if it permits him to find records when they are wanted. But he should have no compunction about rearranging prints, if by such work he can make them more intelligible and more serviceable.

In a small repository, an archivist should organize reference prints in relation to a few subjects that are exclusive of one another. It is difficult to do this, since pictorial records, as we have noted, cut across most subject classes. But there are a few classes that can be established that are fairly exclusive of other classes.

The first of these relates to *persons*. It is usually possible to organize personal prints into a separate class, provided that only prints that relate exclusively to persons are included. Such prints should be arranged alphabetically by name of person.

Another class, which is fairly exclusive of other classes, relates to *places* or geographical areas. Information on place or area provides an important key to the user of pictorial, as it does to the user of cartographic, records. Arranging prints according to area, therefore, is one of the best and easiest ways of arranging them. Thus, the reference prints for Farm Security Administration photographs at the Library of Congress are organized into regional classes, or classes established, more generally, in relation to geographical areas. The Library of Congress classes, in this case, follow fairly closely the regions of the United States as defined by Howard W. Odum in his *American Regionalism.*[9]

Another class, which is fairly exclusive of other classes, relates to *time* or chronological periods. If information on the time to which pictures relate is considered more important to their use than information on place, reference prints should be organized into chronological classes.

Place and *time* classes are often subdivided into topical subclasses in large repositories. Thus, the Library of Congress divides its geographical classes, established for the FSA reference prints mentioned above, into a number of subclasses on the basis of economic and sociological considerations. Within each class it has subclasses for land; towns and cities; people; homes and ways of living; tranportation and agriculture; manufacturing, processing, selling, and government; war; the intellectual world; and amusement and relaxation. Its classification system has been adopted, with modifications, by other pictorial repositories.[10] The degree to which place and time classes should be subdivided topically depends upon the size of a pictorial collection. Generally, curators of pictorial records tend to overclassify, i.e., to establish too many subdivisions, on the mistaken assumption that prints will be easier to consult if organized into fine classes.

Purely *topical* classes have also been established, especially for library files of clippings of pictures and commercial files of reference prints. To date, no classification scheme for pictorial records has been devised that will serve the needs of all repositories. This has been amply demonstrated in the annual workshops held by the Picture Division of the Special Libraries Association for the past ten years. In her introduction to a seminar on the classification of "Pictures in Print," Romana Javitz of the New York Public Library, said: "Methods and systems for the organization of knowledge as recorded in words do not serve for the organization of the pictorial record. As yet, principles have not been established for the handling of the vast masses of pictorial documents that have accumulated in the century of the camera and the decades of photo-mechanical means for the reproduction of the image."[11]

The classification practices with regard to clippings of pictures are best reflected in the work of the New York Public Library. In 1916 the library began collecting clippings, and now has the largest and most comprehensive picture collection in the United States. It consists largely of published pictures clipped from magazines and books and comprises over three million items. The pictures are arranged first by portraits and then alphabetically by subjects. The subject heads are specific and total more than eight thousand. For example, the following specific subjects relating to "hearts" are included:

> Hearts (Anatomical)
> Hearts (Romantic)
> Hearts (Playing Cards)
> Hearts of Lettuce

Specific subject heads are subdivided, or compounded, only when this is unavoidable. If subdivisions must be made, they are made by taking into account various factors, such as name, region, style, type, and year or decade. The subject "dance," for example, is subdivided by region, style, type, and decade. In addition, heads are included for specific types of dances, such as "calypso."

The picture collection of the New York Public Library is maintained in bins or tubs which are directly accessible to users, who serve themselves, working at tables placed beside the bins so that a hundred or more pictures can be spread out for examination and selection. The pictures are maintained loose in folders, open at the top and at one end for facility in handling. The library lends the material in folders and keeps a record only of the number of folders borrowed, regardless of the number of pictures within the folders.

Somewhat similar and equally active, each stored in 250 legal-sized file drawers, are the picture collections at Twentieth Century-Fox and at Warner Brothers in Hollywood. These, and a somewhat smaller collection maintained in the Walt Disney Research Library, are described by Romana Javitz and Polly Magrish of the Picture Division of Special Libraries Association.[12]

Description

The descriptive work that has to be done on pictorial records differs somewhat from that on textual records. Much of the work relates to an identification of the subjects of such records on captions to reference prints. Catalogs, lists, and indexes are ordinarily the only kinds of finding aids that need to be produced for pictorial records. In small repositories, inventories are not needed and lists serve adequately as comprehensive finding aids. Guides are needed only in large repositories.

CAPTIONS TO REFERENCE PRINTS

Subjects are more difficult to identify in pictures than in maps. The subject matter and the source of a map are recorded in the course of its production. Pictorial records are notably deficient in this respect. An individual picture is seldom completely identified as it is produced; partial identification, when obtainable from accompanying descriptive matter, may be misleading, if not actually erroneous. According to Paula M. Strain, "Titles are not the integral part of photographs as they are of books, and yet they are essential in making the photograph available. The title is assigned after the picture is made and whether or not it is adequate depends on the person assigning it. Besides, some pictures cannot be captioned completely even by the man who planned and took the picture." [13]

Subjects of pictures must therefore be identified after the pictures have been produced; if they are not identified immediately, or shortly after production, they are likely to remain unidentified. Thereafter they must be identified either by a visual inspection of the pictures or by an analysis of evidence on the time and place at which they were produced, on the method of production, and on the source from which they were obtained.

By visually inspecting pictorial records, and by analyzing when, where, and how they were produced and whence they were obtained, an archivist can often reveal much of the subject content of even uncaptioned photographs. He can identify well-known subjects, such as famous personages or historic sites and buildings; he can identify classes of things, such as log houses or sailing vessels; and he can usually indicate, in general terms, at least, the time and place to which pictures relate.

The extent to which the archivist should go in identifying

specific subjects in pictures should be considered from a budgetary point of view. The desirability of identifying the personages who stand on the platform of the railroad station at Hanover Junction, Pennsylvania, in the picture mystery of "Is this Lincoln on his way to Gettysburg?" is admitted; but after a reasonable number of hours has been spent in pursuing all available angles, the cost of the activity must be weighed against the chances of identification after a hundred years. With a collection of one thousand pictures of sailboat races covering a period of ten years and lacking identification of the boats by name, the cost of the labor of identifying the boats should be weighed against the value of the accomplishment. Unless there is an excellent chance that an accurate and full identification of specific subjects can be made with a reasonable outlay of money, archivists should not attempt to identify them. Press productions and original productions, however, are usually worth the time spent on identification.

Subjects of pictures should be identified in captions. Normally, a caption should identify the main subject, which may be a person, thing, phenomenon, or place, and should indicate the date of the information recorded in the picture. G. Hubert Smith, curator of the Museum of the Minnesota Historical Society, refers to "the five W's" as important reminders in the description of pictures.[14] These have been phrased very succinctly by Camilla P. Luecke, who says that eight main questions should be answered in a caption: [15]

1. Who?—names and titles of persons; if important, add subject's home town and state, or home town and country if the subject comes from a country other than the United States.
2. What?—the occasion.
3. Why?—the circumstances, reasons for event, why noteworthy.
4. When?—date picture was taken. (Distinguish between this and received or released date. If exact date is not known, say "about" or "between.")
5. Where?—town and state where photograph was made.
6. How?—method, for example, manufacturing process.

7. Source—name of photographer or sources from which the photograph was procured.
8. Negative information—is it an original or copy negative?

Captions should be placed on mounts, if photographs are mounted, or on the back of prints.

INDEXES

Indexes to pictorial records should be like those to textual records in that they identify by symbol, without superfluous descriptive information, the records that relate to particular matters. Such indexes should be keyed to the symbols assigned to negatives and unique prints.

An alphabetically arranged index to persons should be prepared first, followed by a geographically arranged index to places. Thereafter, indexes, arranged by subject, should be prepared to things (physical structures, manufactured articles, and the like) and phenomena (episodes and events) in relation to which an interest exists among users of the pictorial holdings. Modern information retrieval methods, similar to those mentioned in Chapter XVII, should be employed to compile extensive subject indexes.

INDIVIDUAL DESCRIPTIONS

Pictorial records may be described individually in catalogs and lists. Catalogs are designed for use within a repository; lists, for external distribution.

Library rules for cataloging pictures should be followed in preparing lists and catalogs. The most recent and the most useful rules for cataloging are those of the Library of Congress, prepared by an Interdepartmental Committee consisting of staff members from the Library of Congress, with representatives of the National Archives, the People-to-People Program, and the State Historical Society of Wisconsin serving as consultants.[16] The rules prepared by this committee from 1952 to 1954 were revised several times, in order to conform to the established rules of the American Library Association. In 1959 the rules were published by the Library of Congress, with the approval of the American Library Association. They provide for a *main entry* by author, artist, photographer, engraver, corporate body, producer, etc., and provide for information essential in a proper caption for a picture. Such information should normally indicate the maker, the subject to which the picture relates, unless it relates exclusively to persons, the dates of production as well as subject date, and the technical information required for an understanding of its character. The rules provide also for notes that are, seemingly, more essential for pictorial material than for any other class of records.

An example of a Library of Congress catalog entry, compiled according to its own rules, follows:

Rosenthal, Joe, *photographer.*
[U.S. Marines raising the flag on Mt. Suribachi, Iwo Jima, February 23, 1945.]
1 photo 14 x 11 in.
The Marine Corps War Memorial, Arlington, Va., was designed from this picture.
Gift, Associated Press, 1951.

COLLECTIVE DESCRIPTIONS

Collective descriptions should be prepared in large repositories that arrange pictorial records by provenance. Such descriptions may appear in inventories and guides. An inventory should cover all pictures in a particular group; a guide, all groups in a repository.

In preparing an entry for an archival group, an archivist should (*a*) provide a brief history of the photographic or other pictorial activities of the agency that produced the group and (*b*) identify and describe the series within the group.

Administrative histories

In an administrative history of an agency, an archivist should provide brief information on each of its pictorial activities, describing their nature and stating when they began and ended (if they are not continuing activities). He may present this information in the form of a chronological table, listing and describing each activity or development after the date at which it occurred. He should not include information on organizational and functional developments that does not relate to pictorial work.

Guide entries

In compiling guide entries, an archivist should establish pictorial series, group them for descriptive purposes, and prepare separate entries for each of them.

An archivist should establish pictorial series on the basis of the following factors: their serial (or other) arrangement in the agency that produced them; their production in the course of a photographic activity of an agency; or their relation to a common subject, such as a particular event or episode, or a particular person, or a particular place or thing.

Series entries should be grouped, for descriptive purposes, either by the administrative subdivisions that produced them, by the subjects to which they relate, or by type.

Each series entry, normally, should be in two parts, the first consisting of a title line and the second of a descriptive paragraph.

In the *title line*, an archivist should provide the following information about a pictorial series: the subject to which it relates; the date of the information recorded in it; its type; and its quantity.

For purposes of describing pictorial records, four general classes of *subjects* should be noted.

The first general class relates to persons, either individually or collectively. The persons may be notable historical figures, such as Abraham Lincoln and Woodrow Wilson; or groups or classes of persons, such as Indians or members of professional or religious groups of various kinds. When a group of persons is pictured in a series, the kind of group should be indicated as precisely as possible. Examples:

GROVER CLEVELAND'S CHILDREN, 1895–1903
ABRAHAM LINCOLN, n.d.

The second general class of subjects pertains to places, either real or fictional. If an archivist indicates the place to which a picture relates, he is likely to reveal much of its meaning, for often both persons and phenomena are identifiable with places. Examples:

KISKA HARBOR, ALASKA, 1904
"SHANGRI-LA"

The third general class of subjects pertains to things, either man-made or natural. The things may include buildings and other man-made structures and objects, the flora and fauna of an area, its topographic features, and other natural things. Pictures may be identified in relation to a specific thing, such as the White House, or a class of things, such as sod houses or prairie schooners. The location of things should be indicated. Examples:

FEDERAL BUILDINGS, WASHINGTON, D.C., 1893–1914
HANGARS, EUROPEAN WAR THEATER, 1918–19

The fourth class of subjects pertains to phenomena, or happenings to persons or things. The phenomena may be described in general terms, such as rural activities; or in specific terms, such as rubber procurement in Colombia; or in relation to a specific event, such as the Philippine insurrection; or in relation to a specific episode, such as the Battle of the Bulge. Examples:

CONSERVATION ACTIVITIES, 1933
CORROSION TESTS, ENGLISH TORPEDO DESTROYERS, 1909–19
MEXICAN PUNITIVE EXPEDITION, 1914–17
BIKINI BOMB TESTS, 1946

If a series has a title given it by the agency that created it and it is meaningful, it may be placed immediately after the title devised by the archivist. In such cases it should be enclosed in parentheses and quotation marks, as follows:

("Erickson Collection")
("Brady Civil War Collection")

After giving the subject of a series in a title line, an archivist should show the *dates* during which the records were produced. As with textual and cartographic record series, the dates should be inclusive and should indicate significant gaps, if such exist.

After giving the subject and dates of a series, an archivist should indicate its *type* and *quantity*.

Whenever possible, he should identify specific types of photographic negatives, prints, and slides, if this can be done. He need not, however, identify the specific types of original productions; for descriptive purposes the term "painting" is adequate to cover both oils and water colors, and the term "drawing" to cover all kinds of drawings.

If the records consist of photographic copies of original productions (paintings, drawings, and the like) or of press productions (collotypes, etchings, and the like), an archivist should indicate, first, the specific type of photograph and, then, the specific type of original or press production. Thus:

> Prints of paintings
> Negatives of drawings
> Prints of collotypes

After indicating the record type in a title line, an archivist should indicate the quantity of pictorial records in a series in terms of items, if less than six inches, and in terms of linear feet or inches, if more than six inches. The figure that represents the nearest full linear foot should be used unless the quantity is less than one linear foot, in which case the figure should be given in inches.

Examples of complete title lines follow:

SAN FRANCISCO EARTHQUAKE DAMAGE, 1906. 97 prints in one album.
HAYDEN SURVEY, 1868–78. Negatives (3 ft., 6 in.).
LIGHTHOUSES, Calif., Fla., N.Y., 1855–79. 21 prints of drawings.
OKLAHOMA TERRITORY (Anthony Rice Collection), 1893. 24 prints.

In a *descriptive paragraph*, an archivist should present information, if useful in interpreting records, that is not available elsewhere in an inventory or guide. It may pertain to the following matters about a series:

Its *production*, showing its corporate or personal origins, or the circumstances under which it was produced, if not fully explained elsewhere.

Its *subject*, giving details about the persons, places, things, or phenomena that were not included in the series title. If a series relates to a group of persons, for example, an archivist may identify the kind of group more precisely, or mention important persons that are found in it. Or if it pertains to a place, he may identify it more precisely. If, for instance, a title shows that a series relates to California, he may identify the specific cities or parts of the state that are pictured. Or if a series pertains to buildings, ships, or other material objects, he may say what kind they are or what characteristics they have. Or if it pertains to phenomena, he may identify the specific event, episode, or happening that is pictured. Or if it is arranged according to a subject filing system, he may enumerate its significant subheads.

Its *dates*, giving information about time other than that during which the series was produced. If he is describing photographic copies of original and press productions, for example, an archivist may give the dates when the productions were created, or the dates of the subjects recorded in them. Thus, he may give the date of a collotype of George Washington, or the dates of the coverage of a series of lantern slides.

Its *composition*, providing information about the form or type of pictorial records, the file units into which they were brought together, or the files into which they were organized. An archivist may provide certain technical data in the descriptive paragraph, such as:

> Size and kind of prints
> The way prints are maintained, i.e., whether mounted or loose
> Size and kind of negatives, i.e., whether glass, film, paper

He should furnish such data only if they will prove useful to the average run of users. If the pictures chiefly serve technical users, such as is the case in respect to aerial mapping photographs, the technical data should be quite complete. He may also provide information on the character of the file units within a series, showing whether they are portfolios, albums, volumes, scrapbooks, notebooks, binders, or the like. He may also indicate how a series is arranged.

An example of a complete guide entry follows:

OKLAHOMA TERRITORY (Anthony Rice Collection), 1893. 24 prints. "Boomer" activities at Arkansas City, Orlando, Perry, and Wharton as the Cherokee Strip was opened for settlement. Prints were made by the W. A. Flower Photograph Co., collected by Anthony Rice (one time chief of the Homestead Division of the General Land Office), and donated to the government by his daughter. Numbered but unarranged.

NOTES

Part I: Development of Principles and Techniques

The quotation by Adams is from the Massachusetts Historical Society, *Proceedings*, 1899–1900 (Boston, 1900), XIII, Ser. 2, 116. Hereafter cited as MHS, *Proc.*

Chapter I: Development of Library Methodology

1. Justin Winsor, *Narrative and Critical History of America* (8 vols., Boston, 1884–89).

2. MHS, *Proc.*, IV, Ser. 2, 103–5.

3. Justin Winsor to Robert C. Winthrop, Dec. 23, 1890, *ibid.*, VI, Ser. 2, 260.

4. American Historical Association, *Annual Report*, 1894 (Washington, 1895), pp. 281–98. Hereafter cited as AHA, *Ann. Rept.*

5. William F. Poole to James B. Angell, Nov. 23, 1893; Justin Winsor, "Historical Papers, Scraps, etc.," V, 131, in Massachusetts Historical Society.

6. U.S. Bureau of Education, *Public Libraries in the United States of America* (Washington, 1876), pp. 760 ff.

7. *Ibid.*, p. 1011.

8. Statement by John Langdon Sibley, former librarian of Harvard, quoted in *Library Journal*, IV (July–Aug., 1879), 305.

9. Statistics for the periods 1836, 1863, and 1876 were obtained from Bur. of Ed., *Public Libraries*, pp. 764–65; for 1893, from U.S. Bureau of Education, *Papers Prepared for the World's Library Congress* (Washington, 1896), p. 864; and for the 1900s, from articles in *College and Research Libraries*.

10. Robert C. Binkley, review of *The Care and Cataloguing of Manuscripts, as Practiced by the Minnesota Historical Society*, by

Grace Lee Nute (St. Paul, 1936), in *Minnesota History*, XVII (Dec., 1936), 448.

11. AHA, *Ann. Rept.*, 1912, pp. 253–63.

12. William I. Fletcher, *Public Libraries in America* (Boston, 1894), p. 86*n*.

13. Grace O. Kelley, *The Classification of Books* (New York, 1937), p. 29.

14. Thelma Eaton, "The Development of Classification in America," in *The Role of Classification in the Modern American Library* (Champaign, Ill., 1959), p. 24. (Papers presented at an institute conducted by the University of Illinois Graduate School of Library Science, November 1–4, 1959.

15. Bur. of Ed., *World's Library Congress*, pp. 869–70.

16. *Ibid.*, p. 869.   17. *Ibid.*, pp. 872–73.

18. *Library Journal*, XVI (April, 1891), 113. See also Bur. of Ed., *Public Libraries*, pp. 493–94.

19. Bur. of Ed., *Public Libraries*, pp. 467–68.

20. Bur. of Ed., *World's Library Congress*, p. 881.

21. *Library Journal*, XLV (April, 1910), 152.

22. *Ibid.*, VII (June, 1882), 148–66.

23. *Ibid.*, XI (April, 1886), 103.

24. Bur. of Ed., *Public Libraries*, p. 640.   25. *Ibid.*

26. *Ibid.*, pp. 623–48.

27. Library Bureau, *The Story of the Library Bureau* (Boston, 1909), *passim*.

28. *Library Journal*, XI (April, 1886), 100–1.

29. Bur. of Ed., *Public Libraries*, p. 735.

30. *Library Journal*, XI (Feb., 1886), 37–43, and XI (March, 1886), 68–74.

31. Bur. of Ed., *World's Library Congress*, p. 873.

32. *Ibid.*, p. 870.

33. Ernest Cushing Richardson, *Classification: Theoretical and Practical* (New York, 1901), p. 207.

34. *Ibid.*, p. 88.

35. Bur. of Ed., *Public Libraries*, pp. 577–622.

36. M. S. R. James, "The Progress of the Modern Card Catalog Principle," in *The Library and Its Contents*, ed. by Harriet Price Sawyer (New York, 1925), p. 333.

37. Bur. of Ed., *Public Libraries*, p. 512.

38. James, "The Progress of the Modern Card Catalog Principle," in *The Library and Its Contents*, p. 334.

39. Bur. of Ed., *World's Library Congress*, p. 928.

40. Fletcher, *Public Libraries in America*, p. 57.

41. *Ibid.*, p. 89.

Chapter II: Factors Influencing Archival Methodology

1. Leslie W. Dunlap, *American Historical Societies, 1790–1860* (Madison, Wis., 1944).

2. Walter M. Whitehill, *Independent Historical Societies* (Boston, 1962).

3. MHS, *Proc.*, I, Ser. 1, xx.

4. Moses Coit Tyler, "The Neglect and Destruction of Historical Materials in This Country," AHA, *Papers*, II, No. 1, 20–22.

5. AHA, *Papers*, II, No. 1, 91–92.　　6. *Ibid.*, III, No. 1, 75.

7. AHA, *Ann. Rept.*, 1905, I, 255–61.

8. *Historical Societies in the United States and Canada: A Handbook*, comp. and ed. by Christopher Crittenden and Doris Godard (Washington, 1944).

9. *Directory of Historical Societies and Agencies in the United States and Canada, 1956*, comp. by American Association for State and Local History (Columbus, Ohio, 1956).

10. Dunlap, *American Historical Societies*, p. 76.

11. AHA, *Ann. Rept.*, 1893, p. 4.

12. James B. Angell to Justin Winsor, Nov. 24, 1892; Justin Winsor, "Historical Papers, Scraps, etc.," V, 110–12, in Massachusetts Historical Society.

13. William F. Poole to James B. Angell, Nov. 23, 1893, *ibid.*, V, 131.

14. AHA, *Ann. Rept.*, 1900, II, 5–6.

15. University of Virginia Library, *Annual Report of the Archivist, 1939–40* (Charlottesville, 1940), p. 4.

16. Society of American Archivists, State Records Committee, *Guide to State and Provincial Archival Agencies, 1961* (Raleigh, N.C., 1961), pp. 1–2.

17. U.S. Bureau of Education, *Public Libraries in the United States of America* (Washington, 1876), p. 297.

18. *Library Journal*, XI (May, 1886), 131.

19. AHA, *Papers*, III, No. 1, 10.

20. MHS, *Proc.*, X, Ser. 1, 294–95.

21. Bur. of Ed., *Public Libraries*, p. 257.

22. Dorothy S. Eaton and Vincent L. Eaton, "Manuscripts Relating to Early America," in Library of Congress, *Quarterly Journal of Current Acquisitions*, VIII (Nov., 1950), 17–28.

23. MHS, *Proc.*, XX, Ser. 2, 125–26.

24. Robert B. Downs, "Notable Materials Added to American Libraries, 1938–1939," *Library Quarterly*, X (April, 1940), 166.

25. National Historical Publications Commission, *A Guide to Archives and Manuscripts in the United States*, ed. by Philip M. Hamer (New Haven, 1961).

26. Bur. of Ed., *Public Libraries*, p. 326.   27. *Ibid.*, p. 313.

28. *Ibid.*, pp. 332–77 *passim*.

29. MHS, *Proc.*, XIII, Ser. 2, 115–16.

30. AHA, *Ann. Rept.*, 1909, p. 287.

31. MHS., *Proc.*, I, Ser. 1, xii.   32. *Ibid.*, XLVII, 276.

33. *Ibid.*, XLV, 546.   34. *Ibid.*, XLVIII, 364.

35. Justin Winsor, in his address before the American Historical Association in 1887, on "Manuscript Sources of American History," discusses public or semi-public records pertaining to the Revolution that are in private repositories (AHA, *Papers*, III, No. 1, 9–27). Curtis W. Garrison, in an article on "The Relation of Historical Manuscripts to Archival Materials," estimates that 35 of 160 manuscript collections received by the Library of Congress up to July, 1931, answer Hilary Jenkinson's definition of the term "archives" (*American Archivist*, II [April, 1939], 98).

Chapter III: Development of Archival Methodology

1. MHS, *Proc.*, XIII, Ser. 1, 227.

2. *Ibid.*, X, Ser. 1, 256. See also AHA, *Papers*, III, No. 2, 11.

3. Dorothy S. Eaton and Vincent L. Eaton, "Manuscripts Relating to Early America," in Library of Congress, *Quarterly Journal of Current Acquisitions*, VIII (Nov., 1950), 22.

4. MHS, *Proc.*, XIII, Ser. 2, 375–76.

5. AHA, *Ann. Rept.*, 1909, pp. 472–73.

6. *Ibid.*, 1902, I, 357–63. See also *Southwestern Historical Quarterly*, XLIX (July, 1945), 21.

7. W. A. Whatley, "The Historical Manuscript Collections of the University of Texas," *Texas History Teachers' Bulletin*, IX (Nov., 1920), 19–25.

8. MHS, *Proc.*, IV, Ser. 2, 103.

9. New York State Library, *Annual Report*, 1905 (Albany, 1906), p. 16.

10. *Library Journal*, XVII (May, 1893), 149–50.

11. Hubert H. Bancroft, *Literary Industries*, in *The Works of Hubert Howe Bancroft* (San Francisco, 1890), XXXIX, 396.

12. *Ibid.*, p. 409.

13. U.S. State Department, Bureau of Rolls and Library, *Bulletin*, No. 3 (Jan., 1894), pp. 15–17.

14. R. C. Waterston to Charles Dean, Aug. 29, 1870, MHS, *Proc.*, XI, Ser. 1, 347–53. See also U.S. Department of Interior, *Annual Report*, 1880 (Washington, 1881), p. 924.

15. AHA, *Ann. Rept.*, 1905, I, 355–63.

16. MHS, *Proc.*, II, Ser. 1, 16.   17. *Ibid.*, XIV, Ser. 1, 113–16.

18. AHA, *Ann. Rept.*, 1900, II, 48.

19. Richard G. Wood, "Richard Bartlett, Minor Archival Prophet," *American Archivist*, XVII (Jan., 1954), 15.

20. *New England Historical and Genealogical Register*, III (1849), 167–68.

21. New York State Library, *Annual Report*, 1899 (Albany, 1900), p. 22.

22. AHA, *Ann. Rept.*, 1910, p. 285.

23. Herbert Friedenwald, "The Care of Manuscripts," *Library Journal*, XXII (Oct., 1897), 54. See also Fred Shelley, "Manuscripts in the Library of Congress: 1800–1900," *American Archivist*, XI (Jan., 1948), 17, and Herbert Friedenwald, "Historical Manuscripts in the Library of Congress," AHA, *Ann. Rept.*, 1898, pp. 37–45, for a discussion of his plans.

24. Library of Congress, Division of Manuscripts, *Notes on the Care, Cataloguing, Calendaring, and Arranging of Manuscripts*, by John C. Fitzpatrick (1st ed., Washington, 1913), pp. 8–9.

25. Library of Congress, Division of Manuscripts, *Handbook of Manuscripts in the Library of Congress* (Washington, 1918), *passim*.

26. New York Public Library, *The Manuscript Division in the New York Public Library*, by Victor H. Paltsits (New York, 1915), p. 5.

27. Wisconsin State Historical Society, *Proceedings,* 1916 (Madison, 1917), p. 48.

28. New York State Library, *Annual Report,* 1916 (Albany, 1917), p. 28.

29. Pennsylvania State Librarian, *Report,* 1903 (Harrisburg, 1903), p. 18.

30. *Ibid.,* p. 20.

31. *Ibid.,* pp. 21–23. See also AHA, *Ann. Rept.,* 1906, I, 141–45.

32. AHA, *Ann. Rept.,* 1919, I, 155–57.

33. *Ibid.,* 1907, I, 169; 1910, pp. 304–5; 1914, I, 376–80.

34. Cassius C. Stiles, *Public Archives: A Manual for Their Administration in Iowa* (Des Moines, 1928).

35. Dunbar Rowland, "The Importance of the Concentration and Classification of National Archives," *Actes, Congrés de Bruxelles,* ed. by J. Cuvelier and L. Stanier (Brussels, 1912), pp. 567, 570–71.

36. AHA, *Ann. Rept.,* 1914, I, 376.

37. Herman V. Ames, "Resume of the Archives Situations in the Several States in 1907," *ibid.,* 1907, I, 163–87.

38. Douglas Brymner, "Canadian Archives," AHA, *Papers,* III, No. 2, 155–56. See also Bernard Weilbrenner, "The Public Archives of Canada, 1871–1958," *Journal of the Society of Archivists,* II, No. 3 (April, 1961), 101–4.

39. AHA, *Papers,* III, No. 2, 2.

40. AHA, *Ann. Rept.,* 1894, pp. 283–84.

41. D. N. McArthur, "The Dominion Archives," *ibid.,* 1911, I, 345.

42. David W. Parker, "Some Problems in the Classification of Departmental Archives," *ibid.,* 1922, I, 164.

43. *Ibid.,* I, 172.

44. Pennsylvania State Librarian, *Report,* 1903, p. 19.

45. AHA, *Ann. Rept.,* 1909, pp. 342–48.

46. *Ibid.,* 1910, p. 285.   47. *Ibid.,* 1912, p. 267.

48. Waldo G. Leland, "The National Archives: A Programme," *American Historical Review,* XVIII (Oct., 1912), 24.

49. Waldo G. Leland, "Report on the Public Archives and Historical Interests of the State of Illinois," Illinois State Education Building Commission, *Report* (Springfield, 1913), p. 50.

50. AHA, *Ann. Rept.,* 1914, I, 373–74.   51. *Ibid.,* 1912, p. 260.

52. *Ibid.,* 1913, I, 263.   53. Stiles, *Public Archives,* pp. 24–25.

54. MHS, *Proc.,* I, Ser. 1, 16.   55. *Ibid.,* I, Ser. 1, 342 and 373.

56. *Ibid.*, XII, Ser. 2, 162.   57. *Ibid.*, X, Ser. 1, 256.

58. U.S. State Department, Bureau of Rolls and Library, *Bulletin*, No. 3 (Jan., 1894), pp. 15–17.

59. AHA, *Ann. Rept.*, 1894, p. 283.

60. Lester J. Cappon, ed., "Correspondence between Charles Campbell and Lyman C. Draper, 1846–1872," *William and Mary Quarterly*, III, Ser. 3 (Jan., 1946), 95. See also Wisconsin State Historical Society, *Descriptive List of Manuscript Collections of the State Historical Society of Wisconsin*, ed. by Reuben G. Thwaites (Madison, 1906), p. viii.

61. *Library Journal*, XVIII (May, 1893), 149–50.

62. Bancroft, *Literary Industries*, in *Works*, XXXIX, 396 and 431.

63. William L. Clements Library, *Report*, 1928–29 (Ann Arbor, 1930), p. 5.

64. AHA, *Ann. Rept.*, 1910, p. 250.

65. MHS, *Proc.*, II, Ser. 1, 120; IV, Ser. 1, 16.

66. *Ibid.*, XI, Ser. 2, 221; VI, Ser. 2, 418.

67. *Ibid.*, LXX, 304, 341, 365.   68. *Ibid.*, LXXI, 463.

69. *Classified Illustrated Catalog of the Library Bureau* (Boston, 1890).

70. Pennsylvania State Librarian, *Report*, 1903, p. 19.

71. For the various rules adopted by the Massachusetts Historical Society, see its *Proceedings*, II, Ser. 1, 16, 433, and 518; III, Ser. 1, 245; XII, Ser. 1, 145; XIX, Ser. 1, 182–93; IV, Ser. 2, 222; VIII, Ser. 2, 331; and I, Ser. 3, 439–49.

72. *Ibid.*, VIII, Ser. 2, 326.

73. U.S. Bureau of Education, *Public Libraries in the United States of America* (Washington, 1876), pp. 334, 341, 344, 354, 358, 363, and 371.

74. Massachusetts Historical Society, *Catalogue of the Books, Pamphlets, Newspapers, Maps, Charts, Manuscripts, etc., in the Library of the Society* (Boston, 1811). See MHS, *Proc.*, I, Ser. 1, 221, for information on authorship.

75. New-York Historical Society, *Catalogue of the Books, Tracts, Newspapers, Maps, Charts, Views, Portraits, and Manuscripts in the Library of the Society* (New York, 1813). See Bur. of Ed., *Public Libraries*, p. 925, for information on authorship.

76. AHA, *Ann. Rept.*, 1896, I, 481–512, and *ibid.*, 1898, pp. 573–85.

77. New York State Library, *Catalogue of MSS. Received from*

the Office of the Secretary of State and Deposited in the State Library in Pursuance of a Joint Resolution of the Senate and Assembly. Passed December 15, 1847: Catalogue of Historical Papers . . . (Albany, 1849).

78. MHS, *Proc.*, II, Ser. 2, 392.

79. Herbert Friedenwald, "The Care of Manuscripts," *Library Journal*, XXII (Oct., 1897), 54.

80. Harry M. Lydenberg, "Historical Manuscripts and Prints in the New York Public Library, and the Method of Cataloging Them," *Library Journal*, XXIV (June, 1899), 252.

81. The Library of Congress rules were published by John C. Fitzpatrick, *Notes on the Care, Cataloguing, Calendaring, and Arranging of Manuscripts* (Washington, 1913, 1921, 1928, 1934); the Minnesota Historical Society rules by Grace Lee Nute, *The Care and Cataloguing of Manuscripts as Practiced by the Minnesota Historical Society* (St. Paul, 1936), and Lucile Kane, *A Guide to the Care and Administration of Manuscripts* (prepared as a *Bulletin* of the American Association of State and Local History, II [Sept., 1960], 371–82); the Clements Library rules by Howard H. Peckham, "Arranging and Cataloguing of Manuscripts in the William L. Clements Library," *American Archivist*, I (Oct., 1938), 215–27; the Detroit Public Library rules by Dorothy V. Martin, "Use of Cataloguing Techniques in Work with Records and Manuscripts," *American Archivist*, XVIII (Oct., 1955), 317–36; the Houghton Library rules by William H. Bond, "The Cataloguing of Manuscripts in the Houghton Library," *Harvard Library Bulletin*, IV (Autumn, 1950), 392–96; the Harvard School of Business Administration rules by Arthur H. Cole, "Business Manuscripts: Collection, Handling, and Cataloguing," *Library Quarterly*, VIII (Jan., 1938), 93–114; and the Cornell University Library rules by Michael Jasenas, "Cataloging Small Manuscript Collections," *Library Resources and Technical Services*, VII (Summer, 1963), 264–73. Rules for cataloging an amorphous unit, called a "describable item," were also published by Sherrod East, *American Archivist*, XVI (Oct., 1953), 291–304, and Ken Munden, *ibid.*, XIX (Oct., 1956), 291–302.

82. Among the repositories were the William L. Clements Library, the Detroit Public Library, the Minnesota Historical Society, the University of North Carolina, and the Princeton University Library.

83. MHS, *Proc.*, XVIII, Ser. 1, 179–80.   84. *Ibid.*, V, Ser. 1, 60.

85. New York Secretary of State, *Calendar of the New York Colonial Manuscripts, Indorsed Land Papers in the Office of the Secretary of State of New York, 1643–1803* (Albany, 1864); *Calendar of Historical Manuscripts in the Office of the Secretary of State, Albany, N.Y.*, (Part 1, Dutch Manuscripts, 1630–1664; Part 2, English Manuscripts, 1664–1776) (Albany, 1865–66); *Calendar of Historical Manuscripts Relating to the War of the Revolution in the Office of the Secretary of State* (2 vols., Albany, 1868).

86. State of Virginia, *Calendar of Virginia State Papers and Other Manuscripts*, 1652–1869 (11 vols., Richmond, 1875–93).

87. AHA, *Ann. Rept.*, 1905, I, 202.

88. Maryland Historical Society, *Archives of Maryland*, Vol. I (1883) and Vol. II (1884).

89. AHA, *Ann. Rept.*, 1894, p. 284.

90. Worthington C. Ford, "On Calendaring Manuscripts," Bibliographical Society of America, *Papers*, 1909 (Cedar Rapids, Iowa, 1910), IV, 45–56.

91. London University, Institute of Historical Research, "Report on Editing Historical Documents," *Bulletin*, Vols. I and II (1923–25), and "Report on Editing Modern Historical Documents," *ibid.*, Vol. III (1925–26).

92. The Work Projects Administration, Historical Records Survey, Circular of Instructions entitled *Preparation of Inventories of Manuscripts*, issued October, 1940, contains instructions on calendaring. Instructions on calendaring issued by a state office are contained in a *Manual for Copying, Abstracting and Calendaring Historical Manuscripts*, by Flora B. Surles, Columbia, S.C., Aug., 1938.

93. Morris L. Radoff, "A Guide to Practical Calendaring" and "A Practical Guide to Calendaring," *American Archivist*, XI (April and July), 1948, 123–40 and 203–22.

94. MHS, *Proc.*, II, Ser. 1, 436–37, shows that Benjamin R. Nichols first bound and indexed records, in 1822.

95. *Ibid.*, I, Ser. 1, 342; X, Ser. 1, 117.

96. *Ibid.*, I, Ser. 1, 373; II, Ser. 1, 357.   97. *Ibid.*, II, Ser. 1, 433.

98. Pennsylvania State Librarian, *Report*, 1903, p. 18.

99. New York State Library, *Annual Report*, 1854, p. 8; *ibid.*, 1863, p. 6; *ibid.*, p. 7; *ibid.*, 1866, p. 8; *ibid.*, 1870, p. viii; *ibid.*, 1908, Vol. 2, suppl. 5; and University of the State of New York, Division of Archives and History, *The Papers of Sir William Johnson* (Albany, 1921), p. xiii.

100. Lester J. Cappon, ed., "Correspondence between Charles Campbell and Lyman C. Draper, 1846–1872," *William and Mary Quarterly*, III, Ser. 3 (Jan., 1946), 95.

101. M. S. R. James, "The Progress of the Modern Card Catalog Principle," in *The Library and Its Contents*, ed. by Harriet Price Sawyer (New York, 1925), pp. 331–38.

102. MHS, *Proc.*, VI, Ser. 2, 189–90; VII, Ser. 2, 370.

103. John T. Hassam, Boston attorney, to editor, Boston *Herald*, Feb. 9, 1883.

104. Theodore J. Cassady, "Record Holdings of Illinois State Archives," *Illinois Libraries*, XL (April, 1958), 296.

105. West Virginia University, *First Report of the Archivist of the Division of Documents, 1935–36* (Morgantown, 1936), p. 7.

106. William D. McCain, "The Public Relations of Archival Depositories," *American Archivist*, III (Oct., 1940), 239.

107. AHA, *Ann. Rept.*, 1900, II, 5.   108. *Ibid.*, pp. 9–12.

109. The inventories are contained in the following AHA *Annual Reports:*

State	Citation
Alabama	1904, pp. 487–553
Arkansas	1906, II, 23–51
California	1915, pp. 277–309
Colorado	1903, I, 415–37; 1911, I, 365–92
Connecticut	1900, II, 26–36; 1906, II, 52–127
Delaware	1906, II, 129–48
Florida	1905, I, 339–52; 1906, II, 149–58
Georgia	1903, I, 439–74; 1904, pp. 555–96; 1906, II, 159–64
Idaho	1917, pp. 137–72
Illinois	1905, I, 353–66; 1909, pp. 379–463
Indiana	1900, II, 37–38; 1910, pp. 315–30
Iowa	1900, II, 39–46
Kansas	1904, pp. 597–601
Kentucky	1910, pp. 331–64
Louisiana	1912, pp. 275–93
Maine	1908, II, 261–318
Maryland	1905, II, 367–68
Massachusetts	1900, II, 47–59
Michigan	1900, II, 60–63; 1905, I, 369–76
Minnesota	1914, I, 385–476
Missouri	1908, I, 323–64
Montana	1912, pp. 295–303
Nebraska	1900, II, 64–66; 1910, pp. 365–420
New Jersey	1903, I, 479–541; 1916, I, 163–99
New Mexico	1909, pp. 465–90
New York	1900, II, 67–250
North Carolina	1900, II, 251–66; 1901, I, 345–52; 1904, pp. 603–27

State	Citation
Ohio	1906, II, 165–96
Oregon	1902, II, 337–55
Pennsylvania	1900, II, 267–93; 1901, II, 231–344; 1904, pp. 629–49
Rhode Island	1903, I, 543–644
Tennessee	1906, II, 197–238
Texas	1901, II, 353–58; 1902, II, 357–63
Vermont	1915, pp. 311–55
Virginia	1903, I, 645–64
Washington	1908, I, 369–98
Wisconsin	1900, II, 294–97; 1905, I, 377–419
Wyoming	1913, I, 275–317

110. Adelaide R. Hasse, "Materials for a Bibliography of the Public Archives of the Original Thirteen States," AHA, *Ann. Rept.*, 1906, II, 243–561.

111. Library of Congress, Division of Manuscripts, *Guide to the Archives of the Government of the United States*, comp. by Claude H. Van Tyne and Waldo G. Leland (Washington, 1904; 2d ed. rev. and enl. by Waldo G. Leland, 1907).

112. AHA, *Ann. Rept.*, 1909, p. 346.   113. *Ibid.*, 1914, I, 384.

114. Work Projects Administration, Historical Records Survey, *Guide to the Manuscript Collections in the Historical Society of Pennsylvania* (Philadelphia, 1940), p. xi; also, Historical Records Survey, *Guide to Depositories of Manuscript Collections in the United States: New York City* (New York, 1941), p. iii.

115. Works Progress Administration, Survey of Federal Archives, *The Manual of the Survey of Federal Archives* (Washington, Feb., 1936).

116. Works Progress Administration, Historical Records Survey, *The Preparation of Guides to Manuscripts* (Supplement 6 to the Manual of the Historical Records Survey; Washington, Sept., 1937). Issued in revised and expanded form by the Work Projects Administration, Historical Records Survey, Circular of Instructions, *Preparation of Inventories of Manuscripts* (Washington, Oct., 1940).

117. National Archives, *Annual Report of the Archivist*, 1940–41 (Washington, 1942), pp. 65–68.

118. Andrew H. Horn, review of *Booker T. Washington: A Register of His Papers in the Library of Congress* (Manuscript Division, Library of Congress, Washington, 1958), in *American Archivist*, XXII (April, 1959), 229.

119. Katharine E. Brand, "Developments in the Handling of

Recent Manuscripts in the Library of Congress," *American Archivist*, XVI (April, 1953), 99–104, and "The Place of the Register in the Manuscripts Division of the Library of Congress," *ibid.*, XVIII (Jan., 1955), 59–68.

120. Dan Lacy, "The Library of Congress: A Sesquicentenary Review," *Library Quarterly*, XX (Oct., 1950), 251.

121. Frank H. Severance, *Rough List of Manuscripts in the Library of the Buffalo Historical Society* (Reprint from *Publications* of the Society, Vol. XIV; Buffalo, 1910).

122. R. G. Thwaites to Justin Winsor, July 5, 1891; Winsor Letters, VII, 64, in Massachusetts Historical Society.

123. Wisconsin State Historical Society, *Descriptive List of Manuscript Collections*, by Thwaites, p. vii.

124. AHA, *Ann. Rept.*, 1909, p. 346.   125. *Ibid.*, 1912, p. 260.

126. Work Projects Administration, *Preparation of Inventories of Manuscripts*.

127. MHS, *Proc.*, VIII, Ser. 1, 476.   128. *Ibid.*, IX, Ser. 1, 343.

129. AHA, *Papers*, III, No. 1, 27.

130. AHA, *Ann. Rept.*, 1905, I, 270.   131. *Ibid.*, 1938, p. 71.

132. *Ibid.*, 1945, I, 41–46, and 1946, I, 64–71.

133. *American Archivist*, XV (April, 1952), 180; Robert H. Land, "The National Union Catalog of Manuscript Collections," *ibid.*, XVII (July, 1954), 195–208.

Chapter IV: Development of the Archival Profession

1. Bertha E. Josephson, "How Can We Improve Our Historical Societies?" *American Archivist*, VIII (July, 1945), 198.

2. Hilary Jenkinson, "The Problems of Nomenclature in Archives," *Journal of the Society of Archivists*, I (April, 1959), 234.

3. Curtis W. Garrison, review of *Guide to the Manuscripts of the Wisconsin Historical Society*, ed. by Alice E. Smith (Madison, 1944), in *American Archivist*, VIII (April, 1945), 155.

4. MHS, *Proc.*, X, Ser. 1, 157.

Chapter V: Nature of Archival Arrangement

1. Thelma Eaton, *Classification in Theory and Practice* (Champaign, Ill., 1957), p. 18.

2. University of Virginia Library, *Thirteenth Annual Report on Historical Collections*, 1942–43 (Charlottesville, 1943), p. 2.

3. Waldo G. Leland, "The National Archives: A Programme," *American Historical Review*, XVIII (Oct., 1912), 24.

4. University of Virginia Library, *Thirteenth Annual Report*, p. 2.

5. AHA, *Ann. Rept.*, 1910, p. 285.   6. *Ibid.*, 1909, p. 346.

7. Leland, "The National Archives," *American Historical Review*, XVIII, 24.

8. Texas State Historical Association, *The Handbook of Texas* (2 vols., Austin, 1952).

9. Ellen Jackson, "Manuscript Collections in the General Library," *Library Quarterly*, XII (April, 1942), 276–77.

10. Morris Rieger, "Packing, Labeling, and Shelving at the National Archives," *American Archivist*, XXV (Oct, 1962), 417–26.

Chapter VI: Principles of Archival Arrangement

1. Lester K. Born, "Balassare Bonifacio and His Essay *De Archivis*," *American Archivist*, IV (Oct., 1941), 237.

2. Hilary Jenkinson, *A Manual of Archive Administration* (1st ed., London, 1922; 2d ed., London, 1937), p. 11.

3. Ian Maclean, Lecture 1, Archives Division, Commonwealth National Library, Canberra, Australia, mimeographed, *ca.* 1953, p. 1.

4. Hilary Jenkinson, *The English Archivist: A New Profession* (an inaugural lecture for a new course in archive administration delivered at University College, London, Oct. 14, 1947; London, 1948), p. 4.

5. University of Virginia Library, *Thirteenth Annual Report on Historical Collections*, 1942–43 (Charlottesville, 1943), p. 2.

6. National Archives, *European Archival Practices in Arranging Records*, by T. R. Schellenberg ("Staff Information Circulars," No. 5; Washington, 1939), p. 7.

7. *Ibid.*, p. 18.   8. MHS, *Proc.*, I, Ser. 2, 202; VII, Ser. 2, 126.

Chapter VII: Character of a Descriptive Program

1. Frontis W. Johnston, "A Historian Looks at Archives and Manuscripts," *American Archivist*, XIX (July, 1956), 232.

2. Boyd C. Shafer, "Lost and Found," *American Archivist*, XVIII (July, 1955), 223.

3. University of Virginia Library, *Annual Report of the Archivist*, 1938–39 (Charlottesville, 1939), p. 2.

4. Wisconsin State Historical Society, *Descriptive List of Manuscript Collections of the State Historical Society of Wisconsin*, ed. by Reuben G. Thwaites (Madison, 1906), p. vii.

5. John S. Kendall, "Historical Collections in New Orleans," *North Carolina Historical Review*, VII (1930), 464.

6. New York Public Library, *The Manuscript Division in the New York Public Library*, by Victor H. Paltsits (New York, 1915), p. 6.

7. The *Guides to Depositories of Manuscript Collections in the United States* were produced from information obtained by questionnaires which were filled in by custodians of various depositories. Each entry contains a number of paragraphs, one of which related to the "total quantity of all manuscript holdings and status of arrangement and cataloguing."

8. National Archives, *Annual Report of the Archivist*, 1940–41 (Washington, 1942), pp. 65–68.

9. Nannie M. Tilley and Noma L. Goodwin, *Guide to the Manuscript Collections in the Duke University Library* (Durham, 1947), p. v.

10. West Virginia University Library, *Guide to Manuscripts and Archives in the West Virginia Collection*, comp. by Charles Shetler (Morgantown, 1958), pp. iv–v.

11. Katharine E. Brand, "Developments in the Handling of Recent Manuscripts in the Library of Congress," *American Archivist*, XVI (April, 1953), 100.

12. R. B. Haselden, "Manuscripts in the Huntington Library," *Library Journal*, LIII (Sept. 15, 1928), 764.

13. Andrew H. Horn, review of *Booker T. Washington: A Register of His Papers in the Library of Congress* (Manuscript Division, Library of Congress, Washington, 1958), in *American Archivist*, XXII (April, 1959), 229–30.

14. "Report of *Ad Hoc* Committee on Manuscripts Set Up by the American Historical Association in December 1948," *American Archivist*, XIV (July, 1951), 229–40.

15. AHA, *Ann. Rept.*, 1909, p. 346; *ibid.*, 1914, I, 384.

16. National Archives, *Annual Report*, 1940–41, pp. 65–68.

Chapter VIII: Record Attributes

1. Work Projects Administration, Historical Records Survey, *Guide to the Manuscript Collections in the Department of Archives, Louisiana State University Library*, ed. by William R. Hogan (Baton Rouge, La., 1940), p. ii.

2. Alice E. Smith, *Guide to the Manuscripts of the Wisconsin Historical Society* (Madison, 1944), preface. Smith's example is followed by Josephine L. Harper and Sharon C. Smith, *Guide to the Manuscripts of the State Historical Society of Wisconsin: Supplement Number One* (Madison, 1957), p. v.

3. Curtis W. Garrison, review of Smith's *Guide to the Manuscripts of the Wisconsin Historical Society*, in *American Archivist*, VIII (April, 1945), 155.

4. Library of Congress, Descriptive Cataloging Division, *Rules for Descriptive Cataloging in the Library of Congress; Manuscripts* (Prelim. ed., Washington, 1954).

5. William Matthews, comp., *American Diaries: An Annotated Bibliography of American Diaries Written Prior to the Year 1861* (Berkeley and Los Angeles, 1945), p. ix.

6. Lewis E. Atherton, "The Cataloging and Use of Western Mercantile Records," *Library Quarterly*, VIII (April, 1938), 189–99.

7. Thomas Y. Crowell Co., *The Practical Handbook of Business and Finance* (rev. ed., Garden City, N.Y., 1936).

8. Donald T. Clark, *Dictionary of Business and Finance* (New York, 1957).

9. Harold Lazarus, *American Business Dictionary* (New York, 1957).

10. R. J. Schwartz, ed., *Dictionary of Business and Industry* (New York, 1954).

11. John Bouvier, *Bouvier's Law Dictionary*, ed. by William Edward Baldwin (Cleveland, 1934).

12. Work Projects Administration, Historical Records Survey, *Preparation of Inventories of Manuscripts: A Circular of Instructions for the Use of the Historical Records Survey Projects* (mimeographed; Washington, Oct., 1940).

13. Library of Congress, *Rules*.

14. Curtis W. Garrison, review of Smith's *Wisconsin Guide*, in *American Archivist*, VIII, 155.

15. Marguerite J. Pease, review of *Guide to the Western Historical Manuscript Collections* (University of Missouri, *Bulletin*, Columbia, Mo., 1952), in *American Archivist*, XVI (April, 1953), 169–70.

16. Henry P. Beers, review of *A Catalogue of Manuscripts in the Collection of Western Americana Founded by William Robertson Coe, Yale University Library* (New Haven and London, 1952), in *American Archivist*, XVI (July, 1953), 266–67.

17. Nannie M. Tilley and Noma L. Goodwin, *Guide to the Manuscript Collections in the Duke University Library* (Durham, 1947).

18. Elizabeth C. Biggert, *Guide to the Manuscript Collections in the Library of the Ohio State Archaeological and Historical Society* (Columbus, 1953).

19. Tilley and Goodwin, *Duke Guide*.

20. Howard H. Peckham, *Guide to the Manuscript Collections in the William L. Clements Library* (Ann Arbor, 1942), p. xvi.

21. Norma B. Cuthbert, *American Manuscript Collections in the Huntington Library for the History of the Seventeenth and Eighteenth Centuries* (San Marino, Calif., 1941).

22. Oneida Historical Society, *A Catalogue of the Manuscript Holdings at the Oneida Historical Society at Utica, New York* (Utica, 1952).

23. Colton Storm, review of Smith's *Wisconsin Guide*, in *Library Quarterly*, XV (July, 1945), 272–73.

Chapter IX: Notational Systems

1. Anatole France, "The Revolt of the Angels," in *Novels and Short Stories of Anatole France*, ed. by Frederic Chapman and James Lewis (41 vols., New York and London, 1917–), XIX, 19–20.

2. Fred Shelley, "Manuscripts in the Library of Congress: 1800–1900," *American Archivist*, XI (Jan., 1948), 17.

3. New York State Library, *Annual Report*, 1916 (Albany, 1917), p. 30.

4. *Ibid.*, pp. 28–31.

5. Wisconsin State Historical Society, *Proceedings*, 1916 (Madison, 1917), pp. 47–48.

6. Grace Lee Nute, *The Care and Cataloguing of Manuscripts* (St. Paul, 1936), p. 16.

7. Work Projects Administration, Historical Records Survey, *Guide to the Manuscript Collections in the Department of Archives, Louisiana State University Library*, ed. by William R. Hogan (Baton Rouge, La., 1940), p. iii.

8. Great Britain, Public Record Office, *Guide to the Public Records, Introductory* (London, 1949), Part 1, p. 39.

9. Neville Williams, *The British Public Record Office: History and Description* (Richmond, 1960), pp. 50–53 (Virginia State Library, *Publications*, No. 12).

10. National Archives," Information for Searchers Citing Records in the National Archives," Pamphlet (Washington, 1957), p. 1.

11. Roscoe R. Hill, "Classification in the National Archives," American Library Association, *Archives and Libraries*, 1940 (Chicago, 1940), pp. 61–76.

12. H. M. Lydenberg, "Historical Manuscripts and Prints in the New York Public Library, and the Method of Cataloging Them," *Library Journal*, XXIV (June, 1899), 252.

13. Arthur H. Cole, "Business Manuscripts: Collection, Handling, and Cataloging," *Library Quarterly*, VIII (Jan., 1938), 103.

14. Charles A. Cutter, *Expansive Classification* (Boston, 1891–93), preface.

Part II: Application of Principles and Techniques

The quotation by Adams is from MHS, *Proc.*, XIII, Ser. 2, 118.

Chapter X: Arrangement of Archival Groups

1. Hilary Jenkinson, *A Manual of Archive Administration* (1st. ed., London, 1922; 2d ed., London, 1937), p. 11.

2. See T. R. Schellenberg, *Modern Archives: Principles and Techniques* (Melbourne, 1956; Chicago, 1956), pp. 178–84, for a fuller discussion of the considerations that are taken into account in the United States in establishing record groups.

3. National Archives, Archivist's Memorandum No. A-142, Feb., 1941.

4. Roscoe R. Hill, "Classification in the National Archives," American Library Association, *Archives and Libraries*, 1940 (Chicago, 1940), p. 61.

Chapter XI: Arrangement of Manuscript Collections

1. Worthington C. Ford, "Manuscripts," in Charles A. Cutter, *Rules for a Dictionary Catalog* (4th ed., Washington, 1904), p. 135.

2. New York State Library, *Annual Report*, 1916 (Albany, 1917), p. 30.

3. Library of Congress, Descriptive Cataloging Division, *Rules for Descriptive Cataloging in the Library of Congress: Manuscripts* (Prelim. ed., Washington, 1954).

4. Ruth K. Nuermberger, "A Ten-Year Experiment in Archival Practices," *American Archivist*, IV (Oct., 1941), 250.

5. Norma B. Cuthbert, *American Manuscript Collections in the Huntington Library for the History of the Seventeenth and Eighteenth Centuries* (San Marino, Calif., 1941), p. vii.

6. *Ibid.*

7. The guides analyzed are the following: Nannie M. Tilley and Noma L. Goodwin, *Guide to the Manuscript Collections in the Duke University Library* (Durham, 1947); Lucile M. Kane and Kathryn A. Johnson, *Manuscript Collections of the Minnesota Historical Society: Guide Number Two* (St. Paul, 1955); Work Projects Administration, Historical Records Survey, *Guide to the Manuscripts in the Southern Historical Collection of the University of North Carolina* (Chapel Hill, 1941); Work Projects Administration, Historical Records Survey, *Guide to the Manuscript Collections in the Archives of the North Carolina Historical Commission* (Raleigh, 1942); West Virginia University Library, *Guide to the Manuscripts and Archives in the West Virginia Collection*, comp. by Charles Shetler (Morgantown, 1958); and Josephine L. Harper and Sharon C. Smith, *Guide to the Manuscripts of the State Historical Society of Wisconsin: Supplement Number One* (Madison, 1957).

8. Tilley and Goodwin, *Duke Guide*, p. v.

9. Grace Lee Nute, *The Care and Cataloguing of Manuscripts* (St. Paul, 1936), p. 16.

10. Cuthbert, *American Manuscript Collections*, p. vii.

11. Library of Congress, Division of Manuscripts, *Handbook of Manuscripts in the Library of Congress* (Washington, 1918), p. 313.

12. Work Projects Administration, Historical Records Survey, *Guide to the Manuscript Collections in the Department of Archives, Louisiana State University Library*, ed. by William R. Hogan (Baton Rouge, La., 1940), p. iii.

13. Neal Harlow, "Managing Manuscript Collections," *Library Trends*, IV (Oct., 1955), 206.

14. University of Virginia Library, *Thirteenth Annual Report on Historical Collections*, 1942–43 (Charlottesville, 1943), pp. 1–4.

15. MHS, *Proc.*, LX, 208.

16. Harlow, "Managing Manuscript Collections," *Library Trends*, IV, 207.

17. H. C. Schulz, "The Care and Storage of Manuscripts in the Huntington Library," *Library Quarterly*, V (Jan., 1935), 80.

18. Nute, *Care and Cataloguing of Manuscripts, passim*.

19. Historical Society of Western Pennsylvania, *Inventory of the Manuscript and Miscellaneous Collections of the Historical Society of Western Pennsylvania* (Pittsburgh, Pa., 1933), *passim*.

20. University of Wyoming, Archives Department, *University Archives and Western Historical Manuscripts Collection, University of Wyoming* (Laramie, Wyo., 1949), *passim*.

21. Henrietta M. Larson, *Guide to Business History: Materials for the Study of American Business History and Suggestions for Their Use* (Cambridge, Mass., 1948), p. 990.

22. Ford, "Manuscripts," in Cutter, *Rules*, p. 135.

23. Library of Congress, Division of Manuscripts, *Notes on the Care, Cataloguing, Calendaring, and Arranging of Manuscripts*, by John C. Fitzpatrick (1st ed., Washington, 1913), pp. 24–25.

24. Ellen Jackson, "Manuscript Collections in the General Library," *Library Quarterly*, XXII (April, 1942), 276.

25. Harlow, "Managing Manuscript Collections," *Library Trends*, IV, 207.

26. Robert B. Downs, "Organization and Preservation of Manuscript Collections in the University of North Carolina Library," American Library Association, *Public Documents*, 1938 (Chicago, 1938), p. 374.

27. R. B. Haselden, "Manuscript Collections in the Huntington

Library," American Library Association, *Archives and Libraries, 1939* (Chicago, 1939), p. 73.

28. Work Projects Administration, Historical Records Survey, *Guide to the Manuscript Collections in the Historical Society of Pennsylvania,* comp. by Paul Bleyden (Philadelphia, 1940), pp. 22–23.

29. Herbert A. Kellar, "Organization and Preservation of Manuscript Collections in the McCormick Historical Association Library," American Library Association, *Public Documents,* 1938, p. 361.

30. "Report of *Ad Hoc* Committee on Manuscripts Set Up by the American Historical Association in December 1948," *American Archivist,* XIV (July, 1951), 231.

31. Kellar, "Organization and Preservation," *Public Documents,* 1938, p. 364.

32. *Ibid.,* pp. 361 and 364.

Chapter XII: Arrangement of Record Items

1. Ruth K. Nuermberger, "A Ten-Year Experiment in Archival Practices," *American Archivist,* IV (Oct., 1941), 253.

2. Worthington C. Ford, "Manuscripts," in Charles A. Cutter, *Rules for a Dictionary Catalog* (4th ed., Washington, 1904), p. 135.

3. Robert B. Downs, "Organization and Preservation of Manuscript Collections in the University of North Carolina Library," American Library Association, *Public Documents,* 1938 (Chicago, 1938), p. 376.

4. University of Virginia Library, *Thirteenth Annual Report on Historical Collections,* 1942–43 (Charlottesville, 1942), p. 1.

5. Nuermberger, "A Ten-Year Experiment," *American Archivist,* IV, 251.

6. Ford, "Manuscripts," in Cutter, *Rules.*

7. National Association of State Libraries, Committee on Public Archives, *Proceedings and Papers,* 1913–14 (Nashville, 1914), p. 32.

8. Richard C. Berner, "The Arrangement and Description of Manuscripts," *American Archivist,* XXIII (Oct., 1960), 397.

9. Dumas Malone, ed., *Correspondence between Thomas Jefferson and Pierre Samuel du Pont de Nemours, 1789–1817* (Boston and

New York, 1930), and Paul Wilstach, *Correspondence of John Adams and Thomas Jefferson* (Indianapolis, Ind., 1925).

10. National Association of State Libraries, Committee on Public Archives, *Proceedings and Papers,* 1913–14, p. 32.

11. *Ibid.*

12. Herbert A. Kellar, "Organization and Preservation of Manuscript Collections in the McCormick Historical Association Library," American Library Association, *Public Documents,* 1938, p. 360.

13. MHS, *Proc.,* II, Ser. 1, 120.   14. *Ibid.,* XI, Ser. 2, 221.

15. *Library Journal,* II (Nov.–Dec., 1877), 114.

16. Downs, "Organization and Preservation," *Public Documents,* 1938, p. 374.

Chapter XIII: Physical Arrangements

1. The National Archives accession numbers consisted, originally, of two parts, the first reflecting the year during which an accession was made, and the second denoting the numerical sequence of the accession.

2. Great Britain, Public Record Office, *Guide to the Public Records, Introductory* (London, 1949), Part 1, *passim.*

3. Arnold J. Van Laer, "The Lessons of the Catastrophe in the New York State Capitol at Albany on March 29, 1911," AHA, *Ann. Rept.,* 1911, I, 334.

4. Morris Rieger, "Packing, Labeling, and Shelving at the National Archives," *American Archivist,* XXV (Oct., 1962), 417–26, provides a full discussion of National Archives practices.

5. Grace Lee Nute, *The Care and Cataloguing of Manuscripts* (St. Paul, 1936), p. 35.

6. Josephine L. Harper and Sharon C. Smith, *Guide to the Manuscripts of the State Historical Society of Wisconsin: Supplement Number One* (Madison, 1957), p. xii.

7. Society of American Archivists, Committee on State Records, "Returns of 37 State Archives to Questionnaire on Record Preservation," Dec., 1959.

8. Colton Storm, "The Care and Feeding of a Manuscript Collection," *Autograph Collectors Journal,* I (Oct., 1948), 11.

9. Cassius C. Stiles, *Public Archives: A Manual for Their Administration in Iowa* (Des Moines, 1928), p. 18.

10. Waldo G. Leland, "The Archive Depot," in National Association of State Libraries, *Proceedings and Papers,* 1915–16 (Nashville, 1916), p. 62.

11. Stiles, *Public Archives,* p. 19.

12. Work Projects Administration, Historical Records Survey, *Guide to Depositories of Manuscript Collections in the United States: Pennsylvania* (Harrisburg, 1939), p. 59.

13. Library of Congress, Division of Manuscripts, *Notes on the Care, Cataloguing, Calendaring, and Arranging of Manuscripts,* by John C. Fitzpatrick (1st ed., Washington, 1913), pp. 19-20.

14. Norma Cuthbert, "Brief Note on the Classification, Cataloguing, Usage, and Storage of Manuscripts in the Henry E. Huntington Library and Art Gallery," Manuscript, Library, National Archives, pp. 15–17.

15. Arthur H. Cole, "Business Manuscripts: Collection, Handling, and Cataloging," *Library Quarterly,* VIII (Jan., 1938), 101.

16. Society of American Archivists, "Returns to Questionnaire on Record Preservation."

17. National Association of State Libraries, Committee on Public Archives, *Proceedings and Papers,* 1913–14 (Nashville, 1914), pp. 29–33.

18. *Ibid.,* p. 30.   19. *Ibid.,* p. 32.   20. *Ibid.,* p. 30.

21. *Ibid.,* p. 32.

22. Society of American Archivists, "Returns to Questionnaire on Record Preservation."

Chapter XIV: Preparation of Archival Inventories and Guides

1. For a fuller discussion of European inventories see T. R. Schellenberg, *Modern Archives: Principles and Techniques* (Melbourne, 1956; Chicago, 1956), pp. 195–201.

2. National Archives, *Annual Report of the Archivist,* 1940–41 (Washington, 1942), pp. 65–68.

3. *Ibid.*

4. National Archives, *Guide to the Records in the National Archives* (Washington, 1948), p. 614.

5. Donald H. Mugridge, review of *Guide to the Records in the National Archives,* in *American Archivist,* XII (Oct., 1949), 415–18.

6. National Archives, *Preliminary Inventory No. 44, Records of the National Recovery Administration*, comp. by Homer L. Calkin, Meyer H. Fishbein, and Leo Pascal (Washington, 1952).

7. National Archives, *Preliminary Inventory No. 48, Records of the Special Committees of the Senate to Investigate the National Defense Program*, comp. by Harold E. Hufford and Toussaint L. Prince (Washington, 1952).

Chapter XV: Preliminary Description of Private Papers

1. Ruth K. Nuermberger, "A Ten-Year Experiment in Archival Practices," *American Archivist*, IV (Oct., 1941), 257.

2. Katharine E. Brand, "Developments in the Handling of Recent Manuscripts in the Library of Congress," *American Archivist*, XVI (April, 1953), 99–104, and "The Place of the Register in the Manuscripts Division of the Library of Congress," *ibid.*, XVIII (Jan., 1955), 59–68.

Chapter XVI: Description of Manuscript Collections

1. Hubert H. Bancroft, *Literary Industries*, in *The Works of Hubert Howe Bancroft* (San Francisco, 1890), XXXIX, 231.

2 *Ibid.*, p. 233.   3. *Ibid.*, p. 238.   4. *Ibid.*   5. *Ibid.*, p. 239.
6. *Ibid.*, pp. 239–40.   7. *Ibid.*, p. 239.   8 *Ibid.*, p. 240.
9. *Ibid.*

10. Harvard University, Graduate School of Business Administration, *List of Business Manuscripts in Baker Library*, comp. by Margaret R. Cusick (Boston, 1932); later ed., comp. by Robert W. Lovett (Boston, 1951).

11. Nannie M. Tilley and Noma L. Goodwin, *Guide to the Manuscript Collections in the Duke University Library* (Durham, 1947).

12. Grace L. Nute and Gertrude W. Ackermann, *Guide to the Personal Papers in the Manuscript Collections of the Minnesota Historical Society* (St. Paul, 1935), p. viin.

13. Josephine L. Harper and Sharon C. Smith, *Guide to the Manuscripts of the State Historical Society of Wisconsin: Supplement Number One* (Madison, 1957), p. v.

14. Massachusetts Historical Society, *Handbook of the Massachusetts Historical Society, 1791–1948* (Boston, 1949), p. 118.

5. Elizabeth C. Biggert, *Guide to the Manuscript Collections in the Library of the Ohio State Archaeological and Historical Society* (Columbus, 1953), p. vi.

16. Norma B. Cuthbert, *American Manuscript Collections in the Huntington Library for the History of the Seventeenth and Eighteenth Centuries* (San Marino, Calif., 1941), p. vii.

17. Alice E. Smith, *Guide to the Manuscripts of the Wisconsin Historical Society* (Madison, 1944), p. ix.

18. Cuthbert, *Huntington Guide*, p. vii.

19. Nute and Ackerman, *Minnesota Guide*, p. viin.

20. Biggert, *Ohio Guide*, p. vi.

21. Library of Congress, Division of Manuscripts, *Handbook of Manuscripts in the Library of Congress* (Washington, 1918), pp. iv–xvi.

22. Library of Congress, Division of Manuscripts, *Check List of Collections of Personal Papers in Historical Societies, University and Public Libraries, and Other Learned Institutions in the United States* (Washington, 1918), p. 37.

23. Howard H. Peckman, *Guide to the Manuscript Collections in the William L. Clements Library* (Ann Arbor, 1942), pp. 279–82.

24. Work Projects Administration, Historical Records Survey, *Preparation of Inventories of Manuscripts: A Circular of Instructions for the Use of the Historical Records Survey Projects* (mimeographed; Washington, Oct., 1940).

25. Lucile M. Kane and Kathryn A. Johnson, *Manuscript Collections of the Minnesota Historical Society: Guide Number Two* (St. Paul, 1955).

26. Nute and Ackermann, *Minnesota Guide*.

27. Harper and Smith, *Wisconsin Guide*.

28. Smith, *Wisconsin Guide*.

29. Elizabeth Ring, *A Reference List of Manuscripts Relating to the History of Maine* (3 vols., Orono, Me., 1938), I, xii ("University of Maine Studies," 2d Ser., No. 45).

30. New-York Historical Society, *Survey of the Manuscript Collections in the New-York Historical Society*, comp. by Susan E. Lyman (New York, 1941), pp. 1–4, 64–67, 71–72.

31. Harvard University, Graduate School of Business Administration, *List of Business Manuscripts in Baker Library*, comp. by Robert W. Lovett (Boston, 1951).

Chapter XVII: Preparation of Indexes and Item Catalogs

1. U.S. Department of Commerce and Labor, Bureau of the Census, *A Century of Population Growth* (Washington, 1909), pp. 227–70.

2. R. L. Polk & Co., *Standard Cross References of Proper Names* (Detroit, 1928).

3. T. R. Schellenberg, *Modern Archives: Principles and Techniques* (Melbourne, 1956; Chicago, 1956), pp. 86–87.

4. Margaret C. Norton, "The Archives Department of the Illinois State Library: Its Organization and Operation," *Illinois Libraries,* XXV (June, 1943), 231.

5. New York State Library, *Annual Report,* 1855 (Albany, 1856), p.7.

6. *Ibid.* See also *ibid.,* 1881, p. 145, for information on the nature of the calendar.

7. *Ibid.,* 1881, p. 6.   8. *Ibid.*   9. *Ibid.,* p. 145.

10. *Ibid.,* 1883, p. 16.   11. *Ibid.,* 1887, p. x.

12. *Ibid.,* 1898–99, p. 26.

13. Elizabeth A. Ingerman, "A New Method of Indexing Manuscripts," *American Archivist,* XXV (July, 1962), 331–40.

14. Anatole France, "My Friend's Book," in *Novels and Short Stories of Anatole France,* ed. by Frederic Chapman and James Lewis (41 vols., New York and London, 1917–   ), IX, 75.

15. MHS, *Proc.,* LX, 206.   16. *Ibid.,* LXV, 425.

17. Clement M. Silvestro and Richmond D. Williams, *A Look at Ourselves: A Report on the Survey of the State and Local Historical Agencies in the United States* (Bulletin of the American Association for State and Local History, Madison, Oct., 1962), p. 416.

18. R. B. Haselden, "Manuscripts in the Huntington Library," *Library Journal,* LIII (Sept. 15, 1928), 764.

19. New-York Historical Society, *Survey of the Manuscript Collections in the New-York Historical Society,* comp. by Susan E. Lyman (New York, 1941), p. iv.

20. Ruth K. Nuermberger, "A Ten-Year Experiment in Archival Practices," *American Archivist,* IV (Oct., 1941), 251.

21. Work Projects Administration, Historical Records Survey, *A*

Guide to the Manuscript Collection of Duke University (Raleigh, 1939), p. iii.

22. Randolph W. Church, "The Relationship Between Archival Agencies and Libraries," *American Archivist*, VI (July, 1943), 145.

23. See ·Chapter III, note 81, for references to cataloging rules.

Chapter XVIII: Preparation of Lists and Calendars

1. For a full discussion of the calendaring technique, see the articles of Morris L. Radoff, "A Guide to Practical Calendaring" and "A Practical Guide to Calendaring," *American Archivist*, XI (April and July, 1948), 123–40 and 203–22.

2. Worthington C. Ford, "On Calendaring Manuscripts," Bibliographical Society of America, *Papers*, 1909 (Cedar Rapids, Iowa, 1910), IV, 45–56.

3. "Report on Editing Historical Documents," London University Institute of Historical Research, *Bulletin*, Vols. I and II (1923–25), and "Report on Editing Modern Historical Documents," *ibid.*, Vol. III (1925–26).

4. *Ibid.*, III, 18.

Chapter XIX: Arrangement and Description of Cartographic Records

1. Erwin Raisz, *General Cartography* (New York and London, 1938; 2d ed., 1948). Other good general accounts are Lloyd A. Brown, *The Story of Maps* (Boston, 1949), and Library of Congress, Division of Maps, *Maps: Their Care, Repair, and Preservation in Libraries*, by Clara Egli LeGear (Washington, 1949; rev. ed., 1956). References to other books and articles may be obtained from Walter W. Ristow, "Maps in Libraries: A Bibliographical Summary," *Library Journal*, LXXI (Sept. 1, 1946), 1101–7, and LXXI (Sept. 15, 1946), 1121–24.

2. S. Whittemore Boggs and Dorothy C. Lewis, *The Classification and Cataloging of Maps and Atlases* (New York, 1945), pp. 128–40.

3. Arch C. Gerlach, "Geography and Map Cataloging and Classification in Libraries," *Special Libraries*, LII (May–June, 1961), 250.

4. Raisz, *General Cartography* (2d ed.), p. 321.

5. Boggs and Lewis, *Classification and Cataloging of Maps and Atlases*, section on classification.

6. Classification patterns are shown in the following literature: Lloyd A. Brown, *Notes on the Care and Cataloguing of Old Maps* (Windham, Conn., 1940); Wilmer L. Hall, "A Classification for Maps," *Library Journal*, L (March 15, 1925), 257–59; LeGear, *Maps: Their Care, Repair and Preservation in Libraries;* Walter Thiele, "Classification, Cataloguing and Care of Maps," in *Official Map Publications* (Chicago, 1938); J. P. Terrell, *The Williams System of Classification, Cataloguing, Indexing, Filing and Care of Maps as Adopted for the General Staff Map Collection* (2d ed., Washington, 1930); and G. R. Crone, "The Cataloguing and Arrangement of Maps," *Library Association Record*, III (March, 1936), 98–104.

7. Herman R. Friis, "Cartographic and Related Records: What Are They, How Have They Been Produced and What Are Problems of Their Administration?" *American Archivist*, XIII (April, 1950), 135–55.

8. Francis H. Parsons, "The Care of Maps," *Library Journal*, XX (June, 1895), 201.

9. Friis, "Cartographic and Related Records," *American Archivist*, XIII, 153–54.

10. Parsons, "Care of Maps," *Library Journal*, XX, 201.

11. Gerlach, "Geography and Map Cataloging," *Special Libraries*, LII, 250.

12. National Archives, "Special List of Civil War Maps," comp. by Charlotte M. Ashby and Laura E. Kelsay, to be published in *Guide to Civil War Maps*.

13. National Archives, *Preliminary Inventory of the Cartographic Records of the Bureau of the Census*, comp. by James Berton Rhoads and Charlotte M. Ashby (Washington, 1958); National Archives, *List of Cartographic Records of the Bureau of Indian Affairs*, comp. by Laura E. Kelsay (Washington, 1940).

Chapter XX: Arrangement and Description of Pictorial Records

1. Helen L. Davidson, "Handling Pictures and Audio-Visual Materials in Company Libraries and Archives," *Special Libraries*, LIII (July–Aug., 1962), 326–29.

2. Beaumont Newhall, "Photographic Words," *Image*, V (Dec., 1956), 234–35.

3. For a full discussion of the ambrotype and daguerreotype, see Robert Taft, *Photography and the American Scene* (New York, 1938; reprinted 1942), chapters 3, 4, 5, and 7.

4. Library of Congress, Descriptive Cataloging Division, *Rules for Descriptive Cataloging in the Library of Congress: Pictures, Designs, and Other Two-Dimensional Representations* (Prelim. ed., Washington, 1959).

5. W. J. Burke, "The Picture Collection of *Look* Magazine," *Special Libraries*, XXXV (Dec., 1944), 481–85.

6. For a discussion of the storage and preservation of pictorial records, see Minor White, "Care and Preservation of the Old Photographs and Negatives," *Image*, Vol. IV (Nov., 1955), and Paul Vanderbilt, "Notes on the Care and Arrangement of Picture Collections" (Processed manuscript, 1955, available from Mr. Vanderbilt, State Historical Society, Madison, Wisconsin).

7. Ben Melnitsky, "Classifying Negatives and Prints," *Industrial Photography*, Jan., 1954, pp. 34–40; March, 1954, pp. 36–38.

8. Burke, "Picture Collection of *Look* Magazine, *Special Libraries*, XXXV, 481–85.

9. Howard W. Odum, *American Regionalism: A Cultural-Historical Approach to National Integration* (New York, 1938).

10. Elizabeth L. Adams and Marion Lambert, "The Photograph Section of Library of Congress," *Library Journal*, LXXI (Sept. 1, 1946), 1081–87.

11. Romana Javitz, "A Check List on the Organization of Picture Collections," *Special Libraries*, L (July–Aug., 1959), 252.

12. *Picturescope*, IX (Oct., 1961), 32–34.

13. Paula M. Strain, "Photographs in Scientific and Technical Libraries," *Special Libraries*, XXXIX (March, 1948), 79–80.

14. G. Hubert Smith, "Pictures and History," *Bulletins of the American Association for State and Local History*, II (Sept., 1949), 84.

15. Camilla P. Luecke, "Photographic Library Procedures," *Special Libraries*, XLVII (Dec., 1956), 457.

16. Library of Congress, *Rules*.

SELECTIVE BIBLIOGRAPHY

This bibliography lists recent American books and articles that relate to the methods of managing documentary material. It includes only items that provide information that is supplemental to that found in the text of this book. In the citations below the symbol *AA* is used for the *American Archivist* and *LQ* for the *Library Quarterly*.

General Books

Dunlap, Leslie W. *American Historical Societies, 1790–1960.* Madison, Wis., 1944.

Posner, Ernst. *American State Archives.* Chicago, 1964.

Schellenberg, T. R. *Modern Archives: Principles and Techniques.* Melbourne, 1956; Chicago, 1956.

Whitehill, Walter M. *Independent Historical Societies.* Boston, 1962.

Works on the Management of Public Papers

Campbell, Edward F. "Functional Classification of Archival Material," *LQ*, XI (Oct., 1941), 431–41.

Holmes, Oliver W. "Archival Arrangement—Five Different Operations at Five Different Levels," *AA*, XXVII (Jan., 1964), 21–41.

Munden, Kenneth. "The Identification and Description of the Series," *AA*, XIII (July, 1950), 213–27.

National Archives. *Archival Principles: Selections from the Writings of Waldo G. Leland.* "Staff Information Papers," No. 20. Washington, 1955.

—— *The Control of Records at the Record Group Level,* by Philip

M. Hamer. "Staff Information Circulars," No. 15. Washington, 1950.

Rieger, Morris. "Packing, Labeling, and Shelving at the National Archives," *AA*, XXV (Oct., 1962), 417–26.

Works on the Management of Private Papers

Berner, Richard C. "The Arrangement and Description of Manuscripts," *AA*, XXIII (Oct., 1960), 395–406.

Brand, Katharine E. "Developments in the Handling of Recent Manuscripts in the Library of Congress," *AA*, XVI (April, 1953), 99–104.

—— "The Place of the Register in the Manuscripts Division of the Library of Congress," *AA*, XVIII (Jan., 1955), 59–68.

Burke, Robert E. "Modern Manuscript Collections and What to Do with Them," *Manuscripts*, VII (Summer, 1955), 232–36.

Cappon, Lester J. "Historical Manuscripts as Archives: Some Definitions and Their Applications," *AA*, XIX (April, 1956), 101–10.

Cole, Arthur H. "Business Manuscripts: Collection, Handling, and Cataloging," *LQ*, VIII (Jan., 1938), 97–114.

Finch, Jean L. "Some Fundamentals in Arranging Archives and Manuscript Collections," *Library Resources and Technical Services*, VIII (Winter, 1964), 26–34.

Garrison, Curtis W. "The Relation of Historical Manuscripts to Archival Material," *AA*, II (April, 1939), 95–105.

Gordon, Robert S. "Suggestions for Organization and Description of Archival Holdings of Local Historical Societies," *AA*, XXVI (Jan., 1963), 19–39.

Harlow, Neal. "Managing Manuscript Collections," *Library Trends*, IV (Oct., 1955), 203–12.

Ingerman, Elizabeth A. "A New Method of Indexing Manuscripts," *AA*, XXV (July, 1962), 331–40.

Jackson, Ellen. "Manuscript Collections in the General Library," *LQ*, XII (April, 1942), 275–83.

Jasenas, Michael. "Cataloging Small Manuscript Collections," *Library Resources and Technical Services*, VII (Summer, 1963), 264–73.

Josephson, Bertha. "Indexing," *AA*, X (April, 1947), 133–50.

Kane, Lucile M. *A Guide to the Care and Administration of Manu-*

scripts. American Association for State and Local History, *Bulletins*, Vol. II, No. 11. Madison, 1960.

Library of Congress, Descriptive Cataloging Division. *Rules for Descriptive Cataloging in the Library of Congress: Manuscripts.* Prelim. ed. Washington, 1954.

Martin, Dorothy V. "Use of Cataloging Techniques in Work with Records and Manuscripts," *AA*, XVIII (Oct., 1955), 317–36.

Nuermberger, Ruth K. "A Ten-Year Experiment in Archival Practices," *AA*, IV (Oct., 1941), 250–66.

Peckham, Howard H. "Arranging and Cataloging Manuscripts in the William L. Clements Library," *AA*, I (Oct., 1938), 215–29.

Radoff, Morris L. "A Guide to Practical Calendaring" and "A Practical Guide to Calendaring," *AA*, XI (April and July, 1948), 123–40 and 203–22.

Russell, Mattie, and E. G. Roberts. "The Processing Procedures of Duke University Library," *AA*, XII (Oct., 1949), 369–80.

Schulz, H. C. "The Care and Storage of Manuscripts in the Huntington Library," *LQ*, V (Jan., 1935), 80–82.

Storm, Colton. "The Care and Feeding of a Manuscript Collection," *Autograph Collectors' Journal*, I (Oct., 1948), 9–11.

Works on the Management of Cartographic Records

American Geographical Society. *Manual for the Classification and Cataloging of Maps.* New York, 1947.

Boggs, S. Whittemore, and Dorothy C. Lewis. *The Classification and Cataloging of Maps and Atlases.* New York, 1945.

Brown, Lloyd A. *Notes on the Care and Cataloging of Old Maps.* Windham, Conn., 1941.

Friis, Herman R. "Cartographic and Related Records: What Are They, How Have They Been Produced, and What Are Problems of Their Administration?" *AA*, XIII (April, 1950), 135–55.

Library of Congress, Division of Maps. *Maps: Their Care, Repair and Preservation in Libraries*, by Clara Egli LeGear. Washington, 1949; rev. ed., 1956.

Ristow, Walter W. "The Library Map Collection," *Library Journal*, LXVII (June, 1942), 552–55.

Thiele, Walter. "Classification, Cataloging, and Care of Maps," in *Official Map Publications.* Chicago, 1938.

Works on the Management of Pictorial Records

Library of Congress, Descriptive Cataloging Division. *Rules for Descriptive Cataloging in the Library of Congress: Pictures, Designs, and Other Two-Dimensional Representations.* Prelim. ed. Washington, 1954.

Luecke, Camilla P. "Photographic Library Procedures," *Special Libraries*, XLVII (Dec., 1956), 455–61.

Melnitsky, Ben. "Classifying Negatives and Prints," *Industrial Photography*, Jan., 1954, pp. 34–40; March, 1954, pp. 36–38.

Strain, Paula M. "Photographs in Scientific and Technical Libraries," *Special Libraries*, XXXIX (March, 1948), 77–82.

Wisconsin State Historical Society. *Notes on Care and Arrangement of Picture Collections,* by Paul Vanderbilt. Madison, 1955.

INDEX

Academy of Sciences (France), 16
Accessions registers, 200
Adams, Charles Francis, 29
Adams, Herbert B., 23
Adams, Samuel, papers, 35
Ainsworth, Fred C., 275
Alabama Department of History and Archives, 24, 213
Alden, Timothy, 48
Alvord, Clarence W., 35-36, 46
American Antiquarian Society, 21, 46, 48
"American Archival Problems" (Leland), 43
American Archivist, 53, 193, 313
American Association for State and Local History, 280
American Baptist Historical Society, 49
American Business Dictionary (Lazarus), 126
American Historical Association, 3, 4, 21-23, 28, 42, 58, 109, 348; Historical Manuscripts Commission, 21, 23, 65; Public Archives Commission, 23-25, 40, 43-44, 52, 55, 57, 65, 83; *Annual Reports*, 55; Committee on Historical Source Materials, 56, 59; *Ad Hoc* Committee on Manuscripts, 112, 188
American Historical Review, 44
American Library Association, 3-4, 7, 17-18, 337-38; Co-operation Committee, 12; Supply Department, 12; Library Bureau, 12, 16, 18, 47, 207
American Oriental Society, 48
American Philosophical Society, 10, 52
American Regionalism (Odum), 332-33
Amherst College, 7; Library, 10-11; Library Committee, 10

Amory, Thomas C., Jr., 58, 78
Andrews, Charles M., 45
Angell, James B., 23
Anglo-American Historical Committee, 52
Archival groups, 147-48, 161-71, 178, 184-85; establishment, 161-62; for major organizational units, 162-63; general groups, 163; collective groups, 163-64; subgroups, 164, 166-67; arrangement, 164-65, 168-70; physical arrangements, 201-2, 212-13
Archival guides, 234-36; organization, 234-35; entries, 235-39, 249; index, 239
Archival inventories, 55-57, 108, 219-34, 240-42; purpose and scope, 220-22; introduction to, 222-24; entries, 224-33; appendixes, 233
Archival lists, 290-97; of disparate record items, 290-92; organization, 292-93; introduction, 293-95; entries, 293; of items having common attributes, 294
Archival principles and techniques, 5, 61-79 *passim*; defined, 64-74; nature of records, 66-67; applications of, 67-69; and current records, 72-73; standardization of methods, 74-76; correct methodology, benefits of, 77-79
Archival series, 167-71; establishment, 168-69; arrangement, 169-70; record type, 169; activity, 169
Archival subgroups, 161-67; establishment, 164; arrangement, 166-67
Archives, *see* Records
Archives of Maryland, 52
Archivists compared with librarians, 4-5